Takeaway English 系列规划教材

Takeaway English 1

原 著 Peter Loveday
Melissa Koop
Sally Trowbridge
Lisa Varandani

改 编 牛 健 张勇军
赵 茹 许瑞松

（学生用书）

图书在版编目(CIP)数据

Takeaway English.1/(美)洛芙迪(Loveday,P.)等原著;牛健等改编.—合肥:安徽大学出版社,2014.6(2016.7重印)

Takeaway English 系列规划教材.学生用书

ISBN 978-7-5664-0752-8

Ⅰ.①T… Ⅱ.①洛… ②牛… Ⅲ.①英语—教材 Ⅳ.①H31

中国版本图书馆 CIP 数据核字(2014)第 102767 号

Peter Loveday, Melissa Koop, Sally Trowbridge, Lisa Varandani

TAKEAWAY ENGLISH STUDENT BK 1 W/CD; TAKEAWAY ENGLISH STUDENT BK 2 W/CD

978-607-15-0585-9; 978-607-15-0588-0

Copyright © 2012 by McGraw-Hill Education.

All Rights reserved. No part of this publication may be reproduced or transmitted in any form or by any means, electronic or mechanical, including without limitation photocopying, recording, taping, or any database, information or retrieval system, without the prior written permission of the publisher.

This authorized English Adaptation is jointly published by McGraw-Hill Education (Asia) and Anhui University Press. This edition is authorized for sale in the People's Republic of China only, excluding Hong Kong, Macao SAR and Taiwan.

Copyright © 2014 by McGraw-Hill Education (Asia), a division of McGraw-Hill Education (Singapore) Pte. Ltd. and Anhui University Press.

版权所有。未经出版人事先书面许可,对本出版物的任何部分不得以任何方式或途径复制或传播,包括但不限于复印、录制、录音,或通过任何数据库、信息或可检索的系统。

本授权英文改编版由麦格劳-希尔(亚洲)教育出版公司和安徽大学出版社有限责任公司合作出版。此版本经授权仅限在中华人民共和国境内(不包括香港特别行政区、澳门特别行政区和台湾)销售。

版权© 2014 由麦格劳-希尔(亚洲)教育出版公司与安徽大学出版社有限责任公司所有。

本书封面贴有 McGraw-Hill Education 公司防伪标签,无标签者不得销售。

出版发行:北京师范大学出版集团
　　　　　安 徽 大 学 出 版 社
　　　　　(安徽省合肥市肥西路 3 号 邮编 230039)
　　　　　www.bnupg.com.cn
　　　　　www.ahupress.com.cn
印　　刷:合肥华星印务有限责任公司
经　　销:全国新华书店
开　　本:210mm×270mm
印　　张:15
字　　数:285 千字
版　　次:2014 年 6 月第 1 版
印　　次:2016 年 7 月第 2 次印刷
定　　价:37.00 元(含光盘)
ISBN 978-7-5664-0752-8
ISBN 978-7-88105-096-6(光盘)

策划编辑:李 梅　钱来娥　薛淑敏　　　　　装帧设计:李 军　金伶智
责任编辑:李 梅　薛淑敏　　　　　　　　　美术编辑:李 军
责任校对:程中业　　　　　　　　　　　　　责任印制:赵明炎

版权所有　侵权必究

反盗版、侵权举报电话:0551—65106311
外埠邮购电话:0551—65107716
本书如有印装质量问题,请与印制管理部联系调换。
印制管理部电话:0551—65106311

前　言

"Takeaway English系列规划教材"改编自美国McGraw-Hill Education（麦格希教育）2012年出版的TAKEAWAY ENGLISH，是一套在教学理念和教学活动设计方面具有国际领先水平，且又适合我国高职高专院校学生使用的英语教材。本系列教材包括：

Takeaway English 1–3（学生用书 配CD）

Takeaway English 1–3（练习册）

Takeaway English 1–3（教师用书 配DVD）

Takeaway English Online Learning Center（学习网站）

《学生用书》第一、二册由15个单元组成，第三册由10个单元组成，每5个单元后设有一个综合复习单元。每个单元设1个主题，通过12个模块展开：热身（Start）、听力（Listening）、词汇（Vocabulary）、语法（Grammar）、阅读（Reading）、项目（Project）、歌曲/文化（Song/Culture）、语音（Pronunciation）、对话（Conversation）、写作（Writing）、测试（Test）、单元小结（Unit Summary）。

《练习册》是《学生用书》的配套教材，提供了专项补充练习，旨在帮助学生巩固所学知识，强化语言技能训练。

《教师用书》供教师教学使用和参考，内含对《学生用书》中各单元内容的教学指导、教学方法小贴士、对不同水平学生的教学指导、课堂知识拓展、文化知识补充、课文相关背景知识、可能存在的教学问题和可行的解决方案等。

"学习网站"是供学生自主学习的平台，同时也辅助教师课上教学，为教师和学生实施线上、线下相结合的混合式教学模式及翻转课堂教学提供了便利。（注："学习网站"仍以原版教材四册书安排，教师与学生在使用时需与本改编版三册教材对接。）

本系列教材的特色是：

1. 在重视语言知识的基础上，强化语言能力的提高，尤其是口语交流能力。作为口语能力的基础，语音和语调训练在教材中占有一定比例。

2. 选材时尚，体裁广泛，互动活动丰富，富于时代感，话题涵盖日常生活及一般职场，符合高职教学要求。

3. 中文旁注及听、说、读、写策略指导适合学生自学，旨在培养学生的自主学习能力。

4.《学生用书》与《练习册》相互参照，导航明确，方便使用。

5. 线上、线下资源相结合，配套完备，相辅相成，相得益彰。

6. 项目（Project）模块采用项目驱动教学法，引导学生在真实的语境下应用英语，解决实际问题。

7. 歌曲/文化（Song/Culture）模块设计新颖，将语言运用融于歌曲和文化中，既增加了学习趣味性，又帮助学生了解了中西文化异同，提高了跨文化交际意识及能力。

8. 测试（Test）模块独树一帜，在点滴中提高学生的应试能力，增加学生的考试自信心。

9. 单元小结（Unit Summary）模块列出了每单元的单词、短语及表达法，一目了然，方便学生有效学习。

10. 各种附录齐全，能最大程度地满足学生的学习与测试需求。

说明：

1. Takeaway English 1（学生用书），15单元（60学时），达到高等学校英语应用能力考试B级水平；

2. Takeaway English 2（学生用书），15单元（60学时），达到高等学校英语应用能力考试A级水平；

3. Takeaway English 3（学生用书），10单元（40学时），达到大学英语四级水平。

我们希望本系列教材能够助推高职高专英语教学改革，为学生提供优质的教学内容，创设良好的学习平台。由于改编者学识与水平有限，虽经最大努力，教材仍难免有不足之处，敬请使用本系列教材的教师和学生不吝指正。意见和建议请发往邮箱：xsm678@126.com。

编者

2014年5月

CONTENTS

Unit 1	Let's begin!	2
Unit 2	All about me!	14
Unit 3	Tell me about your day	26
Unit 4	Let's go shopping!	38
Unit 5	My family	50
	Review 1	62
Unit 6	Yesterday	66
Unit 7	What are you doing?	78
Unit 8	I'm taking a trip	90
Unit 9	Going out	102
Unit 10	Let's celebrate!	114
	Review 2	126
Unit 11	It's a great job!	130
Unit 12	Great vacations	142
Unit 13	Cities around the world	154
Unit 14	Wildlife	166
Unit 15	All about sports	178
	Review 3	190
	Grammar Takeaway	194
	Irregular Verbs	209
	Key to Phonetic Symbols	210
	Vocabulary	211
	Audioscript	221
	Photo Credits	231
	Audio Track List	232

SCOPE and SEQUENCE

Unit	Start	Listening	Vocabulary	Grammar	Reading
1 Let's begin! page 2	Making introductions	Filling in a registration form *Strategy:* Use what you know	What's your date of birth?	Simple present of *be* and other verbs	A school handbook *Strategy:* Preview the title and photos
2 All about me! page 14	An international school	What's your job? *Strategy:* Preview the task	What's your nationality? / More jobs	Questions with be	E-pals messages *Strategy:* Read more than once
3 Tell me about your day page 26	What time do you have math class?	Teresa's daily routine *Strategy:* Learn new words	Daily activities	Simple present	Daily routines around the world *Strategy:* Reread
4 Let's go shopping! page 38	What's your favorite store?	It's next to the bookstore *Strategy:* Listen for main idea and details	Places to go and things to buy	There is / there are	A news story *Strategy:* Read for the gist
5 My family page 50	Meet my family	Who's that in the photo? *Strategy:* Use pictures	Who's he? What's he like?	Possessive adjectives and possessive nouns	My social network page *Strategy:* Use prior knowledge
Review 1, page 62					
6 Yesterday page 66	What day is it?	Where did they go yesterday? *Strategy:* Make a mental image	Where did you go? How was it?	Simple past	Blogs about a special day *Strategy:* Guess meaning from context
7 What are you doing? page 78	What's the weather like?	Calling home *Strategy:* Preview the questions	Activities	Present continuous	An email home *Strategy:* Make an inference
8 I'm taking a trip page 90	Staying at a hotel	Let's meet up! *Strategy:* Take notes	What's the best way to get downtown?	Simple present and present continuous for the future	Let's get together! *Strategy:* Find the main idea
9 Going out page 102	Entertainment places	What's playing? *Strategy:* Listen for specific information	Places to go and things to do	Prepositions *at, in, on*	What can we do for entertainment? *Strategy:* Scan for specific information
10 Let's celebrate! page 114	Holidays and festivals	A New Year's custom *Strategy:* Use your senses	Celebrations	Count and non-count nouns	Festival of the month *Strategy:* Understand footnotes
Review 2, page 126					
11 It's a great job! page 130	Jobs	About my job	Job descriptions	Review: questions in the simple present Adverbs of frequency	An out-of-this-world job *Strategy:* Guess the meaning of new words
12 Great vacations page 142	Where do you go on vacation?	Favorite vacations	Vacation activities	Go + gerund	A travel blog Strategy: Build vocabulary through antonyms
13 Cities around the world page 154	What's the city like?	Comparing cities	Tell me about the city	Comparatives and superlatives	A world-class city *Strategy:* Preview section titles
14 Wildlife page 166	Endangered animals	An endangered bird	Animal actions	*Can* and *can't* for ability and permission	Animal facts *Strategy:* Skim for general idea
15 All about sports page 178	What sports do you play or do?	My favorite sport	Sports actions	*Must* and *have to*	A great sporting moment *Strategy:* Scan for key words
Review 3, page 190					
Grammar Takeaway, page 194					

SCOPE and SEQUENCE

Song / Culture	Pronunciation	Conversation	Writing	Test
Song: Hello, hello	Syllables	Greeting someone and saying goodbye *Strategy*: Use gestures	Writing a student profile *Strategy*: Use a word map	Multiple choice questions
Culture: English around the world	Intonation in questions	Talking about likes and dislikes *Strategy*: Keep a conversation going	Writing an e-pal message *Strategy*: Use capital letters correctly	Understand words from context
Song: Hard life	Third-person singular *s/es* ending	Using time expressions *Strategy*: Gain time	Writing a description of your daily routine *Strategy*: Sequence the events	Listen for the main idea
Culture: Shopping times around the world	Reduction of *there is / there are*	Asking for help in a store *Strategy*: Express surprise	Writing a description of shopping habits *Strategy*: Answer question words	*True / False* questions
Song: My second family	The sounds /ɪ/ *his* and /iː/ *he's*	Making formal and informal introductions *Strategy*: The use of names and titles	Writing a description of you and your family *Strategy*: Write a topic sentence	Prepare for a listening activity
Culture: The names of the days of the week	Simple past *ed* ending	Describing past experiences *Strategy*: Use conversation fillers	Writing a description of a special day *Strategy*: Summarize the main idea	Choose the correct verb tense
Song: Missing you	Connecting words	Connecting words Inviting and accepting or not accepting an invitation *Strategy*: Be polite	Writing an email home *Strategy*: Use appropriate letter closings	Answer reading comprehension questions
Culture: Hotel breakfasts	The sounds /l/ *light* and /r/ *right*	Asking for and giving travel suggestions *Strategy*: Give feedback	Writing an email to make arrangements *Strategy*: Use appropriate language	Answer vocabulary questions
Song: Let's fall in love	The sounds /uː/ *do* and /əʊ/ *go*	Buying tickets *Strategy*: Ask additional questions	Writing an email to make plans *Strategy*: Use sequential order	Listen for specific information
Culture: New Year's around the world	Stress in long words	Accepting and refusing food *Strategy*: Refuse politely	Writing a description of a festival *Strategy*: Include details	Read for vocabulary
Song: Uncle Bertie's nephew	Intonation in questions	Making excuses *Strategy*: Be polite	Writing a job description *Strategy*: Write a topic sentence	Reading for the main idea
Culture: Holidays and vacation days	The /ŋ/ sound	Making and responding to suggestions *Strategy*: Make suggestions	Writing a travel blog *Strategy*: Use adjectives	Summarizing
Song: All around the world	Sentence stress	Agreeing and disagreeing *Strategy*: Use polite language	Writing a comparison essay about two cities *Strategy*: Write a concluding sentence	Describing a picture
Culture: Wildlife conservation vacations	The sounds /aɪ/ *five* and /ɪ/ *it*	Using measurements *Strategy*: Use shortened word	Writing an essay about an endangered animal *Strategy*: Make a plan with details	Making inferences (drawing conclusions)
Song: The game of life	*Have to / has to*	Talking about rules *Strategy*: Gain time	Writing a description of a sport *Strategy*: Make a word map	Reading for detail

Takeaway English 系列规划教材

"Takeaway English系列规划教材"改编自美国McGraw-Hill Education(麦格希教育)2012年出版的TAKEAWAY ENGLISH,是一套在教学理念和教学活动设计方面具有国际领先水平,且又适合我国高职高专院校学生使用的英语教材。本系列教材包括:
 Takeaway English 1-3(学生用书 配CD)
 Takeaway English 1-3(练习册)
 Takeaway English 1-3(教师用书 配DVD)
 Takeaway English Online Learning Center(学习网站)

1 ▸ Let's begin!

In this unit you...
- make introductions
- ask for and give personal information
- say your date of birth
- give dates
- greet someone and say goodbye

Grammar
- simple present of *be* and other verbs

START

Making introductions

1 Sara and Kris are in English class. Listen to their conversation. Then listen again and repeat.

A: Hello.

B: Hi. I'm <u>Sara</u>. What's your name?

A: My name's <u>Kris</u>.

B: Nice to meet you.

A: Nice to meet you too.

2 Now introduce yourself to four classmates.

Talk about it!

3 Work in a group. Make a list of your classmates in the group.

A: Hi, I'm <u>Alex</u>. What's your name?

B: My name's <u>Eli</u>.

A: How do you spell <u>Eli</u>?

B: <u>E-l-i</u>.

A: OK. Thanks!

4 Now introduce the classmates in your group to the rest of the class.

This is Eli. This is . . .

Classmates
1. Eli
2.
3.
4.
5.
6.

Unit 1

LISTENING

Filling in a registration form

1 Before listening Look at the list of words you see on a registration form. Match the words and the examples.

1. _f_ first name
2. ___ last name
3. ___ city
4. ___ country
5. ___ email address
6. ___ date of birth

a. Seoul
b. Korea
c. sun.2002@smail.co.kr
d. Lee
e. 11/08/1995
f. Sun

ENGLISH express

Email addresses
For "@" we say at.
For "." we say dot.
For "com" we say com.

maria@topmail.com =
Maria at topmail dot com

请注意电子邮件的读法

first name
名
last name
姓

email address
电子邮件地址
date of birth
出生日期

2 Listening 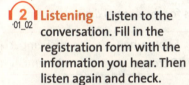 Listen to the conversation. Fill in the registration form with the information you hear. Then listen again and check.

HELP listening

Use what you know
Before you listen, think about what you know. This information helps you understand the conversation.

请注意借助已知信息

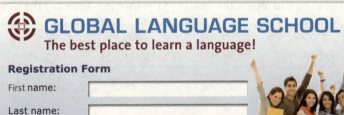

GLOBAL LANGUAGE SCHOOL
The best place to learn a language!

Registration Form
First name:
Last name:
Date of birth: (month/date/year)
Country:
City:
Email address:

3 After listening Read the sentences. Circle *True* or *False*.

1. The name of the school is *Registration*.   True   **False**
2. Her first name is Anita.   True   False
3. Her last name is Valdez.   True   False
4. Miami is in the United States.   True   False

Talk about it!

4 Work with a partner. Ask and answer questions. Fill in the registration form for your partner.

A: What's your <u>first name</u>?
B: My <u>first name</u> is <u>Mike</u>.
A: How do you spell it?
B: <u>M-i-k-e</u>.

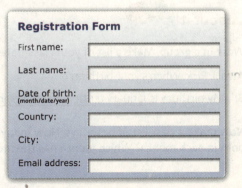

Registration Form
First name:
Last name:
Date of birth: (month/date/year)
Country:
City:
Email address:

WORKBOOK PAGE 1

3

Unit 1

VOCABULARY

What's your date of birth?

1 Listen to the phone conversation. Then practice with a partner.
01_03

A: City Sports Club. May I help you?
B: I want to register for a yoga class.
A: What's your name?
B: Lidia Garcia.
A: What's your date of birth?
B: It's June 21st, 1994.

yoga class
瑜伽课

ENGLISH express

1982 = nineteen eighty-two
2004 = two thousand four
2014 = two thousand fourteen
    OR twenty fourteen

请注意英文年代的读法

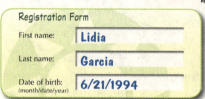

2 Listen to and repeat the names of the months. Then say the months for the special days.
01_04

| January | March | May | July | September | November |
| February | April | June | August | October | December |

1. your birthday   2. your favorite month   3. New Year's Day   4. your favorite holiday

3 Listen to and repeat the ordinal numbers.
01_05

1st first	5th fifth	9th ninth	13th thirteenth	17th seventeenth	21st twenty-first
2nd second	6th sixth	10th tenth	14th fourteenth	18th eighteenth	22nd twenty-second
3rd third	7th seventh	11th eleventh	15th fifteenth	19th nineteenth	23rd twenty-third
4th fourth	8th eighth	12th twelfth	16th sixteenth	20th twentieth	24th twenty-fourth

4 Listen to and write the dates. Then practice saying the dates with a partner.
01_06

1. 2/11/2007   3. _____   5. _____
2. _____   4. _____

ENGLISH express

We write and say dates in this order:
month, day, year.
Write: May 20, 1995 or 5/20/95
Say: May twentieth nineteen ninety-five

请注意英文年、月、日的写法和读法

Talk about it!

5 Work in a group. Make a list of your classmates' birthdays.

A: Hi, Rick. When's your birthday?
B: My birthday is January tenth, nineteen eighty-eight.

Now make a class list of birthdays. How many people are born in each month? Which month has the most birthdays?

Birthdays
Rick 1/10/1988

Unit 1

GRAMMAR

Simple present of *be* and other verbs

ALSO GO TO
Grammar Takeaway
PAGE 194

1 Do you know what a verb is? Look at the charts. Which verb describes an action?

the verb *be*		the verb *speak* and other verbs	
affirmative	negative	affirmative	negative
I am from Chicago.	I'm not from New York.	I speak English.	I don't speak Korean.
You are a teacher.	You aren't a student.	He speaks English.	(don't = do not)
She is nine years old.	He isn't ten years old.		He doesn't speak Korean.
			(doesn't = does not)

2 Read about Rita. Look at the verb forms in red. Write the forms in the correct column.

Hi. My name is Rita Valdez. I am a student at Global Language School. I am from Guatemala, but I don't live there. I live in Miami. I love living in the United States. I don't speak a lot of English, but I study it every day. My teacher often says to me "You are good at English!" She is so nice.

Verb *be*	Other verbs
is	

Global Language School
国际语言学校

3 Write the correct verb forms in the paragraph.

Hi. My name ___is___ (1. be) Julie. My last name _____ (2. be) Park. I _____ (3. be) from Korea. I _____ (4. live) in Los Angeles, California. I _____ (5. be) a student at UCLA. My teachers _____ (6. be) great. L.A. _____ (7. be) a big city. My hometown in Korea _____ (8. be/not) big. My family _____ (9. live) with me in L.A. They _____ (10. speak/not) English.

UCLA
加州大学洛杉矶分校
L.A.
洛杉矶

Talk about it!

4 Tell a partner about you. Say three things that are true and one thing that isn't true. Your partner guesses the thing that's not true.

A: I am from Peru. I live in Lima. I'm a student. I don't have children.

B: You don't live in Lima. You live in Cuzco.

A: Yes! Correct!

5 Now tell the class two things about your partner.

My partner is Manuel. He's from Peru.
He lives in Cuzco.

WORKBOOK
PAGE 3-4

5

Unit 1

READING

A school handbook

HELP reading

Preview the title and photos
Before you read, look at the title and photos. They tell you what the reading is about.

请注意借助标题和图片阅读

1 Before reading Look at the title and the photos of the reading. Circle *True* or *False*.

1. Joshua and Tom are teachers. (True) False
2. Joshua and Tom are English. True False
3. Joshua doesn't like computers. True False
4. Tom loves teaching. True False

2 Reading Read this page from a school handbook. Then check your answers to exercise 1.

01_07

Sao Paolo
圣保罗

Your English teachers

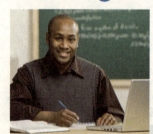

JOSHUA TAYLOR

Hello. My name is Joshua Taylor. I am your teacher. I am from Canada. I am 28 years old. My birthday is February 10th. I live in Sao Paolo, Brazil. I am happy living here. I miss my family. They are not in Brazil. They are in Canada. I love computers. My favorite website is www.takeawayenglish.com. It's great!

TOM MORGAN

Hi. My name is Tom Morgan. I am your English teacher. I love teaching. I am from the United States. I am 45 years old. My date of birth is September 25th, 1967. I live in Sao Paolo. I have a family. They live in Brazil with me. We are happy living here. And you? Where are you from?

Unit 1

3 After reading Read the sentences about Joshua and Tom. Check (✓) the correct names.

	Joshua	Tom	Joshua and Tom
1. He is from Canada.	✓	☐	☐
2. He is a teacher.	☐	☐	☐
3. His family doesn't live in Brazil.	☐	☐	☐
4. He is 45 years old.	☐	☐	☐
5. He is happy living in Brazil.	☐	☐	☐
6. He loves the website www.takeawayenglish.com.	☐	☐	☐

Talk about it!

4 Your teacher gives you his/her personal information. First, complete the sentences.

personal information
个人信息

Teacher's information
1. My name is _____.
2. I live in _____.
3. I am from _____.
4. My family lives in _____.
5. I love _____.

Now work with a partner. Compare your teacher to Joshua and Tom.

A: Tom is from the United States. Our teacher is from the United States too.

B: Joshua loves computers. Our teacher doesn't love computers.

PROJECT

Work in a group. Research personal information about three famous people; for example, each person's first name, last name, date of birth, age, country, etc. Present your information to the class.

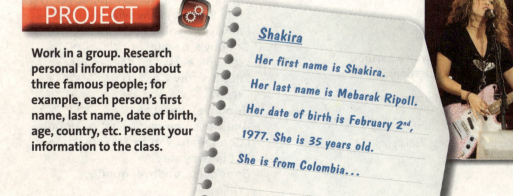

Shakira
Her first name is Shakira.
Her last name is Mebarak Ripoll.
Her date of birth is February 2nd, 1977. She is 35 years old.
She is from Colombia…

Unit 1

SONG

Hello, hello

1 Before listening Read the list of words about songs. Match the words to the definitions. Check your answers with a partner.

_b_ 1. the song title
___ 2. a verse
___ 3. the chorus
___ 4. the lyrics

a. all the words in a song
b. the name of the song
c. part of a song that is repeated
d. part of a song that is not repeated

2 Before listening Complete the tasks.

1. Write the title of the song: _____
2. Circle the chorus.
3. Draw a line (|) next to one verse.
4. Make a box (□) around the lyrics.

3 Before listening Look at the title of the song and the picture.

1. What do you think the song is about?
2. Who are the people in the picture?
3. Do the people know each other? Why?

4 Listening Listen to the song. Read the lyrics. Circle the correct words.
01_08

5 After listening Work with a partner. Ask and answer these questions.

1. Who do you say hello to every day?
2. Who do you say goodbye to every day?
3. Do you like the song "Hello, hello"? Why or why not?

Hello, hello

VERSE 1
Hello, hello.
We (1) always / never say hello.
I don't want you to go.
So I say
Hello, hello.
I see you every (2) day / night.
I don't know what to say
Except
Hello, hello.
And then you say (3) hello / goodbye.
Every day I don't know why
I can only say
Hello, hello, hello.

CHORUS
I don't know where you (4) are / live.
I don't know your name.
I don't know where you're (5) from / at
But I always say the same.

VERSE 2
Hello, hello.
We always say hello.
I don't want you to go.
So I say
Hello, hello.
I see you every day
I don't know what to say
Except
Hello, hello.
And then you say goodbye.
Every day I don't know why
I can only say
Hello, hello, hello.

CHORUS

VERSE 3
Goodbye, goodbye.
I always say (6) hello / goodbye.
I really don't know why
I always (7) play / say
Goodbye, goodbye.
I see you every (8) day / night.
I don't know what to say
Except
Goodbye, goodbye.
And when you say (9) hello / goodbye,
I don't want you to (10) go / know.
But I always say
Goodbye, goodbye, goodbye.

CHORUS

Unit 1

Talk about it!

6 Work with a partner. Ask and answer the questions. Circle the correct answer for you.

1. A: Do you know more songs in English?
   B: (a) No, I don't.
   (b) Yes, I do. I know _____ .

2. A: Do you like singing?
   B: (a) No, I don't.
   (b) Yes, I do.

3. A: Do you like karaoke?
   B: (a) No, I don't.
   (b) Yes, I do.

4. A: What songs do you like now?
   B: (a) I don't like any.
   (b) I like _____ .

5. A: Do singers in your country sing in English?
   B: (a) I don't know.
   (b) No, they don't.
   (c) Yes, they do. For example: _____ .

6. A: Are singers in your country famous around the world?
   B: (a) No, they aren't.
   (b) Yes, they are. For example: _____ .

PRONUNCIATION

Syllables

1 In English, words have syllables—units of sound. Listen to these words.

| desk = 1 syllable | good•bye = 2 syllables | Chi•ca•go = 3 syllables |

2 Listen to the words. How many syllables do they have? Put them in the correct column. Then practice the words.

| ~~one~~ | ~~English~~ | ~~alphabet~~ | computer | eight | language |
| read | student | takeaway | teacher | tomorrow | write |

1 syllable	2 syllables	3 syllables
one	English	alphabet

3 Work with a partner. Add more words to the chart in exercise 2. Then practice saying the words. Clap your hands for each syllable.

clap your hands
拍拍手

Unit 1

CONVERSATION

Greeting someone and saying goodbye

greet someone
与某人打招呼

1 What are different ways of greeting someone and saying goodbye in your language?

2 Listen to each conversation. Then practice with a partner.
01_11

	1	2	3
A:	Hello.	Hi, Carlos.	Goodbye, Jacob.
B:	Hi.	Hello, Bob.	Bye, Emma.
A:	My name's Isabelle. What's your name?	How are you?	See you tomorrow.
B:	My name's Jim.	Fine, thanks. And you?	Yes, see you later.
A:		Not bad, thanks.	

3   the different ways of greeting someone in the conversations in exercise 2. the different ways of saying goodbye.

Talk about it!

4 Work in groups of 5–6. Greet each other and then say goodbye.

A: Hi, John!
B: Hello, Max!
A: How are you?
B: Fine. And you?

CONVERSATION STRATEGY

Use gestures
Conversation is not just words. It's also gestures. When you meet someone, wave and say "Hello!" or shake his/her hand.

请注意借助手势交流

Tell me more!

Visit the Takeaway English Online Learning Center at http://olcs.mcgraw-hill-education.com/takeaway/

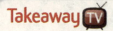 Check out the *Takeaway TV* video.

 Improve your English with the online activities.

Unit 1

WRITING

Writing a student profile

HELP writing
Use a word map
Before you write, make a word map with the most important words and ideas.

请注意借助词汇图进行写作练习

student profile
学生档案

1 Before writing Look at the word map. Write the missing letters to complete the words.

2. F__om: Seoul
3. L__ves: Seoul, Korea
4. Phone nu__ber: 2-555-0164
1. Nam_e_: Ken
5. T__ach__r: Jon Green
6. Jon Green i__ from: Canada
7. e__ail address: kdh@ttcorp.co.kr

2 Writing model Complete the student profile with the words from the box.

| address | live | ~~student~~ | teacher | number |

Hello. My name's Ken. I'm a (1) ___student___ and I'm from Seoul, in South Korea. I (2) _____ and study in Seoul. My phone (3) _____ is 2-555-0164. I'm in class C9. My (4) _____ is Jon Green. He is from Canada. My email (5) _____ is kdh@ttcorp.co.kr.

3 Planning your writing Now make your own word map.

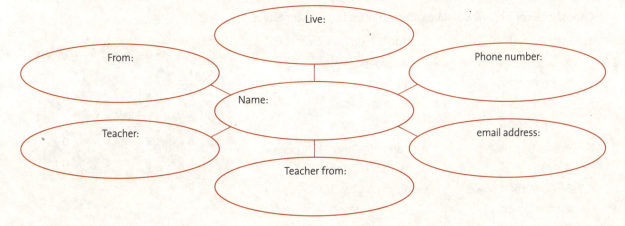

From:
Live:
Phone number:
Name:
Teacher:
email address:
Teacher from:

4 Writing Write your student profile. Use the information in exercises 2 and 3 to help you.

Unit 1

TEST

Test-taking strategy

Multiple choice questions   Many exams include multiple choice questions. You choose the correct answer.

Use these steps to help you choose the correct answer.

1. Read the sentence carefully. Do not look at the multiple choice answers.
2. Try to complete the sentence with words that you know.
3. Then read all of the answers.
4. If you don't know the answer, read the sentence again. Try each answer in the blank.
5. Note the answers that do *not* work.

Example
Choose the correct answer.

1. He _____ in Korea.
   - ~~A.~~ not live   This answer is missing *does*.
   - ~~B.~~ isn't live   This answer uses a form of *be* instead of *does*.
   - C. doesn't live   This is the correct answer.
   - ~~D.~~ don't live   The subject *He* and *don't* don't agree

PRACTICE

Choose the correct answer. Mark the letter on the Answer Sheet.

1. I ___ English.
   - A. am not speak
   - B. don't speak
   - C. isn't speak
   - D. dont speak

2. She ___ Spanish.
   - A. don't study
   - B. does not studies
   - C. doesn't study
   - D. isn't study

3. You ___ in Mexico.
   - A. doesn't work
   - B. isn't work
   - C. aren't work
   - D. don't work

4. John and Tom ___ Chinese.
   - A. doesn't teach
   - B. aren't teach
   - C. don't teach
   - D. isn't teach

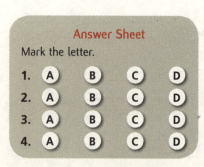

Unit 1

UNIT SUMMARY

Nouns
birthday
city
country
date
date of birth
email address
first name
last name
student
teacher

Nouns—Months
January
February
March
April
May
June
July
August
September
October
November
December

Ordinal numbers
1st first
2nd second
3rd third
4th fourth
5th fifth
6th sixth
7th seventh
8th eighth
9th ninth
10th tenth
11th eleventh
12th twelfth
13th thirteenth
14th fourteenth
15th fifteenth
16th sixteenth
17th seventeenth
18th eighteenth
19th nineteenth
20th twentieth
21st twenty-first
22nd twenty-second
23rd twenty-third

Verbs
be
speak
live
love
say
study
talk

Greet and say goodbye
Bye.
Goodbye.
Hello.
Hi.
OK.
See you later.
See you tomorrow.

Express thanks
Thanks.

Make introductions
I'm (name).
My name's (name).
Nice to meet you.
Nice to meet you too.
This is (name).
What's your name?

Give personal information
How do you spell (name)?
I am from...
I live in...
What's your date of birth?

Ask/say how someone is
And you?
Fine.
How are you?
Not bad.

2 ▸ All about me!

In this unit you...
- identify countries and nationalities
- talk about jobs
- talk about likes and dislikes

Grammar
- *yes/no* and information questions with *be*
- plural nouns

START

An international school

1 Luis is a new student at an international school. Complete the conversation. Use the words from the box. Then listen and check your answers.

| from | meet | ~~student~~ | live | name's |

Luis: Hi, I'm Luis. I'm a new (**1**) _student_ here.
Mei: Hi, Luis. My (**2**) _____ Mei.
Luis: Nice to (**3**) _____ you, Mei. Where are you from?
Mei: Nice to meet you too, Luis. I'm (**4**) _____ China. What about you?
Luis: I'm from Mexico. But I (**5**) _____ in Spain.

2 Write the names of the countries in the chart. Then listen and check your answers.

Argentina	~~Canada~~	France	Mexico	Spain
Australia	China	Japan	New Zealand	the United States
Brazil	England	Korea	Peru	

North America	South America	Europe	Asia	Oceania
Canada				

3 Work with a partner. Add more names of countries to the chart.

Talk about it!

4 Work with a partner. Take turns saying the names of famous people. Your partner says what country they are from.

A: Marie Antoinette.
B: She's from France.

B: Princes William and Harry.
A: They're from England.

Unit 2

LISTENING

What's your job?

at a café
在咖啡馆里

1 Before listening Look at the photo. Then guess the answers. Circle the words.

1. They are old / new friends.
2. They are at a café / school.
3. They talk about jobs / school.

2 Listening Listen to the conversation. Check your answers to exercise 1.
02_03

3 Listening Listen again. Who says each sentence? Circle the correct name.
02_03

	Debra	Marc
1. I'm a new employee.	Debra	**Marc**
2. I'm a computer programmer.	Debra	Marc
3. I'm a manager.	Debra	Marc
4. I work in the sales department.	Debra	Marc
5. I'm from New York.	Debra	Marc
6. I have to go now.	Debra	Marc

HELP listening

Preview the task
Read the sentences in the exercise *before* you listen. This tells you what the listening is about. It also tells you what information to listen for.

请注意听录音前读题

computer programmer
电脑程序设计师

sales department
销售部

4 After listening Read the sentences. Circle *True* or *False*.

1. Debra and Marc work at Tomlin Company.   **True**   False
2. Marc is a computer programmer.   True   False
3. Debra is a new employee.   True   False
4. Debra likes her job.   True   False
5. Marc is from Spain.   True   False

Talk about it!

5 Work with a partner. Role-play a conversation between two people who meet for the first time. Include expressions from the box or your own ideas.

A: Hello! What's your name?
B: My name is... What about you?
A: My name is...
B: Nice to meet you.
A: Nice to meet you too. Where are you from?
B: I'm from... What about you?
A: I'm from... What's your job?
B: I'm a... What about you?

Hello!	My name is...
Where are you from?	I'm from...
Nice to meet you.	My parents are from...
What about you?	Do you work / go to school here?
What's your job?	I'm a...
I like...	I have to go now.
Goodbye.	See you later.

WORKBOOK PAGE 8

15

Unit 2

VOCABULARY

What's your nationality?

1 Write the nationality for each country. Then listen and check your answers.

Country	Nationality
1. Brazil	Brazilian
2. China	_____
3. France	_____
4. Thailand	_____
5. Japan	_____
6. Korea	_____
7. Mexico	_____
8. Spain	_____
9. the U.S.A.	_____

Nationalities

 Mexican American Japanese

French Korean Spanish

 Brazilian Thai Chinese

ENGLISH express

Adjectives are words that describe nouns. We put adjectives between the article and the noun.

a <u>new</u> job   an <u>English</u> school

请注意形容词的位置

2 Work with a partner. Make a list of people and things from each country in exercise 1. Use a nationality adjective.

a Spanish actress: Penelope Cruz   an American city: New York

More jobs

3 Match the jobs to the pictures. Then listen and check your answers.

 A   B   C

1. _B_ student
2. ___ teacher
3. ___ cook
4. ___ hotel manager

5. ___ doctor
6. ___ salesperson
7. ___ factory worker
8. ___ engineer

hotel manager
酒店经理

 D   E   F

Talk about it!

4 Work with a partner. Make a list of other jobs. Use a dictionary if necessary.

Then name people who do the different jobs. Include the nationality if possible.

 G   H

Jobs
businessman/businesswoman
engineer

My mother is an engineer.

Bill Gates is an American businessman.

Unit 2

GRAMMAR

Questions with *be*

ALSO GO TO Grammar Takeaway PAGE 195

1 Look at these questions. What kind of information do they ask for?

Are you Korean?   Where are you from?   What's your job?

2 Notice the word order for questions with the verb *be*.

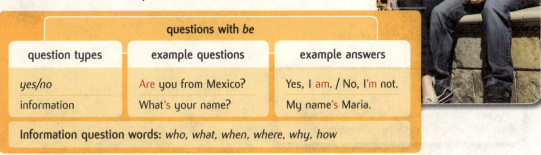

questions with *be*		
question types	**example questions**	**example answers**
yes/no	**Are** you from Mexico?	Yes, I **am**. / No, I**'m** not.
information	**What's** your name?	My name**'s** Maria.

Information question words: *who, what, when, where, why, how*

3 First complete the questions with *am*, *is*, or *are*. Then match the questions with the answers.

1. _**Are**_ you Chinese?   a. _____ Yes, she is.
2. _____ they students?   b. _____ No, I'm not. I'm from Canada.
3. _____ I from the United States?   c. _**1**_ Yes, I am. I'm from Beijing.
4. _____ she a doctor?   d. _____ No, we're not. We're from Australia.
5. _____ he a new employee?   e. _____ Yes, they are.
6. _____ you and Ian from England?   f. _____ Yes, he is.

4 Complete the information questions. Then practice the conversations with a partner.

1. A: _**What**_'s this?
   B: It's a dictionary.
2. A: _____'s she from?
   B: She's from Taiwan.
3. A: _____ is he?
   B: He's my teacher.
4. A: _____ old are you?
   B: I'm 19 years old.
5. A: _____ is your birthday?
   B: It's September 27th.
6. A: _____ is your name spelled?
   B: D-a-n-i-e-l.

Talk about it!

5 Work with a partner. Ask and answer these questions.

1. What's your name?
2. How is your name spelled?
3. When is your birthday?
4. Where are you from?
5. What's your nationality?
6. Who are your teachers?

Unit 2

READING

E-pal messages

1 Before reading Look at the pictures of Yuko and Pedro. Guess the answers to these questions.

1. Where are they from?
2. What are their jobs?
3. What are their favorite sports?

HELP reading

Read more than once
First read the text quickly for the general idea. Then read again for detailed information.

请注意阅读的次数及不同目的

2 Reading Read the e-pal messages. Check your answers to exercise 1.
02_06

the capital city
首都

ENGLISH express

Use **both** to talk about two people.

We're **both** from Japan.
    (after *be*)
They **both** go to English classes.
    (before other verbs)

请注意both的位置

3 Reading Read the messages again. Who says these things? Write *Yuko*, *Pedro*, or *both*.
02_06

1. I'm studying medicine. _Pedro_
2. My brother's an engineer. _____
3. I like to play tennis. _____
4. I listen to music. _____
5. I live with my parents. _____
6. I like to read books. _____
7. My parents both work. _____
8. I have a brother. _____

play tennis
打网球

Real Madrid
皇家马德里队

Yuko

Hello. My name's Yuko. I'm from Japan. I live in Tokyo—it's the capital city. I live with my parents and my brother. My brother is 28 and he's an engineer. I'm 23 and I'm a teacher. My favorite activities are tennis and swimming. I like to read books. I also like to listen to American music—it's good for my English!

Who are you?

Pedro

Hi! I'm Pedro. I'm Spanish. I live with my parents, my brother, and my sister. My brother is 13 and my sister is 10. I'm 19. My birthday is April 2nd. My father's a factory worker and my mother's a cook. We live in Cordoba, in Spain. I'm a student and I'm studying medicine. I want to be a doctor. My favorite sport is soccer, and my favorite team is Real Madrid. I also like to play tennis, but I'm not very good.

Write to me!

Unit 2

4 After reading Find these things in the email messages.

1. five jobs:
   engineer, _____
   _____

2. two countries:
   _____

3. two cities:
   _____

4. three sports:
   _____

Talk about it!

5 Work with a partner. Ask and answer these questions. Use the example conversations to help you.

1. Who is the best e-pal for you—Yuko or Pedro? Why?

   A: Yuko's the best e-pal for me because she is... I am... too. Yuko likes... and I like... too.

   B: Oh, I think Pedro's the best e-pal for me because...

2. Do you have an e-pal?
   - If yes, where is he/she from? What's his/her name? Do you write emails or letters?
   - If no, why not?

   A: I don't have an e-pal. Do you have an e-pal?

   B: Yes, I do. My e-pal's from...

PROJECT

Work in a group. Choose one of these continents: South America, Europe, Asia. Locate and print out or draw a map of the continent. Research the English names and nationalities for all the countries. Write these on the map. Present your information to the class.

Unit 2

CULTURE

English around the world

1 Before reading   What do you know about English? Complete these sentences. Check (✔) the answers you think are correct.

a. Approximately _____ people speak English as a first language.
- [ ] 340 million (340,000,000)
- [ ] 340 billion (340,000,000,000)

b. English is a first language in about _____ countries.
- [ ] 16
- [ ] 36

c. There are about _____ English students around the world.
- [ ] 10 million
- [ ] 1 billion

2 Reading   Read the article "Global English". Check your answers to exercise 1.
02_07

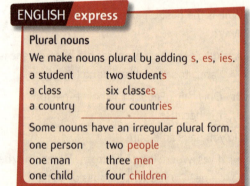

ENGLISH express

Plural nouns
We make nouns plural by adding s, es, ies.
a student — two students
a class — six classes
a country — four countries

Some nouns have an irregular plural form.
one person — two people
one man — three men
one child — four children

请注意名词的复数形式

a billion people
10亿人

3 Reading   Read the article again. Then read these sentences. Check (✔) *True* or *False*.
02_07

one million
100万
all over the world
全世界

1. People speak English in South Africa.
2. English has the most native speakers in the world.
3. There are about one million English students around the world.
4. Words in English are spelled the same all over the world.
5. People in Texas and New York speak differently.
6. People in Hong Kong usually study British English.

Hello! We speak English!

1 English is a global language. It is the first language in about 36 countries. Some countries are: the United States, the United Kingdom,
5 Canada, Australia, Ireland, South Africa, and New Zealand. About 340 million people speak English as their first language.

The number one language in the
10 world is Chinese. A billion people speak Chinese. But English is the

True   False
✔

English

Unit 2

number one foreign language. There are about a billion English students around the world!

In the different English-speaking countries, there are differences in pronunciation, spelling, vocabulary, and grammar. Sometimes there are differences within the same country. For example, in the United States, people in New York speak differently from the people in Texas.

When students study English, they choose between British English and American English. Students in Hong Kong usually learn British English. Students in the Philippines usually learn American English.

4 After reading   In some countries, people speak English and another first language. What do you think is the other first language in these countries? Complete the chart.

| Filipino | ~~French~~ | Irish | Maori | Swahili |

Canada	English and **French**
Ireland	English and
Kenya	English and
New Zealand	English and
The Philippines	English and

Talk about it!

5 Work with a partner. Ask and answer these questions. Explain your answers.

1. Do people speak different languages in your country?
   - **A:** Do people speak different languages in your country?
   - **B:** Yes, there are different languages in Mexico. People speak Spanish and other languages, like Nahuati and Yucatec Maya.
2. Is your language different in different parts of your country?
3. Do you study British or American English?
4. Do you study English for work, school, or because you like studying it?

British English
英式英语
American English
美式英语

PRONUNCIATION

Intonation in questions

1 *Yes/no* questions have rising intonation. Information questions have falling intonation. Listen and repeat.

02_08

Are you a hotel manager? ↗

Where is she from? ↘

rising/falling intonation
升/降调

2 Mark the intonation for each question. Then listen and check.

02_09

1. What's your name?
2. Are you French?
3. Is he a new employee?
4. Where are you from?
5. Who is your English teacher?
6. Is Spanish your first language?

21

Unit 2

go to the movies
去看电影

surf the Internet
上网

play soccer
踢足球(英式)

CONVERSATION

Talking about likes and dislikes

1 Match the pictures to the activities. Then listen and check.

1. _D_ go to the movies
2. ___ swim
3. ___ listen to music
4. ___ meet friends
5. ___ play tennis
6. ___ read
7. ___ surf the Internet
8. ___ watch TV

2 Complete the conversation with expressions from the box. Then listen and check.

Tina: (1) _What do you like to do_ ?
Steve: I like to listen to music.
Tina: (2) _____ to play soccer?
Steve: (3) _____ . I don't like sports. What about you? What do you like to do?
Tina: (4) _____ to go to the movies and to read.
Steve: (5) _____ reading _____ ?
Tina: Yes, it is. How about you?
Steve: My favorite activity is surfing the Internet.

3 Practice the conversation with a partner.

Talk about it!

4 Work in a group. Ask and answer questions about activities you like and don't like. Make a list for each person in the group.

What do you like to do?
  I like to listen to music.
  I don't like to watch TV.
Do you like to play tennis?
  Yes, I do. / No, I don't.
Is swimming your favorite activity?
  Yes, it is. / No, it isn't.

CONVERSATION STRATEGY

Keep a conversation going
Use the expression **What about you?** to keep a conversation going. Another way to say this is: **How about you?**

请注意反问技巧

Matteo	
likes	dislikes

Tell me more!

Visit the Takeaway English Online Learning Center at http://olcs.mcgraw-hill-education.com/takeaway/

 Check out the *Takeaway TV* video.

 Improve your English with the online activities.

Unit 2

WRITING

Writing an e-pal message

1 Writing model Read the e-pal message. Make a list of things you have in common with Manuel.

in common with
与……有共同之处

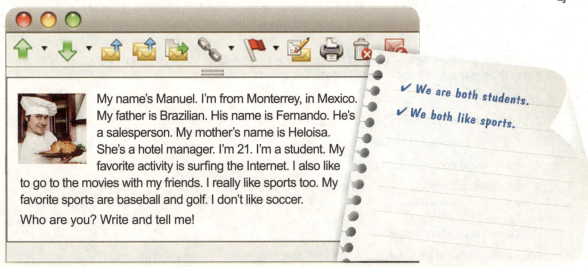

My name's Manuel. I'm from Monterrey, in Mexico. My father is Brazilian. His name is Fernando. He's a salesperson. My mother's name is Heloisa. She's a hotel manager. I'm 21. I'm a student. My favorite activity is surfing the Internet. I also like to go to the movies with my friends. I really like sports too. My favorite sports are baseball and golf. I don't like soccer.
Who are you? Write and tell me!

✓ We are both students.
✓ We both like sports.

2 Before writing Write examples from Manuel's e-pal message.

1. a word at the start of a sentence __My, His,__
2. a subject pronoun _____
3. the names of people _____
4. a nationality _____
5. a city _____
6. a country _____

HELP writing

Use capital letters correctly
Capital letters are used:
• at the start of a sentence
• for the pronoun "I"
• for the names of people, cities, countries, and nationalities

请注意大写字母的用法

3 Planning your writing Complete a chart with ideas for your writing.

my name and age	
my city and nationality	
my job	
activities I like	
activities I don't like	

4 Writing Write an e-pal message. Include the information in exercise 3.

Unit 2

TEST

Test-taking strategy

Understand words from context   In an exam, there are words you don't understand. To guess the meaning of the words, look at the **context**. The context is the words or sentences around a new word. The context gives you information to help you understand the word.

Look at the example below. You don't know the word *principal*. Use these steps to guess the meaning of *principal* and choose the correct answer.

1. Read the sentences carefully.
2. Look at the context of the word *principal*.
3. Ask: What words do I know?
4. You know *teachers* and *students*.
5. So a *principal* probably works with the people at a school.

Example
Choose the correct answer.

Mr. Brown is our principal. He works with teachers, students, and parents every day.

1. A *principal* works at a _____ .

   ~~A.~~ company   Teachers and students don't work and study at a company.

   ~~B.~~ hotel   Teachers and students don't work and study at a hotel.

   ~~C.~~ factory   Teachers and students don't work and study at a factory.

   D. school   This is the correct answer. Teachers, students, and a principal work and study at a school.

PRACTICE

Read the paragraph. Choose the correct answer. Mark the letter on the Answer Sheet.

Karen's father is Chinese and her mother is Australian. Karen speaks <u>perfect</u> Chinese and English. She wants a job as a <u>translator</u> at the United Nations. People at the United Nations speak different languages.

1. *Perfect* means ___ .
   A. bad
   B. excellent
   C. good
   D. terrible

2. A *translator* ___ .
   A. teaches languages
   B. doesn't like languages
   C. doesn't learn languages
   D. speaks more than one language

Answer Sheet
Mark the letter.

1. A   B   C   D
2. A   B   C   D

Unit 2

UNIT SUMMARY

Nouns
book
café
employee
e-pal
friend
job
medicine
music
school
sport
world

Nouns—Countries and continents
Argentina
Asia
Australia
Brazil
Canada
China
England
Europe
France
Japan
Korea
Mexico
New Zealand
North America
Oceania
Peru
South America
Spain
the United States

Nouns—Jobs
businessman/
businesswoman
computer
programmer
cook
doctor
engineer
factory worker
hotel manager
manager
salesperson

Adjectives
both
international
new
old

Adjectives— Nationalities
American
Brazilian
Chinese
French
Japanese
Korean
Mexican
Spanish
Thai

Verbs and verb phrases
go to the movies
like
listen (to music)
meet friends
play (tennis)
read
surf the Internet
swim
watch TV
work

Expressions
Do you work here?
How about you?
I have to go now.
See you later.
What about you?
What's your job?
Where are you from?

Talk about likes and dislikes
Do you like to (play soccer)?
I don't like to (play soccer).
I like to (read).
Is (swimming) your favorite activity?
What do you like to do?
Yes, I do. / No, I don't.
Yes, it is. / No, it isn't.

3 ▶ Tell me about your day

In this unit you...
- tell time
- talk about school subjects
- talk about daily activities
- use time expressions

Grammar
- simple present: affirmative, negative, questions

START

What time do you have math class?

1 What time is it? Write the sentences under the clocks. Then listen and check.
03_01

It's two o'clock.
It's two fifteen.
It's two thirty.
~~It's two forty-five.~~
It's noon.
It's midnight.

A 2:45   B 12:00   C 2:00
It's two forty-five.

D 2:30   E 2:15   F 12:00

2 Listen to the conversation.
03_02

A: What time do you have math class?
B: At 3:00 p.m. How about you?
A: I have math at 11:00 in the morning.

ENGLISH express

7.00 a.m. = seven (o'clock) in the morning
4:00 p.m. = four (o'clock) in the afternoon
6:00 p.m. = six (o'clock) in the evening
10:00 p.m. = ten (o'clock) at night

请注意英文上、下午的区别

have math class
上数学课

3 Match the school subjects with the pictures. Then listen and check.
03_03

1. _G_ English
2. ___ art
3. ___ math
4. ___ social studies
5. ___ science
6. ___ music
7. ___ computer science
8. ___ physical education

social studies
社会学科

computer science
计算机科学
physical education
体育

A   B   C   D

E   F   G   H

Talk about it!

4 Make a schedule of your school subjects. Then ask and answer questions with a partner.

A: What time do you have history class?
B: At 1:45 p.m.

Unit 3

LISTENING

HELP listening

Learn new words
Before you listen, learn new vocabulary words that are related to the content of the listening.

请注意听前掌握有关生词

Teresa's daily routine

1 Before listening   It's Monday morning. Teresa is tired! Put her morning activities in order. Write 1 to 6 for each picture.

get dressed   leave home   eat breakfast   start work   get up   take a shower

get dressed
穿衣服
take a shower
淋浴

2 Before listening   Look at the pictures in exercise 1. Then read the sentences below and circle your guesses.

1. Teresa talks about her morning / evening routine.
2. Teresa wakes up early / late.
3. Teresa starts work at 8:30 a.m. / 8:30 p.m.

wake up
醒来

3 Listening   Listen to a conversation between Teresa and her friend Jane. Check your answers to exercises 1 and 2.
03_04

4 Listening   Listen again. Complete the chart with the times.
03_04

| ~~6:00~~ | 7:30 | 7:30 | 8:00 | 8:00 | 8:30 |

	gets up	leaves home	starts work
Teresa	6:00		
Jane			

Talk about it!

5   Work with a partner. Read the example conversation. Then talk about your morning routine.

A: I get up at 8:00 in the morning. Then I eat breakfast at 8:30.

B: Wow! You wake up late! I wake up at 7:00 a.m.

morning routine
每天早晨的安排

WORKBOOK PAGE 15

Unit 3

VOCABULARY

Daily activities

1 What activities do you like to do? Read? Meet friends? Play soccer?

I like to go to the movies and swim.

2 Here are some daily activities. Write the words under the pictures. Then listen and check.

take a walk
散步

go home	go to bed	eat lunch	do homework	take a walk
~~go to work~~	have dinner	go shopping	watch TV	read my email

1. *go to work* 2. _____ 3. _____ 4. _____ 5. _____

6. _____ 7. _____ 8. _____ 9. _____ 10. _____

3 What are your daily activities? Write them in the chart.

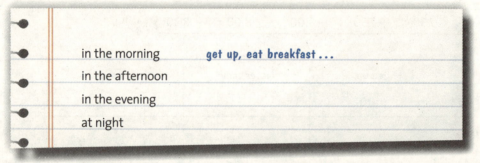

in the morning	*get up, eat breakfast . . .*
in the afternoon	
in the evening	
at night	

Talk about it!

4 Work with a partner. Read the example conversation. Then ask and answer questions about your daily activities.

A: What do you do in the evening?
B: I go home and read my email. Then I eat dinner.
A: And after dinner?
B: After dinner I watch TV. What about you?

GRAMMAR

Simple present

ALSO GO TO
Grammar Takeaway
PAGE 196

1. Look at these sentences about Jim's day. <u>Underline</u> the verbs. What letter do we sometimes add to the end of the verb? When do we add it?

"I get up at 8:00 a.m."   He gets up at 8:00 a.m.
"I leave home at 8:30."   He leaves home at 8:30.

affirmative	negative
I eat lunch late. She eats lunch early.	I don't eat lunch early. She doesn't eat lunch late.

question types	example questions	example answers
yes/no	Do you work here? Does he eat lunch at noon?	Yes, I do. / No, I don't. Yes, he does. / No, he doesn't.
information	Where do you take a walk? What time does she have art class?	I take a walk in the park. She has art class at 3:30 p.m.

2. Complete the chart. Check your answers with a partner.

affirmative	negative
1. She leaves home at 7:30 a.m.	She doesn't leave home at 7:30 a.m.
2. I play soccer in the afternoon.	
3.	He doesn't read his email at night.
4. You watch TV in the evening.	
5.	They don't live in Mexico.

3. Complete the example conversations. Use the words in parentheses. Then practice with a partner.

1. A: _____ soccer? (play/you)
   B: No, _____ .

2. A: _____ work late? (start/she)
   B: Yes, _____ .

3. A: _____ sports? (like/he)
   B: No, _____ .

4. A: _____ lunch at noon? (eat/they)
   B: Yes, _____ .

Talk about it!

4. Work with a partner. Ask and answer five questions about your daily routines.

   A: Do you get up late?
   B: No, I don't. I get up at 6:30 a.m. What about you? When do you get up?

   Now tell the class about your partner.

   A: Kris doesn't get up late. She gets up early. She gets up at 6:30 a.m.

daily routines
日常生活

Unit 3

READING

HELP reading

Reread
If you don't understand a paragraph the first time, reread it. Look for words you know. Then read again with this information in mind. It will help you understand the other words.

请注意借助已知词汇阅读

Daily routines around the world

1 Before reading Work with a partner. Look at the cartoons. Talk about each picture.

Aelaf gets up and eats breakfast. Then he leaves home and...

Name	Country	Daily routine
Aelaf		
Phoung		
Paz		

2 Reading 03_06 Now read the daily routine descriptions. Where is each person from? Complete the chart in exercise 1 with the country names.

My name's Aelaf, and I'm from Ghana. I get up at 7:00 a.m., and I eat breakfast. Then I walk to school. I have class from 8:00 a.m. to 2:00 p.m. In the afternoon, I work as an apprentice carpenter for two or three hours. At night, I eat dinner with my family, and then I do my homework. I go to bed about 9:30 p.m.
Aelaf, 20 years old, Accra, Ghana

My name's Phoung, and I'm from Vietnam. I get up at 6:45 a.m. I get dressed, and I make breakfast for my family. At 8:00 a.m., I go to school. I teach science and math. At noon, the students go home and have lunch. Then at 3:00 p.m., the students have art class and play soccer. We finish school at 6:00 p.m. and go home. My family watches TV, and then we have dinner at 8:00 p.m. I go to bed about 10:30 p.m.
Phoung, 28 years old, Hanoi, Vietnam

My name's Paz, and I'm from Spain. I get up at 7:15, take a shower, and get dressed. After that, I have breakfast and get a ride to school. I finish school at 4:45 p.m. In the afternoon, I play basketball, and then I study at home for an hour or two. I eat dinner around 8:30 p.m., and I go to bed at 10 o'clock.
Paz, 18 years old, Barcelona, Spain

apprentice carpenter
木工学徒

Unit 3

3 Reading Read the descriptions again. Write the correct name for each sentence—Paz, Aelaf, or Phoung.

1. _____Aelaf_____ gets up at 7:00 a.m.
2. _____ plays basketball in the afternoon.
3. _____ finishes school at 6:00 p.m.
4. _____ works in the afternoon.
5. _____ teaches science and math.
6. _____ goes to bed at 10:00 p.m.

4 After reading Say three sentences about Aelaf, Paz, or Phoung. Your partner guesses who it is. Use the example conversation to help you.

A: This person works as an apprentice carpenter. This person doesn't play basketball. This person goes to bed at 9:30 p.m. Who is it?

B: It's Aelaf.

Talk about it!

5 Work with a partner. Compare your routines to Aelaf, Paz, and Phoung. Use the example conversation to help you.

A: Aelaf gets up at 7:00 a.m. I don't. I get up at 7:45 a.m.

B: Paz plays basketball. I don't. I swim.

PROJECT

Work in a group. Make a picture story or cartoon about the daily routine of one person in the group. Use photos or draw pictures. Put a clock with the time for each scene. Write mini-conversations between the person and other people he/she meets.

Judy: Good morning! Do you want to have breakfast with me?

Unit 3

SONG

HARD *life*

Hard life

1 Before listening Look at the picture story and check (✔) the best description.

- A A day in the life of a mother, a father, and two children.
- B A day in the life of a mother with two children.
- C A day in the life of two children.

widowed wife
寡妇

go off
响起来

2 Before listening Match the words to the lettered things in the picture story. Use a dictionary if necessary.

- C kids
- ☐ a factory
- ☐ an alarm (clock)
- ☐ pay
- ☐ pot of coffee
- ☐ tools

3 Listening Read the verses of the song. Number the verses in order so that they match the picture story. Then listen to the song and check.

At a quarter after six.
I <u>wake up</u> the kids.
They have breakfast and they watch TV.
Then they walk to school.
And I <u>pick up</u> my tools.
I take the bus to the factory.

It's a <u>hard</u>, hard life
For a <u>widowed wife</u>.
It's a hard, hard world
For a working girl. **A**

The factory <u>gates</u> at a quarter to eight,
It's not where I want to be.
But I work all day
To earn my pay,
Cos* clothes and food aren't <u>free</u>. **B**

At six o'clock the alarm <u>goes off</u>,
The sun is still asleep.
I get out of bed,
I scratch my head,
I put on a pot of coffee. **C 1**

I leave work at six,
I pick up the kids,
We have dinner when we get home.
When they go to bed,
<u>Poor</u> but <u>fed</u>,
I listen to music <u>alone</u>.

It's a hard, hard life
For a widowed wife.
It's a hard, hard world
For a working girl. **D**

*cos = because

Unit 3

4 After listening Match the underlined words in the song to these definitions.

1. ___gates___ entrances, like doors
2. _____ not with other people
3. _____ when a clock makes a sound
4. _____ for no money
5. _____ a woman whose husband is dead
6. _____ stop sleeping
7. _____ with little money
8. _____ collect
9. _____ difficult
10. _____ with food

Talk about it!

5 Work with a partner. Ask and answer these questions.

1. Do you know anyone (real or from a TV show or movie) who works in a factory? Who? What does he/she do there?

   A: My brother works in a factory. He makes TVs.

2. Do you know anyone (real or from a TV show or movie) who is a single parent? Describe his/her life.

   B: My aunt is a single parent. She works and goes to school.

TV show
电视节目

a single parent
单身父亲/母亲

PRONUNCIATION

Third-person singular s/es ending

1 The *s/es* at the end of third-person singular verbs has three different sounds. Listen and repeat.
03_08

/s/	/z/	/ɪz/
He starts work at 8:00.	She leaves home at 7:00.	She watches TV in the evening.

2 Listen and write the words you hear in the chart. Then practice reading the words with a partner.
03_09

/s/	/z/	/ɪz/
	plays	

33

Unit 3

CONVERSATION

Using time expressions

1 What are different ways of saying the time in your language?

> In English, there are different ways of saying the time.
> 6:15 = six fifteen or quarter past six or quarter after six
> 4:30 = four thirty or half past four
> 1:40 = one forty or twenty to two

2 Match the two ways to say the time. Then listen and check.

1. _e_ 5:05   It's five oh five.
2. ___ 5:15   It's five fifteen.
3. ___ 5:20   It's five twenty.
4. ___ 5:30   It's five thirty.
5. ___ 5:40   It's five forty.
6. ___ 5:45   It's five forty-five.
7. ___ 5:50   It's five fifty.

a. It's twenty after five.
b. It's half past five.
c. It's quarter to six.
d. It's ten to six.
e. It's five past five.
f. It's twenty to six.
g. It's quarter past five.

ENGLISH express
When you say a time, say oh for zero.
请注意时间中"零"的读法

Talk about it!

in order
按顺序；依次

3 Make a list of eight of your daily activities in order. Next to each one, write the time you do the activity. Then, with a partner, ask and answer questions about your lists.

A: What's your first activity?
B: I wake up.
A: What time do you wake up?
B: Let's see... I wake up at quarter to eight.
A: What's your next activity?

CONVERSATION STRATEGY
Gain time
Use Let's see to give yourself time to think before you answer.
请注意说话时争取时间的技巧

My Day
wake up   7:45 a.m.
eat breakfast 8:20 a.m.

Tell me more!

Visit the Takeaway English Online Learning Center at http://olcs.mcgraw-hill-education.com/takeaway/

 Check out the *Takeaway TV* video.

 Improve your English with the online activities.

Unit 3

WRITING

Writing a description of your daily routine

1 Writing model Complete the description of Min's day with the phrases in the box.

> at about   between midnight   I have dinner   I work   In the afternoon   ~~in the morning~~

My daily routine

I get up at 8:00 a.m. (1) _in the morning_. I eat breakfast and read the news online. After that, I take a shower and get ready for work. (2) _____ from 9:00 to 2:00, then I go home for lunch. After lunch, I watch TV. (3) _____, I work on my computer at home. I finish work (4) _____ 7:00 p.m., then (5) _____ and watch the news on TV. After dinner, I meet friends, or I stay home and watch TV. I go to bed (6) _____ and 1:00 a.m.

get ready for work
准备去工作

2 Before writing Look at the underlined words in Min's description. Which ones are nouns? Which ones are subject + verb? Complete the rule with the time words in the box.

| after that | after | then |

Rule: We use a *noun* after _____.

We use *subject* + *verb* after _____ and _____.

> **HELP writing**
> Sequence the events
> Use time words to sequence events and organize your writing.
> 请注意使用时间顺序词

Now circle the correct word(s) to complete each sentence.

1. I get up at 6:00 a.m. After / **After that** I check my email and get ready for work.
2. I play tennis from 9:00 to 11:00, then / after I go home.
3. After / After that dinner, I read a book or watch TV.
4. I finish work at 7:00 p.m., and after / after that I eat dinner.
5. After / Then dinner, I go out with friends.

check email
查阅邮件

3 Planning your writing Make a chart with your daily activities.

4 Writing Write a description of your day. Include these expressions:

in the morning / afternoon   at + (*time*)
after / after that / then   between (*time*) and (*time*)
at noon / at night

Time	Activities
8:00	wake up
8:15	have breakfast read the news

Unit 3

TEST

Test-taking strategy

Listen for the main idea Listening tests often include conversations. In these conversations, speakers ask questions. Listen carefully to key words in the questions. The key words in the questions help you decide the main idea.

Look at the example below. Use these steps to help you decide the main idea.

1. Listen for the questions in the conversation.
2. Listen for the key words in the questions.
3. Write key words from each question. *You write*: learn English, song.
4. Use the key words to help you answer the test question.

Example
You hear this conversation.

Maria:	Hi, Nancy. I'm learning English this year.
Nancy:	How do you learn English?
Maria:	My favorite way is to listen to songs.
Nancy:	What's your favorite song to learn English?
Maria:	It's called *Hard life*. I listen to it every day.

You see this test question.
Listen. What is the conversation about?

~~A.~~ nationalities — The questions include *English*, but not countries.

B. language — This is the correct answer. The key words relate to *language*.

~~C.~~ time — The speaker doesn't talk about *time* in the questions.

~~D.~~ greetings — The speaker doesn't use any *greetings* in the questions.

PRACTICE

Listen. Choose the correct answer. Mark the letter on the Answer Sheet.

1. What is the conversation about?
   - A. Paul's daily routine
   - B. Paul's language class
   - C. Paul's nationality
   - D. Paul's job

2. What is the conversation about?
   - A. clocks
   - B. Saturday classes
   - C. Saturday routines
   - D. breakfast

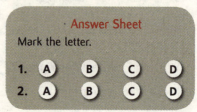

Answer Sheet
Mark the letter.

1. A B C D
2. A B C D

UNIT SUMMARY

Nouns
alarm clock
clock
evening
factory
gate
kid
life
morning
pay
routine
sun
tool
wife

Nouns—School subjects
art
computer science
English
history
math
music
physical education
science
social studies

Adjectives
alone
daily
fed
free
hard
poor
widowed

Verbs and verb phrases
do homework
eat breakfast (lunch, dinner)
get dressed
get up
go home
go off
go shopping
go to bed
go to work
have breakfast (lunch, dinner)
leave home
pick up
read email
start work
take a shower
take a walk
wake up
watch TV

Adverbs
after
after that
early
late
then

Time expressions
a.m.
at night
half past
in the afternoon
in the evening
in the morning
It's (one) o'clock.
It's midnight.
It's noon.
p.m.
quarter after
quarter past
What time...

Expressions
Let's see.
Wow!

4 ▸ Let's go shopping!

In this unit you...
- discuss shopping, stores, and things you buy
- talk about places in a city
- give locations
- ask for help in a store

Grammar
- prepositions of location
- *there is / there are*

START

What's your favorite store?

1 Do you like to shop? Where do you like to shop?

Yes, I like to shop. I like to shop at Ford's Department Store.

Ford's Department Store
福特百货商店

2 Match the store words with the pictures. Then listen and check.
04_01

1. __C__ bookstore
2. _____ department store
3. _____ jewelry store
4. _____ clothing store
5. _____ hardware store
6. _____ electronics store
7. _____ pharmacy
8. _____ shoe store

hardware store
五金店
electronics store
电子产品商店；
家电城

Talk about it!

3 Work with a partner. Read the conversation. Then talk about where you shop.

A: What's your favorite store?
B: My favorite store is Fashionista.
A: What kind of store is it?
B: It's a clothing store. What about you? Where do you like to shop?
A: I like to shop at Gadgets. It's an electronics store.
B: Where is Gadgets?
A: It's on First Street.

Unit 4

LISTENING

It's next to the bookstore

1 Before listening Where do you buy these items? Discuss your answers with a partner.

A an e-reader

B earrings

C sunglasses

D a necklace

E boots

HELP listening

Listen for main idea and details
When you listen more than once, you understand more. The first time, listen for the main idea. Then listen again for details.

请注意听的次数和侧重点

e-reader
电子阅读器

2 Listening 04_02 Alicia and Wanda are shopping. Listen to their conversation. Then listen again and check (✓) the correct answers (2 boxes each).

1. What does Alicia want to buy?
☐ a book ☐ earrings
☐ boots ☐ an e-reader
☐ a pen ☐ sunglasses

2. Where does Wanda say to go?
☐ bookstore ☐ jewelry store
☐ department store ☐ pharmacy
☐ hardware store ☐ shoe store

3 After listening Read the sentences. Circle *True* or *False*.

1. Wanda wants to buy earrings. True (False)
2. The department store is next to the bookstore. True False
3. The bookstore is big. True False
4. Alicia needs to buy books. True False
5. There is a shoe store on Main Street. True False

Talk about it!

4 Work with a partner. Read the conversation. Then talk about places to shop in your city.

A: I like to shop at Latest Electronics.
B: Where is it?
A: It's on Oak Street, next to the hardware store.
B: I like to shop at Bell's. Bell's is a clothing store on Second Avenue.
A: I like to shop at Bell's too.

ENGLISH express

Prepositions of location

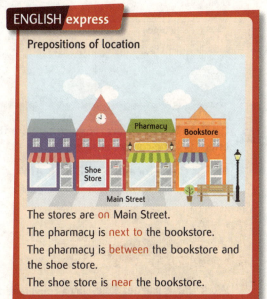

The stores are **on** Main Street.
The pharmacy is **next to** the bookstore.
The pharmacy is **between** the bookstore and the shoe store.
The shoe store is **near** the bookstore.

请注意地点介词的用法

Second Avenue
第二大道

Unit 4

VOCABULARY

Places to go and things to buy

1 Write the names of the places under the pictures. Then listen and check your answers.
04_03

1. café

2. _____

3. _____

4. _____

ATM
bus stop
~~café~~
library
movie theater
post office
restaurant
station

bus stop
公交车站

post office
邮局

5. _____

6. _____

7. _____

8. _____

2 Work with a partner. Put the words in four groups. Use a dictionary if necessary.

| ~~money~~ | candy | coffee | sandwich | cash | envelope |
| ~~popcorn~~ | dollars | package | stamps | tea | ticket |

ATM	café	post office	movie theater
money			popcorn

3 Listen to three conversations. Where are the people? Check (✔) the correct answers.
04_04

pay with cash
用现金支付
credit card
信用卡

1. ☐ movie theater   2. ☐ ATM   3. ☐ post office
   ☐ station   ☐ café   ☐ library

ENGLISH express

The expression **Cash or credit?** means "Do you want to pay with cash or with a credit card?"

cash   credit card

请注意付款方式的表达法

Talk about it!

4 Work with a partner. Role-play a conversation in a place in the city. The class guesses where you are.

A: May I help you?
B: Yes, I want to buy popcorn.
A: Sure. Five dollars, please. Cash or credit?
B: Cash. Here you are.
A: Thank you.
Class: You're at the movie theater.

40

Unit 4

GRAMMAR

There is / there are

ALSO GO TO
Grammar Takeaway
PAGE 197

1 Look at the sentences below. Circle the verb forms. Underline the nouns. When do we use *there is* and when do we use *there are*?

a. There's a jewelry store on Elm Street.
b. There are two shoe stores near here.
c. There isn't a department store.
d. Is there a clothing store near here?

	there is	there are
affirmative	There's a library near here.	There are two cafés near here.
negative	There isn't a library near here.	There aren't any cafés near here.
questions	Is there a library near here?	Are there any cafés near here?
answers	Yes, there is. / No, there isn't.	Yes, there are. / No, there aren't.

2 Complete the sentences. Use *there is/are/isn't/aren't*.

1. __There isn't__ a post office on this street. (no)
2. _____ two stations in the city. (yes)
3. _____ any shoe stores near here?
4. _____ a bus stop near here?
5. _____ any restaurants near here. (no)
6. _____ an ATM across from the library. (yes)

ENGLISH express

Another preposition of location
The man is across from the woman.

请注意 across from 的用法

across from
在……对面

3 Write names for the places in the picture. Then write eight sentences about the city. Use *there is/are/isn't/aren't*. Also use the prepositions of location *on, next to, between, near, across from*.

There's a restaurant across from the post office.
There aren't any department stores on the street.

restaurant   post office

Talk about it!

4 Draw a map of a city street. Write the names of places on the map. Then work with a partner. Describe your picture. Your partner draws what you say.

WORKBOOK
PAGE 24-25

41

Unit 4

READING

A news story

HELP reading

Read for the gist
When you first read a passage, it's not necessary to understand all of the words. Read for the gist—the main idea. Only use a dictionary for words that are important to understand the main idea.

请注意阅读时抓住文章大意

1 Before reading Where do you read the news—in the newspaper or online? What news stories do you like to read?

2 Before reading Match the opposites. Use a dictionary if necessary.

1. _b_ love
2. ___ enthusiastic
3. ___ young
4. ___ alone

a. bored
b. hate
c. with friends
d. old

3 Reading Read the news story. Circle the best title.

Friends hate shopping   A friend to help you shop   A store for your friends

shopping centre
购物中心

play video games
打电子游戏

Good news for people who don't like shopping! There is a <u>Scottish</u> mall that has a new service. This service provides a "shopping friend" for people who don't like shopping <u>alone</u>. The Braehead Shopping Centre in Glasgow also has a <u>lounge</u>. Shoppers can leave their husbands, wives, girlfriends, or boyfriends who don't like shopping in the lounge. Then they can shop with a new "shopping friend" for <u>a few</u> hours. This new shopping friend loves shopping! <u>While</u> you go shopping with your shopping friend, your partner plays video games, reads magazines, or watches TV. "The shopping friend is perfect: friendly, polite, and enthusiastic," said a representative of this new service. She said that a survey <u>showed</u> that "shopping" was one of the things many young <u>British</u> men hate—they say that they are bored when shopping.

4 Reading Read the story again. Check (✓) the picture (A, B, or C) that best illustrates the story.

A

B

C

42

Unit 4

5 After reading Write the underlined words in the story next to the definitions.

1. a place to relax   **lounge**
2. demonstrated   _____
3. from Britain   _____
4. from Scotland   _____
5. not with other people   _____
6. two or three   _____
7. at the same time   _____

6 After reading Read the sentences about the news story. Circle the correct answers.

1. This news story is about _____ .
   a. Scotland   b. the United States
2. Shopping friends are for people who _____ shopping.
   a. love   b. hate
3. _____ can sit in the lounge.
   a. Shoppers   b. The shopper's partner
4. The people in the lounge probably _____ shopping.
   a. love   b. hate

culture matters

In the United States, many teens go to shopping malls as a social activity. They meet friends, play video games, and talk. Sometimes they shop too. Do teens in your country do the same thing?

social activity
社交活动

请注意美国年轻人的逛街目的

Talk about it!

7 Work with a partner. Ask and answer these questions.

1. Do you like shopping? Why or why not?
2. Do you like shopping alone or with friends? Why?
3. When do you go shopping?
4. Do you ever go shopping just for fun? (When you don't need to buy anything.) Explain.
5. What do you like to buy?

PROJECT

Work in a group. Make a shopping guide for your city. Make a list of your ten favorite stores. Write a short description of each store. Where is the store? What can you buy there? Is it expensive or cheap? Who shops there?

ENGLISH express

expensive = costs a lot of money
cheap = doesn't cost a lot of money

shopping guide
购物指南

请注意价格的表达用语

43

Unit 4

CULTURE

Shopping times around the world

1 Before reading What time do stores open in your country? What time do they close? Are they open every day?

2 Before reading Match the words to the parts of the map.

1. _C_ city
2. ___ country
3. ___ state
4. ___ town

3 Reading Read about the store opening times in different countries. Then complete the sentences with the correct country names.
04_06

1. Stores close one day a week in ___Japan___.
2. Stores close in the middle of the day in _____ and _____.
3. Some stores are always open in _____.
4. Small stores normally stay open later than department stores in _____.
5. Store hours are normally 10:00 a.m. to 8:00 p.m. in _____.

public holidays
公共假日

stay open
继续营业

STORE OPENING TIMES

Stores are open at different times in different countries. In some countries, stores are open at the same time all over
5 the country. In other countries, stores are open at different times in different parts of the country. In most countries, stores are closed some days or
10 for some part of the day.

In some parts of Canada, there are no regulations and stores are open 24 hours a day, 365 days of the year. In other parts,
15 stores close on public holidays.

Store hours in Mexico are normally 10:00 a.m. to 8:00 p.m. Some stores stay open until 9:00 p.m. In small towns, stores close early.

In Spain, large stores are open all day, but smaller stores close in the middle of the day. They open at 9:30 or 10:00 a.m. and close at 1:30 p.m. Then they open again at 4:30 and close at 8:00 p.m.

Many stores in Dubai are open from 8:00 a.m. until 1:00 p.m., and then from 3:00 or 4:00 p.m. until 6:00 or 7:00. Large stores are open until 9:00 or 10:00 p.m.

In Japan, department stores and bigger stores open around 10:00 a.m. and close at 7:00 or 8:00 p.m. with no break for lunch. Small stores normally stay open later, while many convenience stores are open 24 hours. Most stores are closed one day a week, not always on Sunday.

Unit 4

4 After reading Work with a partner. Ask and answer the questions.

1. What time do smaller stores open in Spain in the afternoon?
2. Do stores close for lunch in Japan?
3. Where can you go shopping at 9:00 a.m.?
4. On what days do some stores close in Canada?
5. When do stores close in small towns in Mexico?
6. What type of store is open 24 hours a day in Japan?

Talk about it!

5 Write answers to these questions. Then work with a partner. Compare your answers.

1. What time do stores open and close in your country?
2. When do you go shopping for food and clothes?
3. Do you like shopping in department stores or in small stores? Explain.
4. Do you think it's good for stores to be open every day? Why/why not?

PRONUNCIATION

Reduction of *there is* / *there are*

1 In conversation, *there is* and *there are* are reduced, except in short answers. Listen. (04_07)

A: Is there an ATM near the mall?
B: Yes, there is. There's one near the café.
A: Are there any bookstores in the mall?
B: Yes. There are two.

2 Read the sentences to a partner. Use reduction when appropriate.

1. There are no malls in my town.
2. There's a great electronics store near here.
3. A: Is there a jewelry store?   B: Yes, there is.
4. There aren't any ATMs in the mall.
5. There's a clothing store across from the shoe store.

convenience stores
便利店

Unit 4

CONVERSATION

Asking for help in a store

1 When you're in a store, what help do you need?

 2 Complete the conversation. It takes place in a store. Then listen and check your answers.

How much is/are...?	Can I try on this/these...?
~~Do you sell...?~~	Can I see this/these...?

ENGLISH express

This and *these*
We use this with singular nouns and these with plural nouns.
How much is this necklace?
How much are these shoes?

请注意this和these的用法

Salesperson: Hi! Welcome to Dazzle!
Olivia: Thank you!
Salesperson: May I help you with anything?
Olivia: Yes. (1) __Do you sell__ jewelry?
Salesperson: Yes, we do. The jewelry is next to the shoes.
Olivia: Thank you. Oh, (2) _____ necklace?
Salesperson: Sure. Here you go.
Olivia: Thank you. Wow! It's beautiful.
Salesperson: It comes with these earrings too.
Olivia: That's great! And (3) _____ shoes?
Salesperson: Sure. Here you go.
Olivia: Thank you. (4) _____ they?
Salesperson: They're $90.
Olivia: Wow! That's expensive!

CONVERSATION STRATEGY

Express surprise
To express surprise, you can use the expression Wow! Your tone of voice indicates if it is a pleasant surprise or an unpleasant surprise.

请注意 Wow 的用法

Talk about it!

3 Work with a partner. Role-play a conversation between a customer and a salesperson. Use questions to ask for help in the store. Then change roles.

Tell me more!

Visit the Takeaway English Online Learning Center at http://olcs.mcgraw-hill-education.com/takeaway/

 Check out the *Takeaway TV* video.   Improve your English with the online activities.

Unit 4

WRITING

Writing a description of shopping habits

HELP writing
Answer question words
When you write a description, answer the questions who, what, where, when, and why.
请注意在描述文中需要回答的问题

shopping habits
购物习惯

1 Writing model Read about Maria's shopping habits. Then answer the questions.

> **Shopping and Me, by Maria**
> I don't go shopping often, but I like shopping. I go shopping for clothes <u>or</u> accessories like earrings and shoes. Some people like shopping with friends, <u>but</u> I like shopping alone. I spend more time looking at things <u>and</u> I buy more when I'm alone. My favorite store is Chic. This is a clothing store downtown. I like it <u>because</u> it's a big store and it's not expensive. I like to go shopping on Saturday because I have more time then. I don't buy things on the Internet. I like to see things before I buy them.

1. What does Maria buy? _____
2. Who does she like to shop with? _____
3. When does she like to shop? _____
4. Where does she like to shop? _____
5. Why does she like to shop there? _____

2 Before writing Look at the underlined words in the writing model. Write the words next to the functions.

1. ___and___ adds information
2. _____ shows difference
3. _____ gives a reason
4. _____ gives a choice

ENGLISH express
We use the connectors and, but, or, and because to combine sentences or ideas.
请注意连词的用法

3 Planning your writing Answer the questions about your shopping habits.

Do you like shopping? Why or why not?
_____

Where do you normally go shopping?
_____

When do you normally go shopping?
_____

What do you buy?
_____

Who do you normally go shopping with?
_____

4 Writing Write a description of your shopping habits. Use the information in exercises 2 and 3 to help you.

WORKBOOK PAGE 26-27

Unit 4

TEST

Test-taking strategy

True/False questions Many exams include *True/False* questions.

> *Example*
> Circle the correct answer.
> 1. There are stamps, sandwiches, and packages at the post office.   **True**   **False**

Use this information to help you choose the correct answer.

1. Most tests have more *True* answers than *False* answers.
2. If you don't know the answer, guess. You have a 50% chance of getting the correct answer.
3. Look for words like *always* or *never*. These words mean that something has to be 100% true. The correct answer is probably *False*.
4. Look for words like *usually* or *sometimes*. These words mean that something doesn't have to be 100% true. The correct answer is probably *True*.
5. If any part of the sentence is false, the answer is *False*.

> *Example*
> 1 There are stamps, sandwiches, and packages at the post office.
> ~~True~~   This answer is not correct. There are stamps and packages at the post office. But there aren't sandwiches at the post office.
> **False**   This is the correct answer. There aren't sandwiches at the post office.

PRACTICE

Read this short paragraph.

Mark and Tina like to go to the movie theater, but it's expensive! The tickets, popcorn, and candy cost a lot of money. Sometimes they watch movies at home.

Mark T (True) or F (False) on the Answer Sheet.

1.	They hate going to the movie theater.	True	False
2.	The popcorn is expensive.	True	False
3.	The candy is not expensive.	True	False
4.	They always watch movies at home.	True	False

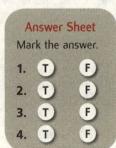

Answer Sheet
Mark the answer.
1. T F
2. T F
3. T F
4. T F

UNIT SUMMARY

Nouns
avenue
boot
candy
cash
coffee
credit card
dollar
earrings
envelope
e-reader
lounge
money
necklace
package
place
popcorn
sandwich
stamp
state
store
street
sunglasses
tea
ticket
town

Nouns—Stores and places
ATM
bookstore
bus stop
café
clothing store
department store
electronics store
hardware store
jewelry store
library
movie theater
pharmacy
post office
restaurant
shoe store
station

Adjectives
bored
British
cheap
enthusiastic
expensive
favorite
few
old
open
Scottish
young

Verbs
buy
close
hate
open
show

Prepositions of location
across from
between
near
next to
on

Conjunctions
and
because
but
or
while

Question words
What…
When…
Where…
Who…
Why…

Expressions
there are
there is
Where is it?

Ask for help in a store
Can I see this/these…
Can I try on this/these…
Do you sell…
How much is/are…

5 ▶ My family

In this unit you...
- talk about your family
- describe people—appearance and personality
- make formal and informal introductions

Grammar
- possessive adjectives
- possessive nouns

START

Meet my family

1 How many people are there in your family? What are their names?

> There are four people in my family. Their names are Mike, Ellen, Paul, and Liz—that's me!

2 Look at the picture of the family. Complete the sentences with the words in the box. Then listen and check.

| grandfather | grandmother | father | ~~mother~~ | brother | sister |

1. I'm Leo. Wendy's my _____mother_____.
2. I'm Sara. Victor's my _____.
3. I'm Leo. Jon's my _____.
4. I'm Sara. Molly's my _____.
5. I'm Leo. Sara's my _____.
6. I'm Sara. Leo's my _____.

3 Who says the sentences? Write the names. Then listen and check.

| Victor and Molly |
| Leo |
| Wendy and Jon |
| ~~Sara~~ |

1. "I have a brother." _____Sara_____
2. "We have two grandchildren." _____
3. "We have two children." _____
4. "Wendy and Jon are my parents." _____

Talk about it!

4 Work with a partner. Ask and answer questions about your family.

A: Do you have any brothers or sisters?
B: I have one brother and two sisters.
A: What are their names?

Unit 5

LISTENING

Who's that in the photo?

1 Before listening Look at the photo of Lily and Amanda and (circle) your guess.

The conversation is about _____ .

a. Lily's family
b. Amanda's family
c. both of their families

HELP listening

Use pictures
Prepare for a listening by looking at any pictures. Guess what the listening is about. Also look for any details, such as people's names, that will help you understand better.

请注意听前借助图片获取信息

2 Listening Now listen to the conversation. Check your guess in exercise 1.
05_03

3 Listening Listen again and write the names of the people in the boxes in the picture.
05_03

Barbara
Jack
Eliza
Madison
Pete

ENGLISH express

Mom is an informal way to say mother. **Dad** is an informal way to say father.

informal way
非正式的方式

请注意英文中"父母"的非正式表达法

4 After listening Write answers to these questions. Check your answers with a partner.

1. How many brothers does Amanda have? _____
2. How old is Pete? _____
3. Who is Madison's mother? _____
4. What does Jack do? _____
5. Who is Bruce? _____

Talk about it!

5 Bring in a picture of your family. If you don't have a picture, draw one. Then talk about the picture with a partner.

This is me with my family. We're at our house. This is my father...

Unit 5

VOCABULARY

Who's he? What's he like?

Rafael — Maria   Luis — Vera
Omar Elsa — Felix Hilda Pancho
Silvia Juanito

1 05_04 Complete the descriptions. Use a dictionary if necessary. Then listen and check.

aunt	brother-in-law	cousins
daughter	husband	mother-in-law
nephew	niece	son	~~uncle~~	wife

1. My name's Omar. Luis is my (a) ___uncle___ and Vera's my (b) _____. Pancho and Hilda are my (c) _____. Silvia's my (d) _____ and Juanito's my (e) _____.

2. My name's Elsa. Felix is my (a) _____. Silvia's my (b) _____ and Juanito is my (c) _____.

3. My name's Felix. Elsa is my (a) _____. Omar is my (b) _____ and Maria is my (c) _____.

2 05_05 Write the words to describe people in the chart. Then listen and check your answers.

~~black hair~~	brown eyes	green eyes	long hair	red hair
blond hair	brown hair	hardworking	outgoing	serious
blue eyes	~~easygoing~~	lazy	quiet	short hair

Describes appearance	Describes personality
black hair	easygoing

ENGLISH express

To describe appearance
A: What does he look like?
B: He has red hair and blue eyes.

To describe personality
A: What's he like?
B: He's very nice.

请注意对外貌和个性提问的方式

Talk about it!

similar to
与……相似

3 Draw your family tree. Then work with a partner. Ask and answer questions about your families similar to this example conversation.

A: Who's Brett?
B: He's my brother-in-law.
A: What does he look like?
B: He has short brown hair and brown eyes.
A: What's he like?
B: He's easygoing.

Unit 5

GRAMMAR

Possessive adjectives and possessive nouns

> ALSO GO TO
> Grammar Takeaway
> PAGE 198

1 Look at the sentences in the chart. What do possessives show?

possessive adjectives	That's **my** sister. Is Silvia **your** niece? That's **his** daughter. Felix is **her** husband. This is my fish. **Its** name is Nemo.	Juanito is **our** son. Luis is **their** uncle.
possessive nouns	My <u>brother has</u> a wife. My brother**'s** wife is outgoing. The <u>students have</u> books. The students**'** books are new.	

ENGLISH express

We use *its* to show possession and *it's* to say *it is*.

请注意 its 和 it's 的区别

2 Complete the conversation with possessive adjectives. Then practice with a partner.

A: Hey, Janet! Is that (1) ___*your*___ husband?

B: No, that's my brother. (2) _____ name is Hiro.
(3) _____ husband isn't here today.

A: Where is he?

B: He's with (4) _____ daughter. She plays basketball on Saturdays.

A: That's nice! What's (5) _____ daughter's name?

B: (6) _____ name is Sonia.

A: Do you have other children?

B: Yes, I do. I have two sons. (7) _____ names are Billy and John.

3 Use possessive nouns to complete the sentences.

1. Julia has three children. ___*Julia's*___ children are hardworking.
2. Phillip has brown hair. _____ hair is short.
3. The teachers have a meeting. The _____ meeting is at 3:00.
4. Tom has a car. _____ car is new.
5. My uncle has two children. My _____ children are my cousins.
6. The girls have blond hair. The _____ hair is long.

Talk about it!

4 Work with a partner. Talk about people you know. Your partner guesses who it is. Use possessive nouns and possessive adjectives.

A: This person's hair is long and brown. His eyes are brown. He's outgoing. He plays soccer for Milan. His number is 80.

B: It's Ronaldinho!

WORKBOOK PAGE 31-32

Unit 5

HELP reading

Use prior knowledge
What do you already know about the reading topic? When you connect this prior knowledge to the new information, you will understand more.

请注意借助题目的信息阅读

READING

My social network page

social network sites
社交网站

1 Before reading Do you use social network sites? What are some of the sites you know?

2 Reading Read and complete Mariana's social network page with the paragraph titles.
05_06

My family   My activities and interests   All about me

Home   Profile   Account

Mariana's page

1. _____

I'm from Venezuela, and I'm 18 years old. I'm a college student. I want to be a doctor. I live with my family in Caracas, the capital city of my country. I'm a quiet, easygoing person.

2. _____

I love my family. My parents are very nice people. My dad, Rodrigo, is a software engineer, and he works for a computer company. My mom's a sales manager. Her name is Cecilia. She has short, brown hair, and she is hardworking. My sister Ana is 10 years old, and she is in high school. She's very outgoing and funny. She has big, brown eyes and long, black hair. My grandmother lives in our house too. She is a teacher, and she teaches in an elementary school. She's quiet, like me, but we talk a lot together.

3. _____

I love medicine and science in general. I think nature is fantastic. In my free time I like to take a walk in natural places—forests, mountains, etc. I also like to listen to music and to read. I'm interested in all kinds of music.

---

software engineer
软件工程师
sales manager
销售经理

elementary school
小学

in general
总体上来说

3 Reading Read Mariana's social network page again. Then read the sentences below.
05_06 Circle *True* or *False*.

1.	Mariana lives in Caracas.	**True**	False
2.	Mariana is outgoing.	True	False
3.	Her mom's an engineer.	True	False
4.	Her sister is in high school.	True	False
5.	Her grandmother is quiet.	True	False
6.	Mariana doesn't like to read.	True	False

in high school
上高中

Unit 5

4 After reading Complete the chart about Mariana's family.

	name	occupation	physical description	personality
father				
mother				
sister		student		
grandmother				

5 After reading Ask and answer questions about Mariana's family. Use the chart in exercise 4 to help you.

A: What does Mariana's sister do?
B: She's a student.
A: What's her name?
B: …

Talk about it!

6 Work with a partner. Ask and answer questions about your families.

A: You have a sister, right?
B: Yes, I do. Her name's Cynthia.
A: What does Cynthia do?
B: She's a biologist.

> **CONVERSATION STRATEGY**
> We use right? to ask a question when we think the answer is yes.
> 请注意交谈中right的用法

PROJECT

Work in a group. Make a list of social network sites on the Internet. Go to three of the sites to answer the questions below. Then report back to your class. As a class, determine the top three social network sites used by students in the class.

1. What kind of information do people share?
2. Do people use it for personal networks, business networks, or both?
3. What language do people use on it?

Social Network Sites
MeBook:
1. personal information, pictures, daily updates
2. mostly for personal networks
3. many languages

personal/business network
个人/商业网络

daily updates
每日更新

Unit 5

SONG

My second family

1 Before listening Match the words to the definitions. Use a dictionary if necessary.

wedding reception 婚宴
get married 结婚
wedding ceremony 结婚典礼
twice as many as 两倍多

1. _f_ wedding reception
2. ___ wedding ceremony
3. ___ honeymoon
4. ___ groom
5. ___ bridesmaid
6. ___ bride
7. ___ best man

a. the man who is getting married
b. the woman who is getting married
c. the trip the bride and groom go on after they are married
d. the woman who helps the bride
e. the ritual in which two people get married
f. the party and meal to celebrate a marriage
g. the man who helps the groom

tell the difference 分清

2 Listening Look at the picture and the words from exercise 1. With a partner, guess the answers to the questions below. Then listen to check your guesses.
05_07

1. Who are the people?
2. What do you think the song is about?

3 Listening Cover the words to the song. Listen and check (✓) the words you hear. Compare your answers with a partner.
05_07

___ aunt
___ daughter
___ nephew
___ son
___ brother-in-law
___ father
___ niece
___ uncle
___ cousin
___ husband
___ sister
___ wife

Your family's very big, it's not like <u>mine</u>.
But when we get married at half past nine,
I'll have <u>twice as many</u> cousins as I had before.
Your mother <u>will be</u> my mother-in-law.
It's time to meet the family and say hello.
But is that Uncle Bill or your cousin Joe?
Is that your Aunt Anita with the dark brown hair?
Or is she the one with the blue eyes sitting over there?

chorus

Mother, father, sister, brother.
They all <u>look like</u> one another.
Niece and nephew, uncle, aunt.
You can <u>tell the difference</u> but I can't.

I know you have four sisters, but which one's that?
Is that your Uncle Robert in the big black <u>hat</u>?
Is that your sister's boyfriend or your cousin's son?
Do you have ten families or just the one?

chorus

We're going for a meal in a big hotel.
At the table I sit next to your Aunt Belle.
I think she's Aunt Anita and I call her that.
Your cousin Billy hears me and he starts to laugh.

chorus

Unit 5

4 After listening Check (✓) the best summary of the song.

a. ___ The bride's family is very small.
b. ___ The bride's family is very rich.
c. ___ The groom doesn't know the names of the people at the wedding.
d. ___ The groom's family is very big.

5 After listening Write the underlined words from the song next to the definitions.

1. __mine__ my family
2. _____ something you wear on your head
3. _____ have the same appearance as   have the same appearance 长相/外观一样
4. _____ identify different people or things
5. _____ a verb referring to the future
6. _____ double the quantity

Talk about it!

6 Read the questions and take notes about your ideas. Then work with a partner. Ask and answer the questions.

1. Do you come from a big family or a small family?
   I come from a small family. I have one…
2. What are the advantages or disadvantages of a big family?
   One advantage of a big family is…
3. What are the advantages or disadvantages of a small family?
4. In your opinion, what is the best age to get married?
5. Describe a wedding you went to recently.

PRONUNCIATION

The sounds /ɪ/ *his* and /iː/ *he's*

1 Be sure to distinguish between the sound /ɪ/, as in *his*, and /iː/, as in *he's*. Listen and repeat.
05_08
His name is Brad. He's from Dallas.

distinguish 区分

2 Write the words in the chart. Then listen and check.
05_09

| this | these | three | listen | she | it |
| cousin | children | niece | green | six | me |

/ɪ/ his	this,
/iː/ he's	these,

57

Unit 5

informal situation
非正式场合

CONVERSATION

Making formal and informal introductions

CONVERSATION STRATEGY

The use of names and titles
In informal situations, use first names.
  Sally, this is my sister, Alice.
In formal situations, use first and last names together or a title (Mr., Mrs., Ms., or Dr.) with a last name.
  Dad, this is my teacher, Mr. Hall.
  Mr. Hall, this is my father, Bob Green.

请注意不同场合称呼语的用法

1 How do you introduce people in your language? When do you use first names? When do you use last names? When do you use titles?

2 (05_10) Listen to the introductions. Notice the red words. Are the introductions formal or informal? Circle the correct answers.

A formal   informal

Lily: Omar, this is my husband, Pat.
Omar: Nice to meet you, Pat.
Pat: Welcome to New York, Omar!

B formal   informal

Stephen: Tara, I'd like to introduce you to Dr. Venn. He's a new doctor at the hospital. Dr. Venn, this is Tara Johnson.
Dr. Venn: Pleased to meet you, Ms. Johnson.
Tara: Likewise, Dr. Venn.

3 Practice the conversations in groups of three.

Talk about it!

4 Work in groups. Role-play four introductions. Make some introductions formal and others informal. Then perform your introductions for the class. The class says if each one is formal or informal. You can use these photos for ideas.

Tell me more!

Visit the Takeaway English Online Learning Center at http://olcs.mcgraw-hill-education.com/takeaway/

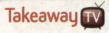 Check out the *Takeaway TV* video.

 Improve your English with the online activities.

Unit 5

WRITING

Writing a description of you and your family

HELP writing
Write a topic sentence
The first sentence of a paragraph is usually the topic sentence. The topic sentence gives the main idea. When you write, start each paragraph with a topic sentence.
请注意写好主题句

1 Writing model Complete Fernando's description with the topic sentences.

| I have a great family. | I have many interests. | I'm from Peru, and I'm 20 years old. |

Home   Profile   Account   Sign Off

Fernando's page

About me
_____. I'm a student, and I study computer science at college. I live with my family in Cuzco, a big city in my country. I have short, brown hair and brown eyes. I'm an outgoing and hardworking person.

Family
_____. My father, José, is a doctor, and he works for a hospital. He has black hair and brown eyes. My mom's a teacher. Her name's Margarita. She has short, brown hair and green eyes. My brother is 18 years old, and he goes to college too. He's very outgoing and funny. He is tall and has black hair. My grandfather lives in our house too. He's short and has gray hair. He likes to tell stories, and we play dominoes together.

Activities and interests
_____. I love computers and technology. I think computers are fantastic. In my free time I like to learn about new programs and applications. I also like to listen to music and read science fiction books.

play dominoes
玩多米诺骨牌

learn about
学习关于……
science fiction books
科幻书籍

2 Planning your writing Complete the chart about you and your family.

family member	name	occupation	physical description	personality
me				

3 Writing Make a webpage about you and your family. Use the information in exercises 1 and 2 to help you.

Unit 5

TEST

Test-taking strategy

Prepare for a listening activity Listening questions on tests often include clues. Clues are information that help you prepare for the listening and find the right answers.

Use these steps to help you prepare for a listening activity.

1. Look at any pictures with the activity.
2. Look for details, like people's names, that help you understand better.
3. Read the directions and the questions carefully before you listen.
4. Try to guess what the listening is about before you listen.

> *Example*
> **You see this test question and picture.**
>
> **Listen to Jeremy talk about his dog. Read the sentence. Mark T (True) or F (False) on the Answer Sheet.**
>
> 1. Rocky is very serious.   True   False

> **You hear this paragraph.**
>
> My name is Jeremy. This is my dog. His name is Rocky. He has brown hair and brown eyes. He's very easygoing, but he doesn't like cats. He's my best friend in the whole world.

> **You answer the question.**
>
> 1. Rocky is very serious.   True   False
>
> ~~True~~   This answer is not correct. Jeremy says his dog is easygoing.
> **False**   This answer is correct. Rocky is not serious. He's easygoing.

PRACTICE

Listen to Abigail talk about her daughter. Read the sentences. Mark T (True) or F (False) on the Answer Sheet.

1. Abigail is 18 years old.   True   False
2. Becky is Abigail's mother.   True   False
3. Abigail and Becky both have brown hair.   True   False
4. Becky is very serious.   True   False

Answer Sheet
Mark the answer.

1. T   F
2. T   F
3. T   F
4. T   F

UNIT SUMMARY

Unit 5

Nouns
appearance
best man
bride
bridesmaid
ceremony
groom
hat
honeymoon
people
personality
reception
wedding

Nouns—Family
aunt
brother
brother-in-law
children
cousin
daughter
family
father
grandchildren
grandfather
grandmother
husband
mother
mother-in-law
nephew
niece
parent
sister
son
uncle
wife
mom
dad

Adjectives—Possessive adjectives
her
his
its
my
our
their
your

Adjectives—Describing personality
easygoing
hardworking
lazy
nice
outgoing
quiet
serious

Verbs and verb phrases
have
look alike
tell the difference

Pronoun
mine

Describing hair and eyes
He/She has...
black hair.
blond hair.
blue eyes.
brown eyes.
brown hair.
green eyes.
long hair.
red hair.
short hair.

Expressions
How old is...
twice as many
What does he/she look like?
What's he/she like?
Who's he/she?

Meeting new people
I'd like to introduce you to...
Likewise...
Nice to meet you.
Pleased to meet you.
This is...
Welcome...

Review 1

VOCABULARY

Put the words and phrases in the seven groups. Compare your answers with a partner. Then write more words that you know in each group.

math	an engineer	a station	eat breakfast	meet friends	Mexican	get up
a wife	swim	a brother	surf the Internet	Chinese	art	Korean
an ATM	science	go to bed	a post office	a cousin	a doctor	a cook

school subjects	jobs	places in a city	family words	daily activities	other activities	nationalities
math						

A: I think "math" goes in "school subjects".
B: Yes, that's right. I think "a cook" goes in "family words".
A: I don't think so. I think it goes in "jobs".

GRAMMAR

Circle the correct answer to complete each sentence.

1. Fred: _____ is this?   Ellen: It's an e-reader.
   A Where   B When   C How   D What

2. He _____ to bed at 10:00 p.m.
   A go   B gos   C goes   D going

3. _____ you go to bed early?
   A Do   B Is   C Does   D Why

4. Tina: Is there a bus stop on this street?   Leo: Yes, _____ .
   A there's   B there is   C it is   D there's it

5. Patrick is my friend. This is _____ wife, Julia.
   A Patrick   B Patricks   C Patrick's   D Patricks'

Review 1

LISTENING

Listen to three short conversations. What are the people talking about in each conversation? Circle the correct answers. Then listen again and check your answers.

Conversation 1	A work	B a vacation	C an animal	D family
Conversation 2	A a sport	B a store	C a movie	D a book
Conversation 3	A food	B a daily routine	C a country	D a song

READING

Read Jagjit's blog. Then circle *True* or *False* for each sentence below.

Jagjit's Blog

My name is Jagjit and I'm from Manchester, in England. My parents are from India. Jagjit is an Indian name. It means "conqueror of the world". I'm a student and I take classes at the university every day. I leave home at 8:30 a.m., and I get home at about 5:00 in the afternoon. I have dinner with my mum, dad, and sister at 6:00 p.m. My sister Ananti is 15, and she looks like me. We both have brown eyes and long, dark hair. We are both outgoing. My family lives in a small house downtown. There are lots of stores and a movie theater near our house. In the evening, I like to surf the Internet and to meet my friends at the café on Park Street.

1. Jagjit is from India.
   True   **False**
2. Jagjit is a student.
   True   **False**
3. Jagjit has lunch with his family.
   True   **False**
4. Jagjit's sister has long, dark hair.
   True   **False**
5. Jagjit likes to meet his friends at the movies.
   True   **False**

Talk about it!

Match the questions to the answers. Then ask and answer the questions with a partner.

1. What's your last name? __c__
2. Where are you from? _____
3. How old are you? _____
4. Do you have any brothers and sisters? _____
5. Is there a library in your town? _____
6. What time is it? _____

a. I'm from Canada.
b. I'm 28.
c. Brady.
d. It's quarter past three.
e. No, I don't. I'm an only child.
f. Yes, there is. It's on Oak Street.

63

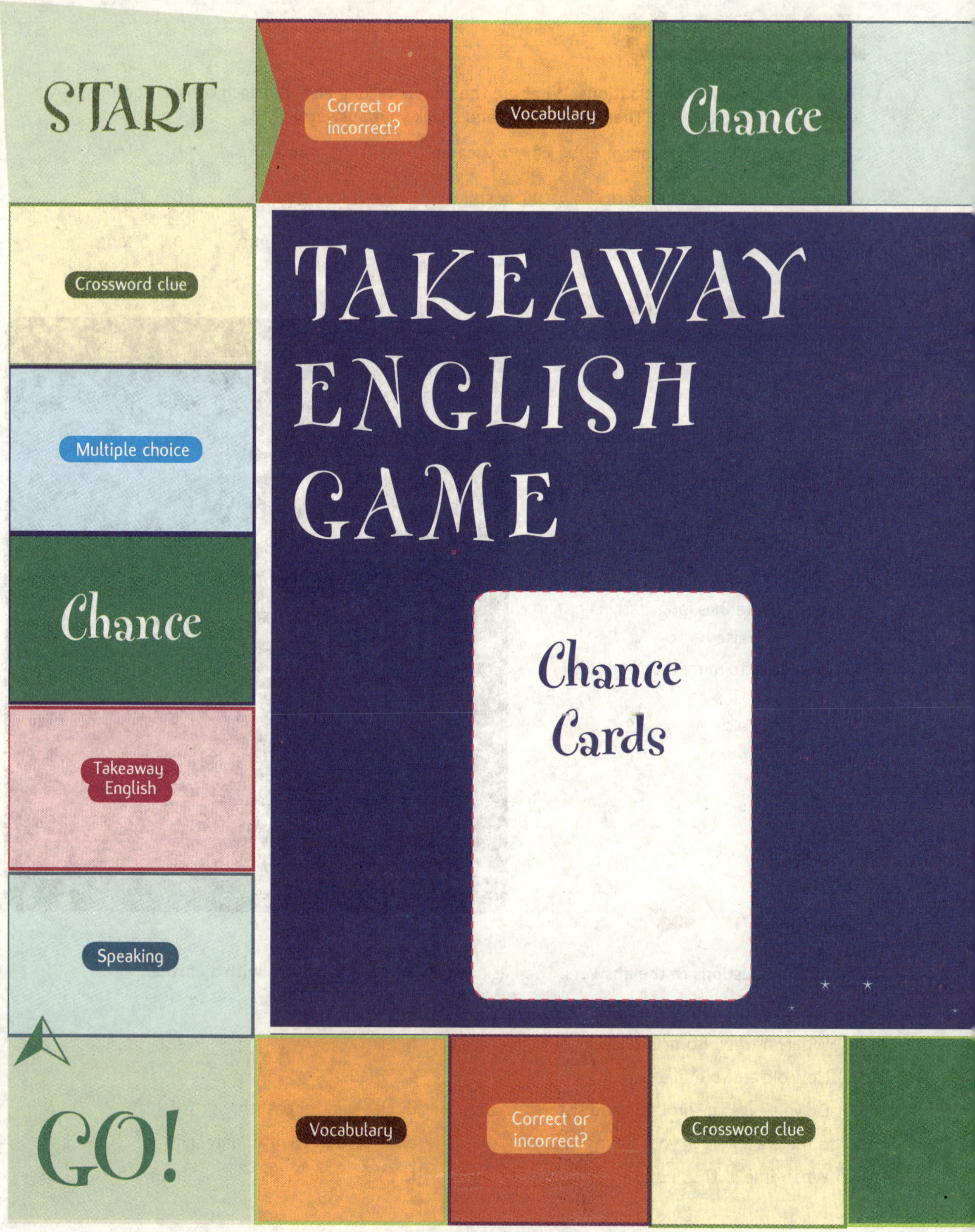

Review 1

START

Correct or incorrect? | Vocabulary | Chance

Crossword clue

Multiple choice

Chance

Takeaway English

Speaking

GO!

Vocabulary | Correct or incorrect? | Crossword clue

TAKEAWAY ENGLISH GAME

Chance Cards

Review 1

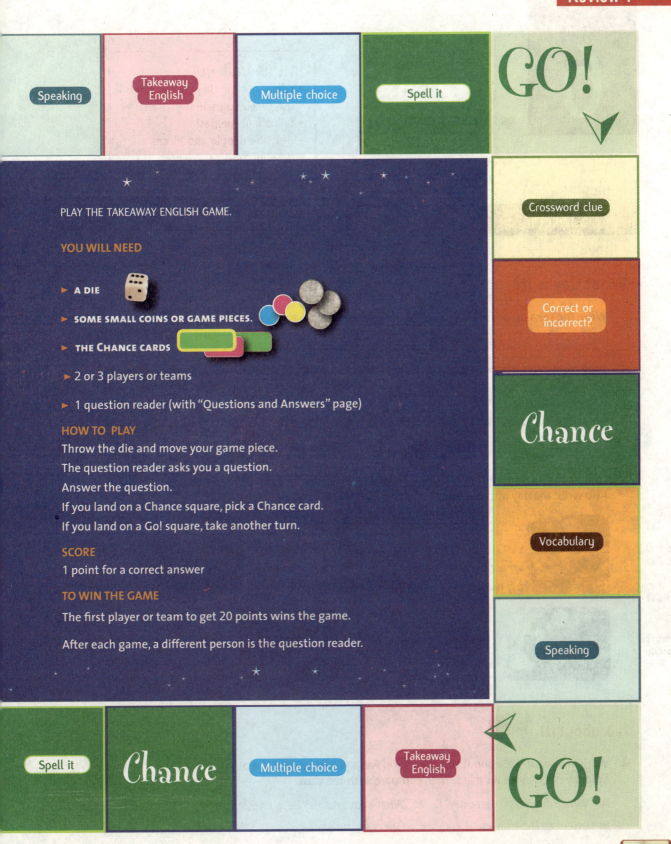

PLAY THE TAKEAWAY ENGLISH GAME.

YOU WILL NEED
- A DIE
- SOME SMALL COINS OR GAME PIECES.
- THE CHANCE CARDS
- 2 or 3 players or teams
- 1 question reader (with "Questions and Answers" page)

HOW TO PLAY
Throw the die and move your game piece.
The question reader asks you a question.
Answer the question.
If you land on a Chance square, pick a Chance card.
If you land on a Go! square, take another turn.

SCORE
1 point for a correct answer

TO WIN THE GAME
The first player or team to get 20 points wins the game.

After each game, a different person is the question reader.

6 ▶ Yesterday

In this unit you...
- talk about the days of the week
- use time expressions
- talk about the past
- describe people and places
- describe past experiences

Grammar
- simple past of the verb *be* and other verbs

START

What day is it?

1 Write the missing days of the week in the calendar. Listen to check your answers.
06_01

| ~~Tuesday~~ | Saturday | Monday | Thursday | Wednesday |

| Sunday | | Tuesday | | Friday |

2 What day is it today? What was yesterday? What was the day before yesterday?

Today is...   Yesterday was...   The day before yesterday was...

3 Look at the pictures of Lenny's week. Put the events in order from 1 to 5.
06_02 Also write the day of the week. Then listen to check your answers.

have an accident
出事故

break down
出故障

the day before
yesterday
前天

 Last night, I had an accident in my new car.

 This morning, I went to work by bus.

 1   Tuesday
Three days ago, my old car broke down.

 Yesterday afternoon, I drove my new car. I was very happy.

 The day before yesterday, I went shopping for a new car. That night, I bought one.

Talk about it!

4 Work in a group. Talk about the places you went yesterday and the day before yesterday. Make a list. Then compare with the class.

A: Where did you go yesterday?
B: I went to the movies.

A: What about the day before yesterday?
B: I went to the mall.

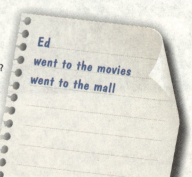
Ed
went to the movies
went to the mall

66

Unit 6

LISTENING

Where did they go yesterday?

1 Before listening Write the name of the place under each photo.

| store   office   ~~factory~~   train station   school   restaurant   cafeteria   museum |

train station
火车站

factory _____ _____ _____ _____

HELP listening

Make a mental image

As you listen, try to *imagine* what is happening. Make a picture in your mind. This helps you remember information.

make a mental image
想象一幅画面

2 Listening Listen to the interviews with Amelia, Daniel, and Tammy. Check (✔) the places they went.
06_03

请注意听力练习时的图像记忆法

	restaurant	office	train station	cafeteria	school	museum	factory	store
Amelia					✔			
Daniel								
Tammy								

3 After listening Match the people with their jobs.

1. ___ Amelia   a. teacher
2. ___ Daniel   b. factory worker
3. ___ Tammy   c. engineer

Talk about it!

4 Work with a partner. Talk about the places you went this week and the time you went.

A: Where did you go on Sunday?
B: On Sunday, I went to an electronics store at 2:30 in the afternoon.
A: What about Monday?
B: On Monday, I went to school from 9:00 to 3:15. I went to a museum at 4:00.

WORKBOOK PAGE 42

Unit 6

VOCABULARY

Where did you go? How was it?

1 Complete the descriptions of where people went on Saturday. Then listen to check your answers.

> beautiful   ~~crowded~~   delicious   excited   happy   bored   terrible   sad

food court
(商场内)美食区

1. We went to a *concert*. It was very ___crowded___.

2. Jim and Beth went to *the movies*. Beth was _____ and Jim was _____.

3. They went to the *food court* in the *mall*. The cake was _____.

4. We went to Pearl's birthday *party*. She was _____ and _____.

5. I went to a *wedding*. The bride was _____.

6. I had the worst day! I didn't do anything. It was a _____ day.

2 Work with a partner. Describe places in your town/school or people you know. Your partner guesses who/what you are describing.

A: It's in the school. It's crowded at noon. The food is *not* delicious.
B: It's the cafeteria!

ENGLISH express

the worst = very bad
the best = very good

请注意最高级表示程度的用法

Talk about it!

3 Work with a group. Talk about places you went yesterday, the day before yesterday, and two days ago. Answer the question *How was it?*.

A: Yesterday, I went to the electronics store.
B: How was it?
A: I bought a new phone. I was happy. What about you?
B: Yesterday, I...

Unit 6

GRAMMAR

Simple past

ALSO GO TO
Grammar Takeaway
PAGE 199

1 Read the email. Write the verb forms in the chart. Then complete the rule.

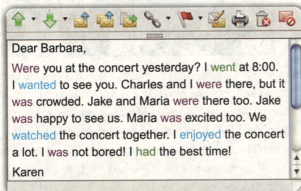

Dear Barbara,

Were you at the concert yesterday? I went at 8:00. I wanted to see you. Charles and I were there, but it was crowded. Jake and Maria were there too. Jake was happy to see us. Maria was excited too. We watched the concert together. I enjoyed the concert a lot. I was not bored! I had the best time!

Karen

be		regular verbs	
I _____		want: I _____	
you _____		watch: we _____	
he _____		enjoy: I _____	
she _____		**irregular verbs**	
it _____		go: I _____	
we _____		have: I _____	
they _____			

watch the concert
观看演唱会

Rule: For regular verbs, add _____ .

be	affirmative	I was at a wedding.	negative	I wasn't at the museum.
	question	Were you at the concert?	answer	Yes, I was. / No, I wasn't.
other verbs	affirmative	I went to the museum.	negative	Kathy didn't go to the museum.
	question	Did Lee enjoy the party?	answer	Yes, he did. / No, he didn't.

2 Complete the conversation about Sam's vacation. Write the verbs in the simple past. Then listen and check.

Gina: How ___was___ (1. be) your vacation?

Sam: We _____ (2. have) the best time!

Gina: Where _____ (3. you / go)?

Sam: Let's see... We _____ (4. go) to Florence and Venice.

Gina: Wonderful! _____ (5. you / go) to any museums?

Sam: Yes, we did. We _____ (6. go) to lots of museums.

Gina: _____ (7. you / eat) Italian food?

Sam: Well, of course! We _____ (8. eat) it every day!

Gina: Which city _____ (9. you / like) best?

Sam: I _____ (10. like) Venice. We _____ (11. take) a boat ride in the canals.

Florence
弗罗伦萨
Venice
威尼斯

Italian food
意大利菜

take a boat ride
乘船游玩

Talk about it!

3 Work with a partner. Ask your partner questions about a vacation he/she took in the past. Use exercise 2 as a model. Then tell the class about your partner's vacation.

Unit 6

READING

Blogs about a special day

1 Before reading Read about blogs. Then circle the best answer to complete each sentence below.

> A **blog** is a type of website, usually written by one person. Some blogs talk about one topic. Others are like a diary, where a person talks about his/her life. Many blogs have both stories and pictures.

1. You find blogs _____ .
   a. on the Internet
   b. in a notebook

2. People use blogs to _____ .
   a. talk about life
   b. keep secrets

2 Reading 06_06 Read the two blogs. Circle the best picture for each one.

3 Reading 06_06 Read the blogs again. Check (✓) the correct name.

Kauai 考艾岛 (美夏威夷群岛之一)
beauty salon 美容院
fix my hair 做头发
wedding gown 婚纱
be related to 与……相关
water polo 水球运动

My Life   by sheryl H.

May 5th

 A    B

Yesterday, I got up early. I was so excited. I had breakfast in the garden of the hotel. It was a special day. I was in Hawaii, on an island called Kauai. It was my wedding day! After breakfast, I got ready. I went to the beauty salon to fix my hair. I put on my wedding gown. Hank called me at 11:00. "Are you ready?" he asked. "Of course I am," I said. "I love you," he said. At noon, Hank and I got married. We got married on the beach. It was beautiful. Our friends and family were there. I was so happy. The photographer took lots of pictures. After lunch, we went for a boat ride. It was the best day of my life!

HELP reading

Guess meaning from context
Guess the meaning of a new word by looking at the words around it. These words are usually related to the new word. They can help you understand.

请注意阅读过程中根据上下文猜词义的方法

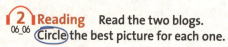

	Sheryl	Jamal	Both
1. Who took a bus to the city?		✓	
2. Who had breakfast in a garden?			
3. Who got up early?			
4. Who went to the beauty salon?			
5. Who was excited?			
6. Who got married?			
7. Who played in the water polo final?			
8. Who was happy?			

Unit 6

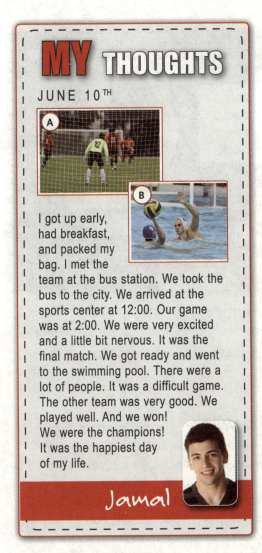

MY THOUGHTS

JUNE 10TH

I got up early, had breakfast, and packed my bag. I met the team at the bus station. We took the bus to the city. We arrived at the sports center at 12:00. Our game was at 2:00. We were very excited and a little bit nervous. It was the final match. We got ready and went to the swimming pool. There were a lot of people. It was a difficult game. The other team was very good. We played well. And we won! We were the champions! It was the happiest day of my life.

Jamal

4 After reading Answer the questions. Then compare your answers with a partner.

1. What time did Sheryl and Hank get married?
2. Where is Kauai?
3. What is a *photographer*?
4. Who was at the wedding?
5. How did Jamal get to the game?
6. What is a *team*?
7. What time was the game?

Talk about it!

5 Work with a partner. Make a list of special days. Choose a special day for you and make notes. Then ask and answer questions.

A: What was the special day?
B: It was the day I went to the Alexis Steel concert.
A: When was it?
B: Two years ago. It was in the summer.
A: What happened?

the final match
决赛

1. first day of school
2. first day at a new job
3. playing in a sports game
4. a birthday
5. going to a concert

PROJECT

Work with a partner. Decide on a topic that interests you (for example, travel, soccer, cooking, etc.). Do an Internet search for blogs about that topic. Choose a blog that you like. Find answers to these questions.

- What is the title of the blog?
- Who is the author?
- What is the topic of the blog?
- What kind of information can you learn in the blog?
- How many people follow the blog?

Report to the class about the blog you chose.

Our Blog

Unit 6

CULTURE

The names of the days of the week

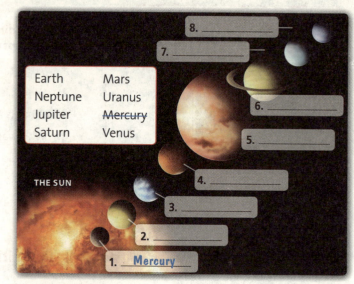

1 Before reading Write the names of the eight planets. Listen to check your answers.

Earth Mars
Neptune Uranus
Jupiter ~~Mercury~~
Saturn Venus

2 Before reading What do you think? Circle *True* or *False* for each statement.

1. In all languages, the names of the days of the week are related to planets. True False
2. In some countries, Monday is the first day of the week. True False
3. Saturday and Sunday are weekend days everywhere in the world. True False

3 Reading Now read the information to check your guesses.

--- **The days of the week** ---

In many languages, the names of the days of the week come from numbers or planets. In Chinese, for example, the days of the week are numbers. Monday is called *day one*. In Spanish, many of the days of the week have the names of planets. Monday is *lunes*, which comes from the word for *moon*. Tuesday is *martes*, which comes from the planet Mars. Wednesday is *miercoles*, which comes from the planet Mercury. Thursday is *jueves*, which comes from the planet Jupiter. Finally, Friday is *viernes*, which comes from the planet Venus. In English, Sunday is from the sun, Monday from the moon, and Saturday from the planet Saturn. In Japanese and Korean, the names of days are also associated with planets and different elements like fire or water.

In some parts of the world, like the United States and Canada, Sunday is the first day of the week. In other parts of the world, Monday is the first day of the week. In many countries, most people don't work on Saturday and Sunday, the weekend. They are days of rest and relaxation. Monday to Friday are called the weekdays. In some Muslim countries, Friday and Saturday are days of rest. In Iran, the weekend is only one day, Friday, and the week starts on Saturday. Other Muslim countries have weekends on Thursday and Friday.

Spanish 西班牙语

be associated with 与……相关联

Muslim countries 穆斯林国家
Iran 伊朗

Casual Friday 星期五便装日

vote for 投票(选举)

4 After reading Look at the map on page 73. Match the two parts of the sentences.

1. Casual Friday __d__
2. Monday and Friday ___
3. In Thailand, green is ___
4. People vote for politicians ___
5. Tuesday the 13th is ___

a. on Saturday in New Zealand.
b. bad luck in Spain.
c. are the two most popular days to *not* go to work.
d. is a day when you can dress informally at work.
e. the color for Wednesday.

72

Unit 6

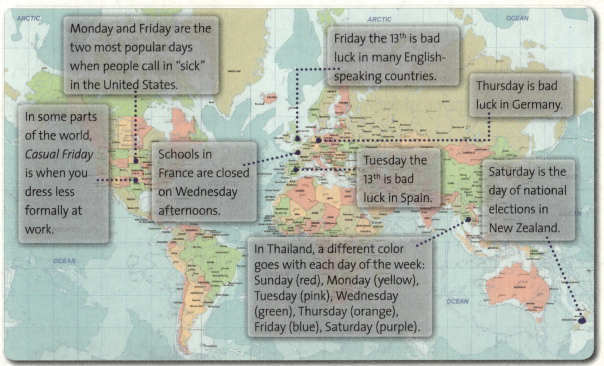

call in "sick"
打电话请病假

national elections
全国大选

Talk about it!

5 Work with a partner. Ask and answer the questions.

1. What is the first day of the week in your country? What are the weekend days?
2. On what days do you have good or bad luck in your culture?
3. People say TGIF (thank goodness it's Friday) in English because they are happy it's Friday. Do you have any expressions about the days of the week in your language?

PRONUNCIATION

Simple past *ed* ending

1 The simple past *ed* ending has three sounds. Listen and repeat.

/d/	/t/	/ɪd/
I studied last night.	He watched TV yesterday.	The concert started at 6:00.

2 Listen and write the words you hear in the chart. Then practice saying the words.

/d/	/t/	/ɪd/
		started

73

Unit 6

CONVERSATION

Describing past experiences

Pirates of the Caribbean
《加勒比海盗》
（电影名）

1 Listen to the conversation between Lori and Kate. How was Kate's weekend? How was Lori's weekend?

Lori: Hey, Kate. How was your weekend?
Kate: It was OK.
Lori: What did you do?
Kate: I had a lot of work to do, so I stayed home. But I also saw a pretty good movie on TV last night.
Lori: Really? What movie?
Kate: You know... the one with Tom Reed and Pam Gold... *A Long Ago Love*...
Lori: You liked that movie? I thought it was awful!
Kate: It's true that the acting was only so-so, but I love romantic movies.

romantic movie
爱情片

Lori: I don't. I get bored when I watch romantic movies.
Kate: So, what about you? How was your weekend?
Lori: Oh, it was fantastic! I went to a concert with Leo on Saturday, and I went to the beach on Sunday.
Kate: That sounds like fun!

CONVERSATION STRATEGY

Use conversation fillers

Use you know... when you think the other person knows what you are talking about.

What's the name of that actor? You know... the one in *Pirates of the Caribbean*...

请注意口语中you know的用法

2 Write the red words from exercise 1 below the faces.

OK

Talk about it!

3 Work with a partner. Talk about last weekend. Use exercise 1 as a model. Be sure to use the words from exercise 2.

Tell me more!

Visit the Takeaway English Online Learning Center at http://olcs.mcgraw-hill-education.com/takeaway/

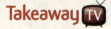 Check out the *Takeaway TV* video.

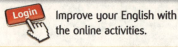 Improve your English with the online activities.

Unit 6

WRITING

Writing a description of a special day

1 Before writing / Writing model Complete the description of Alba's special day.

| met | got ready | ~~Last year~~ | station | went |
| crowded | had | fantastic | walked | woke up |

HELP writing

Summarize the main idea
At the end of your paragraph, write a concluding sentence. This sentence summarizes your main idea.

请注意总结句的写法

The Alexis Steel Concert

I love the singer Alexis Steel. (1) __Last year__ I went to see her concert. That morning, I (2) _____ early. I was excited. I had breakfast and went to work. After work, I went home and I (3) _____ for the concert. Then I (4) _____ Elena at the (5) _____. We took the train to the city. In the city, we (6) _____ to the stadium. There were lots of people. It was very (7) _____. The concert was (8) _____! Elena and I sang all the songs. Finally, when the concert finished, we (9) _____ to a café. We (10) _____ the best time. It was a very special day!

stadium
体育场

2 Planning your writing Now write about a special day. You can use the same one you talked about on page 71, exercise 5, or choose a new one. Take notes in the chart.

What was the special day?	
When was it?	
Who were you with?	
What happened?	
How did you feel?	

3 Writing Write about your special day. Illustrate your writing with a photo or drawing and present it to the class.

Unit 6

TEST

Test-taking strategy

Choose the correct verb tense   For some test questions it is important to pay attention to the verb tense. Is the verb in the present tense? Or is it in the past tense?

Use these steps to help you choose the answer with the correct verb tense.

1. Look for words or phrases that show the verb tense. For example: *yesterday* and *last week* indicate past tense; *usually* and *every day* indicate present tense.
2. What is the tense of the verbs in the complete sentence?
3. Do you see the auxiliary verb *do*? How is it used?
4. Is the incomplete sentence affirmative or negative? Or is it a question?
5. Pay attention to irregular verbs.

Example
Choose the correct answer.

1. **Pam:** Where did you go last week?
   Sue: I _____ to my grandmother's house.

   ~~A.~~ was   This is the past tense of *be*, not *go*.
   B. went   This is the correct answer. The phrase *last week* indicates past tense.
   ~~C.~~ am   This is the present tense of *be*.
   ~~D.~~ go   This is the present tense of *go*, not the past tense.

PRACTICE

Choose the correct answer. Mark the letter on the Answer Sheet.

1. I was tired yesterday.
   I ___ go to the party.
   A. wasn't
   B. don't
   C. didn't
   D. am

2. Sam ___ to work at 8:00 every morning.
   A. went
   B. go
   C. goes
   D. is

3. ___ you walk or drive to school every day?
   A. Are
   B. Do
   C. Did
   D. Was

4. Did you ___ to the concert last night?
   A. go
   B. went
   C. goes
   D. going

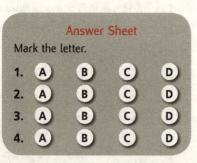

UNIT SUMMARY

Nouns
blog
cafeteria
calendar
concert
day
factory
food court
mall
museum
office
party
past
planet
restaurant
school
store
today
train station
wedding
week
yesterday

Nouns—Days of the week
Sunday
Monday
Tuesday
Wednesday
Thursday
Friday
Saturday

Adjectives
awful
beautiful
bored
crowded
delicious
excited
fantastic
happy
OK
pretty good
sad
so-so
terrible

Time expressions
the day before yesterday
last night
this morning
three days ago
yesterday afternoon

Expressions
How was it?
the best
the worst
What day is it?
You know...

7 ▸ What are you doing?

In this unit you...
- talk about the weather
- talk about what you are doing right now
- invite and accept or not accept invitations

Grammar
- present continuous

Temperature scales
温度计
Fahrenheit
华氏度
Celsius
摄氏度

START

ENGLISH express

Temperature scales
F = Fahrenheit
C = Celsius

请注意两种温度的表达法

What's the weather like?

1 What's the temperature? What's the weather? Write the descriptions. Then listen and check.
07_01

It's warm.
It's freezing.
It's cold.
~~It's hot.~~
It's cool.

1. It's 90 degrees. It's hot.
2. _____
3. _____
4. _____
5. _____

2 Match the pictures to the words. Then listen and check.
07_02

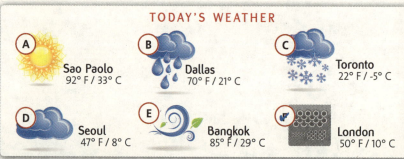

TODAY'S WEATHER

A Sao Paolo 92° F / 33° C
B Dallas 70° F / 21° C
C Toronto 22° F / -5° C
D Seoul 47° F / 8° C
E Bangkok 85° F / 29° C
F London 50° F / 10° C

1. _F_ It's foggy.
2. ____ It's cloudy.
3. ____ It's sunny.
4. ____ It's windy.
5. ____ It's raining.
6. ____ It's snowing.

Talk about it!

3 Look at the weather chart in exercise 2. Ask and answer questions about the weather and temperature in the cities. Then ask about your city.

A: What's the weather like in London?
B: It's cool and foggy.

A: What's the temperature?
B: It's 50 degrees Fahrenheit. That's 10 degrees Celsius.

ENGLISH express

Windy, cloudy, sunny, and *foggy* are adjectives. *Raining* and *snowing* are verbs.

请注意描述天气的词及词性

Unit 7

LISTENING

HELP listening
Preview the questions
Read the exercise questions before you listen. This will tell you what specific information to listen for.
请注意听力练习前读题

Calling home

1 Before listening When do people call home? What do they talk about?

call home
打电话回家

2 Listening Listen to a phone conversation between Kylie and her brother Ben.
07_03 Circle the correct answers.

1. Kylie is in...   2. Ben is in...
   a. San Jose, Costa Rica   a. San Jose, Costa Rica
   b. Brisbane, Australia   b. Brisbane, Australia

San Jose
圣约瑟(首都)
Costa Rica
哥斯达黎加
Brisbane
布里斯班
(澳大利亚东部城市)

3 Listening Listen again and circle *True* or *False* for each statement.
07_03 Then compare your answers with a partner.

1. Kylie is at a restaurant.   True   **False**
2. It's 1:00 p.m. in San Jose.   True   False
3. It's 5:00 p.m. in Brisbane.   True   False
4. Kylie is studying English.   True   False
5. It isn't raining in Brisbane.   True   False
6. Ben is chatting with his new girlfriend.   True   False
7. Melanie is teaching English in Mexico.   True   False
8. It's not really hot in San Jose.   True   False

San Jose, Costa Rica
Brisbane, Australia

chat with sb.
与某人聊天

4 After listening Match the sentences from the conversation to their meanings.

1. _b_ How's it going?   a. I can hear a sound similar to rain.
2. ___ I'm just hanging out.   b. How are you?
3. ___ It sounds like it's raining. c. I'm writing something on my computer.
4. ___ I'm typing.   d. I'm not doing anything special.

hang out
闲逛

Talk about it!

5 Work with a partner. You are studying in another country. Role-play a phone call home. Use the expressions in exercise 4.

WORKBOOK PAGE 49

79

Unit 7

VOCABULARY

Activities

1 What are your favorite activities? Number these activities from 1 (the activity you like best) to 6.

___ study   ___ go to the movies   ___ listen to music
___ watch TV   ___ talk on the phone   ___ shop

talk on the phone
煲电话粥

2 Kylie is thinking about what her family is doing. Match the sentences to the pictures. Then listen to check your answers.

1. _E_ Ali, her sister, is sitting on a train.
2. ___ Her father is wearing an apron and cooking dinner.
3. ___ Ben is chatting with his girlfriend.
4. ___ Her mother is lying on the sofa and watching TV.
5. ___ Tim, her little brother, is walking home from school.

wear an apron
系围裙
cook dinner
做晚餐
lie on the sofa
躺在沙发上

Other activities

Bill is riding a bike.

Sue is running.

Pam is driving a car.

3 Some activities are good for sunny days. Other activities are good for rainy days. Write the activities from exercises 1 and 2 in the chart.

sunny day activities	rainy day activities
walking to school	going to the movies

Talk about it!

4 Work with a partner. Compare your charts for exercise 3. Then decide on your favorite sunny day activities and your favorite rainy day activities.

As a class, decide on the best sunny day activity and the best rainy day activity.

WORKBOOK PAGE 50

Unit 7

GRAMMAR

Present continuous

1 Listen to the conversation. The verbs in red are in the present continuous.

A: What are you doing?
B: I'm talking on the phone with you.
A: What are Liz and Jim doing?
B: They're watching TV. Liz is lying on the sofa and Jim is sitting on the chair.

sit on the chair
坐在椅子上

Now complete the rules. Circle the correct words.

Rules:
1. We use the present continuous to talk about something that is happening in the past / as a routine / now.
2. To form the present continuous, we use the verb do / be / go with the main verb.
3. We add ed / s / ing to the end of the main verb.

Spelling of -ing form

walk	→	walking
do	→	doing
write	→	writing
sit	→	sitting

as a routine
作为常规

affirmative	negative	question
I'm talking with Jasmine.	She's not watching TV tonight.	What are you doing?

2 Complete the conversation. Write the verbs in the present continuous. Then listen to check your answers.

A: Hey, Ed. Where are you?
B: Hi, Steve. I'm at the beach.
A: What ___are you doing___ (1. you / do)?
B: I _____ (2. walk) by the water.
A: Who are you with?
B: I'm with Tina, Matt, and Kelly. Matt and Kelly _____ (3. play) volleyball. Tina _____ (4. play / not). She _____ (5. talk) on the phone. She _____ (6. sit) on a beach chair.
A: Who _____ to? (7. she / talk)
B: Her boyfriend, I think. She _____ (8. smile).

at the beach
在海滩上

Some places	Some activities
at a concert	listening to music
in the mountains	skiing
at home	playing video games
at the beach	sitting in the sun
in China	visiting my family

sit in the sun
晒太阳

Talk about it!

3 Imagine that your partner calls you on the phone. You are at your favorite place. Answer these questions.

1. Where are you? — I'm at the mall.
2. What are you doing? — I'm shopping.
3. What's the weather like? — It's sunny.
4. Who are you with? — I am with my friends.

Unit 7

READING

An email home

1 Before reading Tida is a student from Thailand. Look at the pictures and answer the questions.

1. Where do you think Tida is?
2. What's the weather like?
3. What do you think she's doing there?
4. What do you think she does in her free time?

2 Reading Read Tida's email and check your guesses to exercise 1.

the Empire State Building
帝国大厦
(美国纽约市)
high up
在高处
the Museum of Modern Art
现代艺术博物馆
lunch break
午休

Hi Phim,

How are you? I'm having fun here, and I'm learning lots of English. There are so many places to visit and things to do. New York is a fantastic city and the people are great. On Saturday, we went to the top of the Empire State Building. It was <u>amazing</u> to be so high up. The view was great! Tomorrow there's a visit to the Museum of Modern Art.

My English class is very intensive! I don't have much free time, because we have six hours of class every day and we have homework every night. <u>Right now</u> I am on my lunch break. I am eating a sandwich and writing to you. The other students in the course are nice, but I <u>miss</u> my friends, like you, of course! The weather here isn't very good. It's raining right now. Everyone says that the food here is great, but <u>actually</u> I miss food from home. My time here is going really quickly. I only have three more weeks before I come home. Write and tell me what everyone is doing. <u>See you soon</u>.

Love,

Tida

Unit 7

3 Reading Read Tida's email again. Then read the sentences below. Circle the correct answers.
07_07

1. The email is to her **friend** / father.
2. Tida is studying **English** / Thai.
3. Tida thinks New York is a terrible / **nice** city.
4. She has / **doesn't have** a lot of free time.
5. She probably eats Thai / **American** food every day in New York.
6. Right now, it's **raining** / cloudy in New York.
7. She has three more **weeks** / months in New York.

HELP reading

Make an inference
The answers to some questions cannot be found in the text. For these questions, use logic (make an inference) to figure out the answer.

请注意运用逻辑推理解答问题

4 After reading Write the underlined words in the email next to the definitions.

1. at the present time ___right now___
2. in fact; really _____
3. goodbye _____
4. wonderful; very great _____
5. feel sad because a person or thing isn't with you _____

Talk about it!

5 Work with a partner. Talk about studying in a different country. Where would you go? What would you do? What would you miss? Use this conversation as a model.

A: Do you want to study in another country?
B: Yes, I do.
A: Where do you want to study?
B: I want to study in...
A: Why do you want to study in...
B: Because I...

A: What would you do there?
B: I would...
A: What would you miss?
B: I'd miss my family, the food, my cat...

ENGLISH express

We use **would** + verb to talk about situations we imagine.
I **would miss** my friends and my car. **Would** you **miss** your family? Yes, I **would**.

请注意在表达设想的情景时 would 的用法

PROJECT

Work in a group. Make a list of countries you can visit to study English.
Then choose one place to research on the Internet. Choose a city and a school.
Then make a poster with information about the school and the experience of studying there. Answer these questions:

1. What is the name of the school?
2. Where is the school?
3. Where do students live?
4. How many hours a week do students have classes?
5. How much does it cost to study there?
6. What activities can students do?

Present your poster to the class. The class chooses the favorite country and school.

make a poster
做海报

have classes
上课

Unit 7

SONG

Missing you

1 Before listening How do you feel when you miss someone? What do you do?

2 Before listening Match the words that go together. Use a dictionary if necessary.

and drink	and fall	and go
and stand	and sleep	~~and write~~
and turn	and listen	

1. read _and write_
2. wake _____
3. come _____
4. eat _____
5. speak _____
6. rise _____
7. sit _____
8. twist _____

3 Listening Listen to the song. Number the verses (1–6) in the order you hear them.
07_08

4 Listening Listen again. Circle the main idea.
07_08

A. The singer is very busy and wants to be with a special person.

B. The singer is not very busy and wants to be with a special person.

C. The singer is very busy and doesn't want to be with a special person.

pajamas
睡衣
the Bahamas
巴哈马群岛

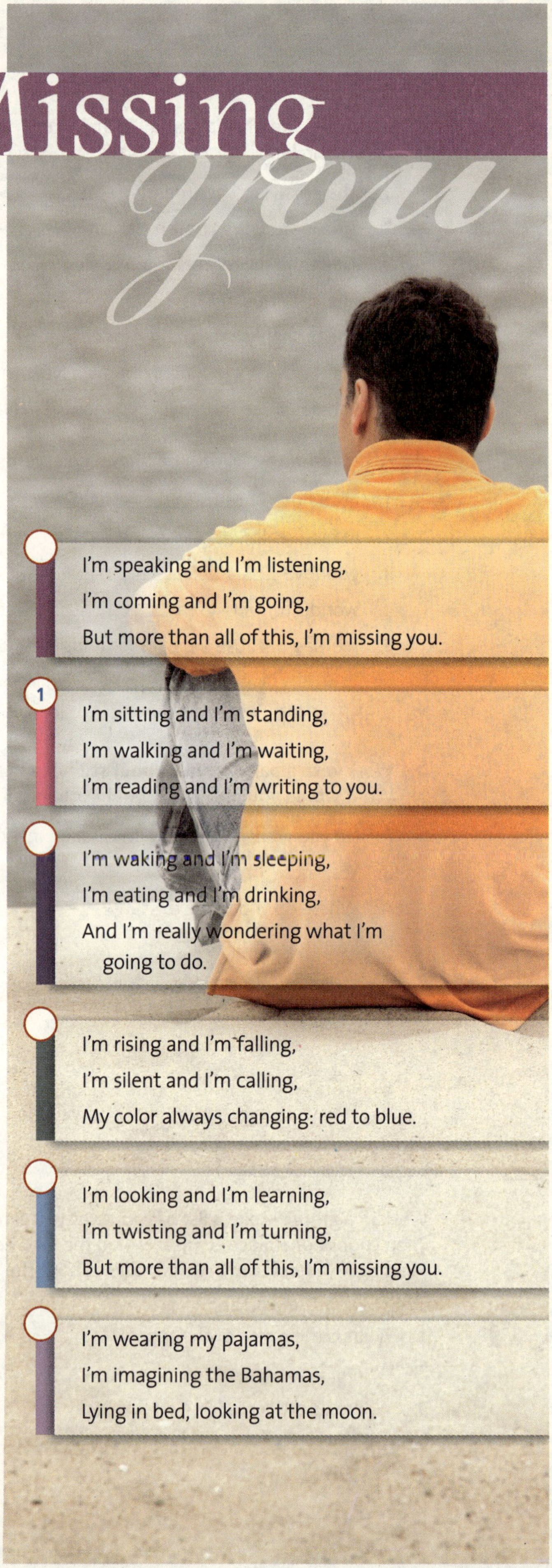

Missing you

I'm speaking and I'm listening,
I'm coming and I'm going,
But more than all of this, I'm missing you.

1
I'm sitting and I'm standing,
I'm walking and I'm waiting,
I'm reading and I'm writing to you.

I'm waking and I'm sleeping,
I'm eating and I'm drinking,
And I'm really wondering what I'm going to do.

I'm rising and I'm falling,
I'm silent and I'm calling,
My color always changing: red to blue.

I'm looking and I'm learning,
I'm twisting and I'm turning,
But more than all of this, I'm missing you.

I'm wearing my pajamas,
I'm imagining the Bahamas,
Lying in bed, looking at the moon.

Unit 7

5 After listening Look at the pictures below. Which one do you think is the singer of the song? Circle your answer. Explain why you chose this picture.

A

B

C

Talk about it!

6 Work with a partner. Tell your partner about a time when you missed someone or something. Answer the questions.

- When was it?
- Who/What did you miss?
- Where were you?
- Where was the other person/thing?
- How did you feel?
- What did you do?

PRONUNCIATION

Connecting words

1 (07_09) We connect words when they are next to each other and have the same sounds. When there's also a contraction, three words can sound like one. Listen.

I am missing you. = I'm missing you.   You are reading. = You're reading.

She is singing. = She's singing.   They are running. = They're running.

2 (07_10) Listen and write the missing words. Then practice saying the sentences.

1. <u>　She's sitting　</u> in the first row.
2. _____ to New York.
3. _____ our bikes.
4. _____ in line.
5. _____ an email.
6. _____ him at 3:00.

the first row
第一排

in line
成一直线; 有秩序

Unit 7

CONVERSATION

Inviting and accepting or not accepting an invitation

1 What are some things that people invite you to do? When do you accept? When don't you accept?

2 Listen to people invite friends to do something.
07_11

① A: Hey, Lily. Let's eat at the outdoor café today.
   B: Sure! Great idea! It's warm and sunny.

② A: Hey, Tara. How about going for a walk?
   B: Sorry, but I'm reading a good book right now.

③ A: Hey, Bob. Would you like to come to the movies with me?
   B: Thanks, but I'm studying for an exam.

> **CONVERSATION STRATEGY**
>
> **Be polite**
> When you don't accept an invitation, it is not polite to just say "no." Thank the person first. You can also begin with Sorry, I'm sorry, or I'm afraid I can't.
>
> 请注意如何礼貌地拒绝邀请

outdoor café
户外咖啡馆
accept an invitation
接受邀请

3 Write the phrases in red from exercise 2 in the chart.

inviting	accepting	not accepting

Talk about it!

make invitations
发出邀请

4 Practice making invitations with a partner. Accept or don't accept your partner's invitations.

A: Would you like to meet my family?
B: Yes. Great idea! How about tomorrow?

A: How about going to the mall?
B: Sorry, but I have a class now.

Tell me more!

Visit the Takeaway English Online Learning Center at http://olcs.mcgraw-hill-education.com/takeaway/

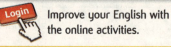

Unit 7

WRITING

Writing an email home

1 Before writing / Writing model Read the email from Kylie to her mother. Answer the questions.

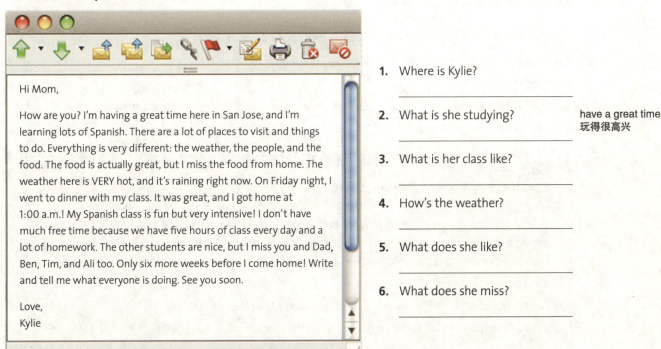

Hi Mom,

How are you? I'm having a great time here in San Jose, and I'm learning lots of Spanish. There are a lot of places to visit and things to do. Everything is very different: the weather, the people, and the food. The food is actually great, but I miss the food from home. The weather here is VERY hot, and it's raining right now. On Friday night, I went to dinner with my class. It was great, and I got home at 1:00 a.m.! My Spanish class is fun but very intensive! I don't have much free time because we have five hours of class every day and a lot of homework. The other students are nice, but I miss you and Dad, Ben, Tim, and Ali too. Only six more weeks before I come home! Write and tell me what everyone is doing. See you soon.

Love,
Kylie

1. Where is Kylie?
2. What is she studying?
3. What is her class like?
4. How's the weather?
5. What does she like?
6. What does she miss?

have a great time
玩得很高兴

2 Planning your writing Imagine you are studying in another country. Complete the chart with ideas for your writing.

Where are you?	
Who are you writing to?	
Where is he/she?	
What are you doing?	
How's the weather?	
What things do you like/not like?	
What do you miss?	

HELP writing

Use appropriate letter closings

When you say goodbye at the end of an email or letter, write Love or Hugs if the letter is to a family member or close friend. Write Sincerely, Best wishes, or Best if the letter is to someone you don't know well.

请注意写信对象不同应使用不同的结束语

3 Writing Write an email to a family member or a friend. Use the information in exercises 1 and 2 to help you.

Unit 7

TEST

Test-taking strategy

Answer reading comprehension questions Some tests have a reading passage and reading comprehension questions. The questions ask about the main idea and details.

Use these steps to help you answer reading comprehension questions.

1. Read the passage quickly for general understanding.
2. Read the questions.
3. Then reread the passage. Look for answers to the questions. Underline the information.
4. Time is limited. Be careful with your time in a reading comprehension test.

Example
Read the paragraph and answer the questions.
I like my Korean class, but it's very intensive! I have no free time. We have five hours of class every day and we have homework every night. Right now I'm having my lunch. I'm eating a sandwich and writing to you. I like the other students in the class, but I miss my friends. How are Hank, Rosa, Abby, Dan, Kim, Sun, Mike, Eric, and Tony?

1. The writer has no _____ .

   ~~A.~~ homework   The writer says, "we have homework every night."

   B. free time   This is the correct answer. The writer says, "I have no free time."

   ~~C.~~ friends   The writer says, "I miss my friends" and writes eight names.

PRACTICE

Answer more comprehension questions about the *Example* reading passage. Choose the correct answer. Mark the letter on the Answer Sheet.

1. What is the writer doing now?

   A. studying   B. doing homework   C. eating and writing

2. The writer has _____ hours of class every day.

   A. five   B. much   C. seven

3. The writer misses his _____ .

   A. students   B. friends   C. homework

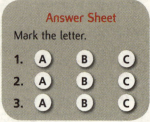

UNIT SUMMARY

Unit 7

Nouns
apron
beach
Celsius (C)
degree
Fahrenheit (F)
mountain
temperature
weather

Adjective
amazing

Verbs and verb phrases
chat
cook
drink
drive
fall
hang out
lie
miss
play video games
ride
rise
run
sit
sit in the sun
ski
sleep
stand
turn
twist
type
visit
walk
watch
wear

Adverb
actually

Weather expressions
It's cloudy.
It's cold.
It's cool.
It's foggy.
It's freezing.
It's hot.
It's raining.
It's snowing.
It's sunny.
It's warm.
It's windy.
What's the weather like?

Expressions
How's it going?
right now
See you soon.

Inviting and accepting/ not accepting an invitation
Great idea!
How about (verb)ing…
I'm afraid I can't.
I'm sorry.
Let's…
Sorry, but…
Sorry.
Sure!
Thanks, but…
Would you like to…

Letter closings
Best
Best wishes
Hugs
Love
Sincerely

8 ▶ I'm taking a trip

In this unit you...
- talk about trips
- talk about staying at a hotel
- identify transportation
- make plans to meet up
- ask for and give travel suggestions

Grammar
- simple present and present continuous for the future

START

Staying at a hotel

take a trip
去旅行

1 Where do you stay when you take a trip? When do you stay in a hotel? What are the names of some good hotels?

2 Write the words for hotel facilities under the pictures. Then listen and check.
08_01

business center
商务中心
fitness center
健身中心
front desk
前台

business center	fitness center
gift shop	(guest) room
conference center	front desk
~~lobby~~	swimming pool

3 Which hotel facilities do these people use?
1. a family with children
2. a businessperson
3. a person who likes sports

Talk about it!

4 Make a list of four hotel facilities that are important to you. Put them in order from 1 to 4 (1 = very important). Explain your answer to a partner.

A: I have <u>business center</u> as number 1. I need to use a computer, and I don't like to bring mine with me.

B: I have <u>swimming pool</u> as number 1. I like to swim every day.

hotel facilities
饭店设施

As a class, decide on the three most important hotel facilities.

1. _lobby_   2. _____

3. _____   4. _____

5. _____   6. _____

7. _____   8. _____

Unit 8

LISTENING

Let's meet up!

1 Before listening Look at the pictures. Who are the women? What are they talking about?

2 Listening Listen to Kelly and Angie's conversation. Check your guesses to exercise 1.
08_02

3 Listening Listen to the conversation again. Circle the words to complete the sentences.
08_02

1. The women are talking about the past / **future**.
2. Kelly knows / doesn't know the hotel.
3. The wedding is at 12 p.m. / 3 p.m.
4. Kelly's tennis class ends at 12 p.m. / 2 p.m.
5. Angie is busy / free on Friday night.
6. The women are meeting on Friday / Saturday / Sunday.

HELP listening

Take notes
When you listen, take notes. Don't write sentences. Write only the important information. Use your notes to help you answer questions.

请注意听录音时学会做笔记

4 After listening Answer the questions about the conversation. Then compare your answers with a partner.

1. Where does Kelly live? Where does Angie live?
2. When is Angie coming to Boston?
3. Why is Angie coming to Boston?
4. When is Angie leaving Boston?

Talk about it!

5 Work with a partner. Tell your partner about a future trip. Ask and answer the questions.

1. Where are you going?   I'm going to China.
2. When are you going?   I'm going in February.
3. Where are you staying?   I'm staying at the Central Hotel.
4. Why are you going?   I'm visiting my family.

the Central Hotel
中央酒店

WORKBOOK PAGE 56

91

Unit 8

VOCABULARY

What's the best way to get downtown?

1 What forms of transportation do you use? Put them in order: 1 = I use this the most; 6 = I use this the least. Compare with a partner.

___ bus   ___ car   ___ airplane   ___ subway   ___ taxi   ___ train

2 Write the transportation places under the pictures. Then listen and check.

rental car company
租车公司
subway station
地铁站
taxi stand
出租车站

airport   bus stop   rental car company   subway station   ~~taxi stand~~   train station

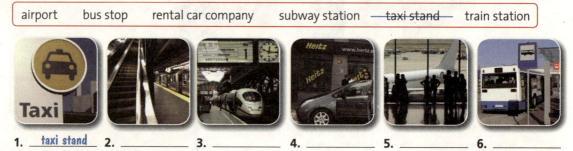

1. _taxi stand_   2. _____   3. _____   4. _____   5. _____   6. _____

3 Complete the travel information. Check your answers with a partner.

get downtown
到市区

terminal building
航站楼

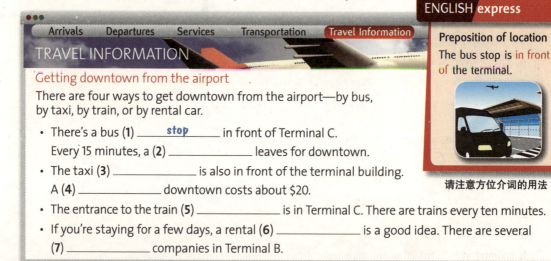

Arrivals   Departures   Services   Transportation   Travel Information

TRAVEL INFORMATION

Getting downtown from the airport
There are four ways to get downtown from the airport—by bus, by taxi, by train, or by rental car.

- There's a bus (1) _stop_ in front of Terminal C. Every 15 minutes, a (2) _____ leaves for downtown.
- The taxi (3) _____ is also in front of the terminal building. A (4) _____ downtown costs about $20.
- The entrance to the train (5) _____ is in Terminal C. There are trains every ten minutes.
- If you're staying for a few days, a rental (6) _____ is a good idea. There are several (7) _____ companies in Terminal B.

ENGLISH express

Preposition of location
The bus stop is in front of the terminal.

请注意方位介词的用法

Some places

school	train station
downtown	swimming pool
airport	shopping mall
gym	supermarket
library	movie theater

Talk about it!

4 Work with a partner. Choose five places in your city. Talk about the best way to get to each one from your home.

A: What's the best way to get to the gym from your home?
B: There are two ways for me to get to the gym—by bus or by car. How about you?

Unit 8

GRAMMAR

Simple present and present continuous for the future

ALSO GO TO
Grammar Takeaway
PAGE 201

1 Read the conversation. The future events are underlined. Which events are arrangements? Which events are scheduled events?

Angie: I'm calling you because I'm coming to Boston next weekend!
Kelly: You are? That's great! Where are you staying?
Angie: I'm staying at the Park Hotel. I'm going to my cousin's wedding.
Kelly: When is the wedding?
Angie: It's on Saturday. It starts at three. What are you doing Saturday morning?
Kelly: Actually, Saturday morning I'm busy. Jack and I are taking a tennis class.
Angie: What time does it end?
Kelly: It ends at noon.

scheduled events
已经计划好的/
安排好的活动

cousin
堂/表兄弟姐妹

> There are two types of future events in the conversation—arrangements and scheduled events.
>
> Arrangements are planned events, usually with other people. We use the present continuous.
> I'm having dinner with friends.
>
> Scheduled events include travel and activity times and meetings. We use the simple present.
> My train arrives at 3:25 p.m.

2 Ken is going to Chicago for the weekend. His friend Jim lives in Chicago. Look at their schedules and complete the conversation. Then listen and check your answers.

Ken: I'm coming to Chicago this weekend! My flight (1) __arrives__ at 7 p.m. on Friday.
Jim: You are? That's great! My family (2) _____ to the beach on Sunday. Do you want to come?
Ken: Oh, thanks, but my flight (3) _____ at 3 p.m.
Jim: That's too bad. I (4) _____ dinner with Bill Friday night at 7 p.m., but maybe we can meet up after.
Ken: Sorry, but I (5) _____ with my friend Kim at 9 p.m. How about Saturday?
Jim: I (6) _____ a haircut at 10 a.m. How about noon?
Ken: Actually, Kim and I (7) _____ lunch together, but I don't have plans Saturday night.
Jim: I (8) _____ to a concert with Tara, but you can come with us! The concert (9) _____ at 8 p.m.

Ken's Schedule
Friday
7 p.m. flight arrives
9 p.m. meet up with Kim
Saturday
1–4 p.m. have lunch with Kim
Sunday
3 p.m. flight leaves

meet up
见面

Jim's Schedule
Friday
7 p.m. have dinner with Bill
Saturday
10 a.m. get a haircut
7 p.m. go to a concert with Tara
8 p.m. concert starts
Sunday
12–5 p.m. go to the beach with family

get a haircut
剪发

Talk about it!

3 Make a schedule for your weekend activities. Then work with a partner and role-play a phone conversation. Make plans to meet up.

WORKBOOK
PAGE 58-59

Unit 8

READING

Let's get together!

HELP reading

Find the main idea
Before you read an email, read the subject line. This will tell you the main idea.

请注意找到邮件主题的方法

1 Before reading When you want to visit a friend or family member, how do you contact them—by phone, email, letter, or text message? Why do you contact the person this way?

2 Reading Ben and Haluk wrote several emails to each other. Read the first email Ben wrote to Haluk. Circle the words to complete the sentences.

Istanbul
伊斯坦布尔

go skiing
去滑雪

From: Ben
To: Haluk
Subject: Meet up in Istanbul?
Date: Tuesday, December 10

Dear Haluk,
How are you? How was your trip to Austria last weekend? Did you go skiing? I'm coming to Istanbul this week for a business meeting. I arrive on Thursday afternoon, and I leave on Monday. The meeting is on Friday. How about dinner one evening?

1. Ben lives / doesn't live in Istanbul.
2. Haluk lives in Istanbul / Austria.
3. Ben is writing to Haluk because he wants to go skiing / meet up with him.
4. Haluk and Ben work together / are friends.

3 Reading Now read the rest of the emails between Ben and Haluk. Put them in order from 1 to 5.

cell phone
手机
the Marmara Hotel
马尔马拉酒店
Taksim Square
塔克西姆广场

A Dear Ben,
I'm going away for the weekend, so we can't meet on Saturday. What are you doing on Thursday night?

B Dear Ben,
The Marmara Hotel at 7:00 p.m. sounds good. Call me on my cell phone if there's a problem. If not, see you on Thursday.

C Dear Haluk,
How about doing something on Saturday night? I'm having dinner with people from the office on Friday night.

D **1** Dear Ben,
Good to hear from you. Austria was fantastic. It's great that you are coming to Istanbul. Yes, let's meet for dinner one evening. Then you can see my pictures!

E Dear Haluk,
I'm free on Thursday night. I'm staying at the Marmara Hotel in Taksim Square. Let's meet at 7:00 at the front desk.

94

Unit 8

4 After reading Answer the questions. Then compare answers with a partner.

1. When did Haluk go to Austria?
2. When are Haluk and Ben having dinner?
3. When is Ben's business meeting?
4. When is Ben having dinner with people from work?
5. Is Haluk staying in Istanbul over the weekend?
6. What's the name of the hotel Ben is staying at?
7. How long is Ben staying in Istanbul?

Talk about it!

5 Make a list of the top five places in the world that you want to visit. Then talk with a partner. Tell your partner why you want to visit these places. Then decide on the best place to visit from your two lists.

A: My number one place to visit is Paris because it's an exciting city with lots to see and do. Also, I love art and the Louvre is a great museum.

B: That's true. French food is good too! But my number one place to visit is Tokyo because I love Japanese culture and food.

Top 5 places I want to visit
1. Paris, France
2. Buenos Aires, Argentina
3. Alaska, USA
4. Seoul, Korea
5. Tahiti

the Louvre
卢浮宫

PROJECT

Work in a group. Decide on a place you all want to visit. Then look up information on the Internet about that city/location and create a travel brochure. Present your travel information to the class.

Include the following in your presentation and brochure:

- the best way to get there from where you live
- the best way to get around once you're there (for example, rent a car, take the subway, etc.)
- places to stay
- things to do and see
- places to eat

look up information
查找资料
travel brochure
旅游手册

get around
到处走走
rent a car
租一辆车

Unit 8

CULTURE

Hotel breakfasts

1 Before reading Match the breakfast descriptions to the pictures.

1. _____ Middle Eastern breakfast
2. _____ continental breakfast
3. _____ American breakfast
4. _____ Japanese breakfast

Middle Eastern
中东的

rice tea soup

juice croissant coffee

coffee pita bread cheese

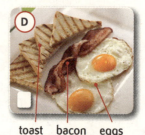
toast bacon eggs

pita bread
皮塔饼；圆面饼

2 Before reading Put the hotel breakfasts in exercise 1 in order for you: 1 = very delicious, 4 = not delicious. Compare with a partner.

A: I have American breakfast as number 1. Eggs and bacon taste good, and then I'm not hungry.

B: Really? I have Japanese breakfast as number 1. I drink tea every day.

travel for leisure
休闲旅行
The Ritz
丽兹酒店
the Place Vendome
旺多姆广场
be popular with…
受……欢迎

Sunday brunch
周日早午餐
the Burj Al Arab hotel
伯瓷酒店(帆船酒店)
be located in
座落于
Dubai
迪拜
the United Arab Emirates
阿联酋
Al Muntaha
顶层餐厅
Arabian Gulf
阿拉伯湾
wear jeans
穿牛仔裤
wear sneakers
穿运动鞋
dress code
着装要求

3 Reading Look at the pictures of the hotels. Where do you think they are? Then read to see if your guesses were right.

What's for breakfast?

A group in the United States studied people who travel for business and leisure. They found that hotel breakfasts are important when people choose a hotel.

5 The Ritz in the Place Vendome in Paris, France, is a very luxurious and elegant hotel. It's popular with celebrities and royalty. This hotel has many different kinds of breakfasts. You can have an American, Japanese, or continental breakfast. You
10 can also try the hotel's Sunday brunch. A brunch is a meal that combines breakfast and lunch. Brunch is served later than breakfast, but earlier than lunch.

The Burj Al Arab hotel is located in Dubai in the
15 United Arab Emirates. At 1,053 feet (321 meters) high, it's the world's tallest hotel. All the rooms in this spectacular hotel are suites with bedrooms and living rooms. This hotel has eight restaurants including Al Muntaha, which has views of the
20 Arabian Gulf. The breakfast at Al Muntaha offers a buffet of Middle Eastern and international food. Everyone that eats at the buffet pays the same price. Then you serve yourself and eat as much as you like. Make sure you aren't wearing jeans or
25 sneakers. This restaurant has a dress code, even for breakfast.

96

Unit 8

4 Reading Read the article again. Match the descriptions and the hotels. Write *R* (Ritz) or *B* (Burj Al Arab).

1. __R__ This hotel serves a Sunday brunch.
2. _____ This hotel serves a Japanese breakfast.
3. _____ This hotel is the tallest in the world.
4. _____ There are eight different places to eat here.
5. _____ This hotel doesn't have an Arabic breakfast.
6. _____ You can't wear jeans at breakfast here.
7. _____ Famous people like this hotel.

5 After reading Write the underlined words and phrases from the text next to the definitions.

1. deluxe; very comfortable _____
2. a meal that combines breakfast and lunch _____
3. rules about the clothes people can wear _____
4. large hotel rooms _____
5. amazing _____
6. vacation _____
7. people serve themselves this meal _____
8. famous people _____

Talk about it!

6 Read the questions and make notes. Then ask and answer the questions with a partner.

1. Which hotel would you like to have breakfast in? Why?
2. What do you usually eat for breakfast?
3. What do people usually eat for breakfast in your country?
4. Some people say that breakfast is the most important meal of the day. Do you agree? Why or why not?

PRONUNCIATION

The sounds /l/ *light* and /r/ *right*

1 Be sure to distinguish between the /l/ sound and the /r/ sound. Listen and repeat.

| light / right | lock / rock | load / road | gloom / groom | Kelly / Kerry |

2 Listen and  the words you hear.

	1	2	3	4	5	6	7
/l/	flight	alive	lock	lent	pilot	dear	loom
/r/	fright	arrive	rock	rent	pirate	deal	room

97

Unit 8

travel agent
旅行社
online travel site
在线旅游网站

CONVERSATION

Asking for and giving travel suggestions

1. Where do you get travel suggestions from? Your family? A travel agent? An online travel site?

2. Look at the expressions in the box. Complete the conversation below. Then listen and check.

Ask for travel suggestions	Give travel suggestions
Where do you think I should go?	I think you should go to Ireland. You could visit Singapore. Why don't you check out Peru?
What do you suggest I do?	I suggest you try paragliding. How about going skiing?
How should I go there?	You would go by train.

paragliding
滑翔伞运动

Croatia
克罗地亚

Amy: Where do you think I (1) __should__ go for my vacation?
Ben: Why don't you (2) _____ Croatia. I hear it's spectacular!
Amy: That sounds interesting. What do you (3) _____ I do there?
Ben: Well, (4) _____ going paragliding? That's fun!
Amy: I'm not so sure about that! Do you have any other suggestions?
Ben: You (5) _____ visit Australia. There are some fantastic places there.
Amy: That's a great idea! How should I go there? By boat or plane?
Ben: I (6) _____ go by plane.

CONVERSATION STRATEGY

Give feedback

When someone gives you a suggestion, let the other person know what you think. Some expressions are:
That sounds good.
That's a great idea.
I'm not so sure about that.

请注意对别人的提议如何作出回应

Talk about it!

3. Work in a group. Ask for and give each other suggestions for a trip. Use the expressions and conversation in exercise 2 to help you. Each person decides on one trip.

Tell me more!

Visit the Takeaway English Online Learning Center at http://olcs.mcgraw-hill-education.com/takeaway/

Takeaway TV — Check out the *Takeaway TV* video.
 Login — Improve your English with the online activities.

Unit 8

WRITING

Writing an email to make arrangements

1 Before writing Read the email from Phil. Write the missing words.

- are
- ~~coming~~
- I'm
- leave
- meet up

Hi Tom!
How are you? I have some good news. I'm (1) _coming_ to visit next week! I found a cheap flight on the Internet. (2) _____ staying at a hotel downtown. I arrive on Wednesday at 11:30 a.m., and I (3) _____ on Sunday at 1:00 p.m. What (4) _____ your plans for those days? When can we (5) _____? Also can you tell me the best way to get downtown from the airport?
See you soon!
Phil

HELP writing

Use appropriate language
When you write an email to a friend, you can use informal language. For example, you can end your email with one of these closings:
See you soon!
Talk to you soon!
Looking forward to hearing from you!

请注意给熟悉的朋友写邮件时结束语的写法

look forward to
期待

2 Writing model Read the email from Tom. Fill out the calendar with Tom's schedule.

Hi Phil!
That's great news that you're coming to visit next week! I am working on Wednesday, Thursday, and Friday, but I'm free for most of the weekend. I have a soccer game on Sunday that starts at 12 p.m. Also, I'm playing golf on Wednesday night with my friend Bob.
What are your plans for your trip? How about meeting up on Saturday? Or if you're busy on Saturday, let's have dinner together on Thursday or Friday.
Looking forward to seeing you!
Tom
P.S. The best way to get downtown is to take the subway. You can also take a taxi, but it's expensive.

fill out
填写

play golf
打高尔夫

Wednesday	Thursday	Friday	Saturday	Sunday
____ ; play ____ with Bob	_____	work	free	_____

3 Planning your writing Fill out a calendar with your schedule.

Wednesday	Thursday	Friday	Saturday	Sunday

4 Writing Imagine you received the email in exercise 1 from Phil. Write to him. Use the information in exercises 2 and 3 to help you.

Unit 8

TEST

Test-taking strategy

Answer vocabulary questions   Many tests have vocabulary questions. You choose the best word to complete a sentence. You need to understand the meaning of the word to answer the question.

Use these steps to help you answer vocabulary questions.

1. Look at the context of the missing word. What words come before or after?
2. What part of speech is the missing word? Is it a verb? Is it a noun?
3. If you don't know the answer, read the sentence again. Try each answer in the blank.
4. Note the answers that do not work.
5. If necessary, make your best guess.

> **Example**
> **Choose the correct answer.**
>
> 1. A _____ travels under the ground.
>   - ~~A.~~ airplane   An airplane travels above the ground, not under it.
>   - ~~B.~~ taxi   A taxi travels on the ground, not under it.
>   - ~~C.~~ bus   A bus travels on the ground, not under it.
>   - **D.** subway   This is the correct answer.

PRACTICE

Choose the correct answer. Mark the letter on the Answer Sheet.

1. Most _____ have a business center and a swimming pool.
   - A. factories
   - B. hotels
   - C. schools
   - D. companies

2. A fitness center is a great place to _____ .
   - A. study
   - B. eat
   - C. sleep
   - D. exercise

3. I'm from Austria. I speak _____ .
   - A. German
   - B. every day
   - C. language
   - D. exciting

4. Did you hear Shakira's new _____ ?
   - A. book
   - B. magazine
   - C. song
   - D. theater

Answer Sheet
Mark the letter.

1. A B C D
2. A B C D
3. A B C D
4. A B C D

UNIT SUMMARY

Unit 8

Nouns
airplane
airport
bacon
brunch
buffet
bus
bus stop
business center
car
celebrity
cheese
coffee
conference center
croissant
downtown
dress code
egg
facility
fitness center
front desk
future
gift shop
guest room
gym
hotel
juice
leisure
lobby
pita bread
rental car company
rice
soup
subway
subway station
suite
supermarket
swimming pool
taxi
taxi stand
tea
terminal
toast
train
train station
transportation
trip

Adjectives
busy
free
luxurious
spectacular

Verbs and verb phrases
arrive
end
get together
know
leave
meet up
stay

Preposition
in front of

Expression
by car (bus, train).

Ask for and give travel suggestions
How about going...
How should I go there?
I suggest you try...
I think you should go to...
I would go by...
What do you suggest I do?
Where do you think I should go?
Why don't you check out...
You could visit...

Give feedback
I'm not so sure about that.
That sounds good.
That's a great idea.

Informal email closings
Looking forward to hearing from you!
See you soon!
Talk to you soon!

9 ▶ Going out

In this unit you...
- talk about places to go and things to do
- talk about things in a theater
- buy tickets for an event

Grammar
- prepositions *at*, *in*, *on*

START

Entertainment places

1 When do you go out to have fun? Where do you go? Who do you go with?

2 Write the names of the places under the pictures. Then listen and check your answers.
09_01

| gallery | movie theater | museum | concert hall | stadium | ~~theater~~ |

A. theater
B.
C.
D.
E.
F.

3 Write the events in the chart. You can write an event more than once.

music concert
音乐会
sculpture exhibit
雕塑展

| a music concert | ~~a painting exhibit~~ | a play | a movie | a baseball game |
| a science exhibit | a soccer match | a ballet | an opera | a sculpture exhibit |

gallery	movie theater	museum	concert hall	stadium	theater
a painting exhibit					

Talk about it!

4 Work with a partner. Talk about a time you went to the places in exercise 2.

A: When did you go to a stadium?
B: I went to a stadium two months ago.
A: What did you see?
B: I saw a tennis match.

Unit 9

LISTENING

What's playing?

1 Before listening Look at the pictures. Where do you think the people are? What is happening? Discuss your guesses with a partner.

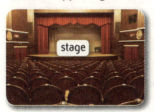   

box office
售票处

2 Listening Listen to check your guesses to exercise 1.

3 Listening Listen again. Write the missing information in the announcement.

> The Rose (1) ___Theater___ presents *The Hairdresser*
> with Brad Benson and Paloma Sanchez.
> Opening party, April (2) _____ at (3) _____ p.m.
> Show and opening party: (4) $ _____ . Buy tickets at
> the Rose Theater box office,
> (5) _____ Jackson Street in Springfield.
> Box office hours: Monday–Saturday
> 11:00 a.m. to (6) _____ p.m. Closed (7) _____ .

HELP listening

Listen for specific information

The first time, just listen for the main idea. The second time, listen for specific information. Know what information you need before you listen. Look at the task in exercise 3 to guide you.

The Hairdresser
《理发师》

请注意如何听关键信息

4 After listening Answer the questions about the announcement. Then compare your answers with a partner.

1. Do you think the Rose Theater sounds like a good theater? Why or why not?
2. How long is *The Hairdresser* playing at the Rose Theater?
3. How can you get tickets to *The Hairdresser*?
4. Would you go to the opening party? Why or why not?

opening party
开幕派对

Talk about it!

5 Work with a partner. Talk about what's playing in a theater near you or at the movies.

A: What's playing at the movies now?
B: Well, *(movie title)* is playing at *(movie theater)*. I'd like to see it. *(Actor)* is in it.
A: He's great! I like him a lot!
B: What about you?

Unit 9

VOCABULARY

Places to go and things to do

1 Look at the pictures in exercise 2. (Circle) the word(s) to complete this sentence.

I think the people are going to a show at a stadium / museum / movie theater.

2 Write the letters next to the words. Then listen and check.
09_03

1. _H_ arcade   3. ___ emergency exit   5. ___ popcorn   7. ___ row   9. ___ seat
2. ___ box office   4. ___ snack bar   6. ___ restroom   8. ___ line   10. ___ ticket

emergency exit
紧急出口
snack bar
小卖部

3 Write *P* for place and *T* for thing.

1. _P_ arcade   3. ___ emergency exit   5. ___ popcorn   7. ___ row   9. ___ seat
2. ___ box office   4. ___ snack bar   6. ___ restroom   8. ___ line   10. ___ ticket

Talk about it!

4 Work with a partner. Ask and answer these questions.

twice a month
一个月两次

1. How often do you go to the movies?   *I go to the movies about twice a month.*
2. Who do you usually go with? When do you usually go?
3. Do you usually get to the movie theater early, on time, or late? Why?
4. Do you buy your tickets online or at the box office? Why?
5. Do you buy anything from the snack bar? Why or why not? What do you buy?
6. Do you like to sit in the front, middle, or back row of the theater? Why?

WORKBOOK PAGE 64

Unit 9

GRAMMAR

Prepositions *at*, *in*, and *on*

ALSO GO TO
Grammar Takeaway
PAGE 202

1 Read the sentences. Circle the prepositions *in*, *on*, and *at*. Underline the words after the prepositions. Then complete the rules below.

1. The Rose Theater announces their grand opening party on Saturday night at 6:00 in the evening.
2. The play opens on April 6th and plays until April 27th.
3. Buy tickets at the Rose Theater box office. It is located at 215 Jackson Street in Springfield.

rules for the prepositions *at, in, on*		
We use _____ before:	We use _____ before:	We use _____ before:
• a time (five o'clock)	• a month (July)	• a day (Friday)
• a place (the stadium)	• time of day (the evening)	• a date (January 16th)
• an address (number + street: 45 Elm Street)	• a city (Bangkok)	• a street (no number: Oak Street)
	• a country (Thailand)	

2 Complete the concert advertisement. Write *at*, *in*, or *on*. Then listen and check.

ALICIA KEYS
in concert

Radio City Music Hall,
New York City
June 3 to June 10, 7:00 p.m.
(Doors open 6:30 p.m.)

Box office: Monday to Saturday
11:30 a.m. to 6:00 p.m.
Tickets on sale March 15
$55–$225

(1) __In__ June, Alicia Keys will be playing (2) _____ Radio City Music Hall (3) _____ New York City. Opening night is (4) _____ June 3rd, and closing night is (5) _____ Friday, June 10th. The concert starts (6) _____ 7:00 (7) _____ the evening. Doors open (8) _____ 6:30 p.m.

closing night
闭幕夜

You can buy tickets (9) _____ the box office. The box office opens every day (10) _____ 11:30 (11) _____ the morning and closes (12) _____ 6:00 (13) _____ the evening. The box office is closed (14) _____ Sundays. Tickets go on sale (15) _____ March 15th.

Radio City Music Hall is located (16) _____ 1260 Avenue of the Americas (17) _____ New York. The Radio City Music Hall box office is located (18) _____ the main lobby of the Music Hall; the entrance is (19) _____ Sixth Avenue.

Talk about it!

3 Work with a partner. Describe an event you went to. Use the correct prepositions to talk about it. Be sure to include the following information in your description:

- where (name of the place, street, and city)
- when (day, date, time, time of day)

Unit 9

READING

What can we do for entertainment?

HELP reading

Scan for specific information
When you scan, you read quickly for specific information. You don't read every word. Read the questions in exercise 3. Then scan.

请注意阅读时快速查读的技巧

1 Before reading How do you find out what entertainment is going on in your town or city? Number each item with how often you use it: 1 = I use it often; 2 = I sometimes use it; 3 = I never use it. Then compare your answers with a partner.

___ magazine ___ Internet ___ newspaper ___ radio ___ TV

2 Reading Read the newspaper section and check (✔) the correct picture for each event.

Sunset Film Festival
落日电影节

Sunset Film Festival

A    B    C

Modern Australia

D    E    F

3 Reading Read the newspaper section again. Circle the correct words to complete the sentences.

Sunset Film Festival

1. The Sunset Film Festival is playing outside / inside.
2. They are showing only old / only new / both old and new movies at the festival.
3. People can / cannot bring food to the festival.
4. Tickets cost $10 / $12 in advance.

Modern Australia

5. Both of the artists in the exhibit are from the U.S. / Australia.
6. Mickson was born in 1948 / 1944.
7. The exhibit is at the gallery on 6/23 only / from 6/23 to 9/15.
8. People buy their tickets at the door / in advance.

at the gallery
在美术馆

in advance
提前

ENTERTAINMENT

This weekend:
What's going on around town?

Sunset Film Festival

It's warm again! It's time to watch a movie <u>under the stars</u>! This year's Sunset Film Festival is on Friday and Saturday, June 23rd and 24th. It <u>features</u> a mix of classic movies, such as *Grease* and *Breakfast at Tiffany's*, plus <u>new releases</u> including *The Brain* and *Spider 3*. Bring a <u>picnic</u>, or order a picnic basket at (507) 555-6528 (please order at least 24 hours in advance).

You can find the Sunset Film Festival in Jackson Park. Please see our website (www.sunsetfilmfest.com) for show times. Tickets are $10 in advance or $12 on the day of the event. Buy tickets at the Jackson Park box office Monday–Friday, 10 a.m.–4 p.m.

• •

Modern Australia

The Loft Gallery is having an opening for their exhibit called *Modern Australia*. This art exhibit features the paintings and drawings of the <u>celebrated</u> Australian artists Robin Mickson and Robin Boyle. Boyle, one of the fathers of modern art, needs no introduction. Robin Mickson, another <u>well-known</u> Australian painter, was born four years after Boyle, in 1948. However all of the works on display are ones he painted in recent years.

The Loft Gallery is located downtown at 752 Davis St. The opening is on Friday, June 23rd, 7–9 p.m. The exhibit will be at the gallery until September 15th. Admission to the event is $7.00 for adults and $4.00 for students with identification. Buy tickets at the door on the day of the event.

Unit 9

4 After reading   Write the <u>underlined</u> words and expressions in the article next to their definitions.

1. cold food to eat outside _____
2. has _____
3. famous _____
4. new movies _____
5. respected and famous _____
6. at night, outside _____

Talk about it!

5 Ask and answer questions about entertainment in your town/city.

A: What can I do for entertainment this weekend? Can you recommend a good movie?

B: Yes, there's a good movie playing at the Rex Theater. It's called "Man and Field". It's a new release this month. It's about life in the north of England.

A: That sounds great! Can you recommend a good art exhibit?

B: Yes, I can. The Sunset Gallery.

PROJECT

Work in a group. Choose two different events that are going on in your town/city (movie, sports, concert, ballet, exhibit, festival, etc.) Look up information about the events in the newspaper, a magazine, or on the Internet. Make two posters with the important information. Then present your events to the class. Be sure to include:

• the name and type of event
• where it's playing/showing
• what days and hours it's open
• how much it costs
• how to get tickets
• any other important information

under the stars
露天

new releases
新片

on display
展出

Unit 9

SONG
Let's fall in love

1 Before listening Look at the title of the song and the pictures. Guess what the song is about.

2 Listening Now listen to the song to see if your guess was correct.

3 Listening Listen to the song again. Complete the lyrics with the words below. Then listen and check.

days	fun	idea	~~late~~
life	love	me	play

4 After listening Circle the best summary of the song. Then compare with a partner.

A. Do different things, but don't fall in love with me.

B. Do different things and fall in love with me.

C. Don't do different things. Only fall in love with me.

fall in love with sb.
爱上某人

see the sights
欣赏风光

Let's fall in love

You can get up early.
You can get up (1) __late__ .
You can go to work or stay at home.
Go to the movies, watch a (2) _____ ,
Go for a walk,
Or stay here.
But if you don't
think that's a good (3) _____ ,

You could fall in love with (4) _____ .
Why don't we fall in love?
Would you like to fall in love with me?
Let's fall in (5) _____ .

You can live your (6) _____
In different ways —
Go around the world, see the sights.
And all in eighty (7) _____ .
Climb a mountain.
Lie in the sun.
But if you don't think that would be
   much (8) _____ ,

You could fall in love with me.
Why don't we fall in love?
Would you like to fall in love with me?
Let's fall in love.

5 After listening Match the two parts of the phrases.

1. watch __d__
2. climb ____
3. fall ____
4. get up ____
5. go ____
6. lie ____
7. stay ____
8. live ____

a. early / late
b. in love
c. for a walk
d. a play
e. a mountain
f. in the sun
g. your life
h. at home

Talk about it!

6 What are the most important things in life? Number these things from 1 (the most important) to 5 (the least important) for you. Then discuss your answers with a partner.

____ love   ____ money   ____ having fun   ____ work   ____ other: _____

Tell the class about your discussion. As a class, decide on the most important thing in life.

PRONUNCIATION

The sounds /uː/ do and /əʊ/ go

1 There are different spellings for the sounds /uː/ and /əʊ/. Listen and repeat.

/uː/ = do / true   /əʊ/ = go / toe

2 Listen to the underlined sounds. Write the words in the correct column. Then practice saying the words.

| ~~restroom~~ | ~~open~~ | gr<u>ou</u>p | s<u>ou</u>venir | cl<u>o</u>se | r<u>ow</u> |
| ag<u>o</u> | bl<u>ue</u> | Oct<u>o</u>ber | kn<u>ow</u> | tw<u>o</u> | m<u>o</u>vie |

/uː/ do	/əʊ/ go
restroom	open

109

Unit 9

CONVERSATION

Buying tickets

entertainment events
娱乐活动

the Phoenix Art Museum
凤凰艺术博物馆

1 How do you usually buy tickets for entertainment events—in person, on the phone, on the Internet?

2 Listen to the conversation. Then practice with a partner.
09_09

Ms. Tan: Welcome to the Phoenix Art Museum. Can I help you?
Ted: Yes, I'll take three tickets, please.
Ms. Tan: Is that three adult tickets?
Ted: No, I'd like two adult tickets and one child's.
Ms. Tan: And would you like tickets for the special exhibit?
Ted: That would be great. Actually, how much are the tickets for the special exhibit?
Ms. Tan: They're $10 for adults and $6 for children. And we have guided tours at 2:00, 3:00, and 4:00.
Ted: Let's see... I'll take tickets for the 3:00, if that's possible.
Ms. Tan: OK. Then that comes to $60. And is that cash or credit?
Ted: Credit. Here's my card.

CONVERSATION STRATEGY

Ask additional questions
When you speak, you can use And to start another question.

请注意谈话时如何追问

3 Write each red phrase from the conversation next to the correct meaning.

Phrase	Meaning
1. how much are	what's the price
2.	do you want
3. (a) (b)	I want
4.	the total price is
5.	if I can
6.	Yes!

Talk about it!

4 Work with a partner. Pretend you are buying tickets to an event. Your partner works at the box office. Role-play a conversation. Use the phrases in exercise 3.

Tell me more!

Visit the Takeaway English Online Learning Center at http://olcs.mcgraw-hill-education.com/takeaway/

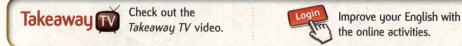

Unit 9

WRITING

Writing an email to make plans

1 Before writing Read the email from Silvia. Write the missing words.

| at | going | have | ~~in~~ | on |

HELP writing

Use sequential order
When writing to someone to make plans, organize the possible events in sequential order. This helps the reader make decisions about which events to choose.

请注意描述计划时的顺序性

Hi Margo,

It's going to be great to spend the day with you (1) __in__ San Francisco (2) _____ Saturday. My train arrives (3) _____ 9:25 in the morning (just 10 minutes after your train arrives). Do you have any ideas for the day? I'm not sure what's (4) _____ on. I would like to go to a museum, (5) _____ lunch, and maybe see live music. What about you?

Silvia

live music
现场音乐会

2 Writing model Read the email. Put Margo's plans in the correct order.

Hi Silvia,

I can't wait for Saturday in San Francisco with you! I have lots of ideas for places to go and things to do. Let's go to an art exhibit in the morning. There's an Eva Hesse exhibit at The Museum of Modern Art. She was a painter and sculptor. There's also the Aztec exhibit at the SOMART center. It costs about $20, but my friend said it was fantastic. There are lots of Chinese restaurants in the area, so let's have Chinese food for lunch.

There's a baseball game at the Scottsdale stadium in the afternoon. Do you like baseball? On Saturday night, there's an Australian band named George playing in Union Square. If you want to see a movie later, we can go to the Strand Movie Theater and see a new release.

Can we do all these things in one day? Tell me what you think.

Margo

the Scottsdale stadium
斯科茨代尔体育场
Australian band
澳大利亚乐队

Margo's plans

___ Chinese food for lunch
___ an Australian band
_1_ Museum of Modern Art
___ the Aztec exhibit
___ Strand Movie Theater
___ a baseball game

3 Planning your writing You are spending next Saturday in your city with a friend. Find out what entertainment events are going on that day. Fill out the chart with details about at least four events. Organize the events in sequential order.

	Event	Time	Place	$
1.				
2.				
3.				
4.				

4 Writing Now write an email to your friend to make plans for the day. Use the information in exercises 2 and 3 to help you.

Unit 9

TEST

Test-taking strategy

Listen for specific information Some tests have a listening passage followed by questions. These questions can ask for specific information.

Use these steps to help you listen for specific information.

1. Read the questions and possible answers before listening.
2. Know what specific information you are listening for.
3. Skim the questions and possible answers while listening.
4. Listen for details in the listening. Write down key words that can help you remember.
5. Choose the best answer. Do not choose an answer just because it is true.

> **Example**
> **You will hear this listening passage.**
> The new stadium is in Central Park. You can buy tickets for soccer games at the box office. It's located on Grand Avenue. The box office is open Monday to Saturday from 9 to 5. It's closed on Sunday.

You see this test question.
Listen to information about a stadium box office. Choose the correct answer.

The box office is open _____.

A. six days a week	This is the correct answer. The box office is open Monday to Saturday
~~B.~~ every day	The box office is closed on Sunday.
~~C.~~ from noon to five	The box office is open from nine to five.

PRACTICE

Listen to information about a theater. Choose the correct answer. Mark the letter on the Answer Sheet.

1. The theater is located ____ 795 Main Street.
   A. at   B. near   C. by

2. The box office entrance is on ____ .
   A. Main Street   B. January 7th   C. 1st Avenue

3. The theater is in ____ .
   A. Los Alamos   B. Los Padres   C. Los Angeles

4. Tickets go on sale on January ____ .
   A. 5th   B. 7th   C. 1st

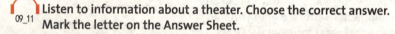

Answer Sheet
Mark the letter.
1. A B C
2. A B C
3. A B C
4. A B C

Unit 9

UNIT SUMMARY

Nouns
arcade
ballet
baseball game
box office
concert hall
emergency exit
entertainment
entrance
event
gallery
inside
line
movie
movie theater
museum
opening party
opera
outside
painting exhibit
picnic
play
popcorn
restroom
row
science exhibit
sculpture exhibit
seat
snack bar
soccer match
stadium
stage
theater
ticket

Adjectives
celebrated
well-known

Prepositions
at
in
on

Verbs and verb phrases
buy
climb
feature
have fun

Expressions
at the door
in advance
new release
under the stars
What's playing?

Buy tickets
How much are…
I'd like…
I'll take…
if that's possible
That comes to…
That would be great.
Would you like…

10 ▶ Let's celebrate!

In this unit you...
- talk about holidays and festivals
- discuss celebrations
- accept and refuse food

Grammar
- count and non-count nouns

START

Holidays and festivals

1 Look at the picture. Who are the people? What are they doing?

2 Match the descriptions to the pictures. Then listen and check.
10_01

Diwali
(印度)排灯节
Hindu festival
印度教节日
the Chinese
calendar
中国农历

1. __D__ Diwali is a five-day Hindu festival in October or November. Homes are decorated with candles. People give gifts and eat special food.

2. ____ The Chinese Moon Festival is in the eighth month of the Chinese calendar (usually in September). On this day, people look at the moon with their family and friends. They eat moon cakes and drink Chinese tea.

Ramadan
斋月
the Islamic
calendar
伊斯兰日历
fasting
斋戒
the Day of the
Dead
亡灵节
St. Patrick's Day
圣帕特里克日
patron saint
守护神

3. ____ Ramadan is a holiday of the Muslim year. It is in the ninth month of the Islamic calendar. People celebrate with prayer and fasting (not eating) during the day.

4. ____ The Day of the Dead is a traditional Mexican holiday. It is celebrated on November 2nd. People go to the cemetery to bring food to their loved ones that have died. They decorate the graves with orange and yellow flowers.

5. ____ St. Patrick's Day is celebrated in March to honor Ireland's patron saint. On this day, people wear green clothes. There are parades in the street.

a feast
大餐

6. ____ Thanksgiving is a national holiday in the United States and Canada. In the United States, people celebrate it in November. In Canada, people celebrate it in October. People spend the day with their family and friends. They eat a feast of turkey, potatoes, and vegetables. They say thank you for the food and good things in their lives.

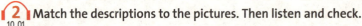

Talk about it!

3 Work with a group. Talk about your favorite holidays and festivals. Make a list. Which one is the group's favorite? Why?

National Holiday
国庆节

My favorite holiday is our National Holiday. I like to watch parades. What about you?

Report to the class about your group's favorite holiday or festival. As a class, decide on the most popular one.

Unit 10

LISTENING

A New Year's custom

1 Before listening People all over the world celebrate the New Year. Look at the picture. Where do you think this New Year's custom is from?

- A Japan
- B Switzerland
- C New Zealand

□ evil spirits
1 a village
□ a group of men
□ a noise
DING DONG
□ a cowbell

evil spirit
幽灵；恶魔

2 Listening Listen to the conversation. Number the words in the picture from 1 to 5 as you hear them.
10_02

3 Listening Listen again and check your answers to exercise 2.
10_02

4 After listening Read the sentences. Circle the correct words.

1. The custom is connected with the New Year / Christmas.
2. There are groups of women / men.
3. They have cows / cowbells.
4. The bells make a loud / quiet noise.
5. The evil spirits like / don't like the noise.
6. The men do this for seven hours / days.

HELP listening

Use your senses
When you listen, use your senses. Listen for what you can see, hear, smell, touch, or taste. This will help you understand the main idea and details of the listening.

请注意听力练习中充分调动五官感受

ENGLISH express

Countries that celebrate New Year's Day on January 1st call December 31st New Year's Eve.

make a loud noise
发出很大的响声

请注意了解12月31日是什么节日

Talk about it!

5 Work with a partner. Talk about what you did last year to celebrate the New Year.

A: What did you do last year to celebrate the New Year?

B: On New Year's Eve, I went to dinner at my friend's house. Then we went to a party at a club. We listened to music and danced. At midnight, we made a lot of noise. On New Year's Day, I did not get up until noon! Then I had breakfast and went to my grandmother's house for dinner.

Unit 10

VOCABULARY

Celebrations

1 Think about celebrations. What do you usually eat and drink? What do you wear?

2 Write the words associated with celebrations under the pictures. Then listen and check.
10_03

costume
戏装
fireworks
焰火；烟花

| balloons | cake | costume | ~~hat~~ | parade |
| bread | candles | fireworks | mask | turkey |

A ____hat____   B _____   C _____   D _____   E _____

F _____   G _____   H _____   I _____   J _____

3 Write the words from exercise 2 in the chart. Then compare with a partner.
Add two more words to each column.

things at a celebration	things people eat at a celebration	things people wear at a celebration
parade,		

Talk about it!

4 Work with a partner. Describe a holiday or festival. Talk about what people do, eat, drink, and wear. Your partner guesses the holiday.

A: On this day, there are parades in the street. People wear green clothes. They eat and drink green food.

B: It's St. Patrick's Day!

A: Right!

Unit 10

GRAMMAR

Countable and uncountable nouns

ALSO GO TO
Grammar Takeaway
PAGE **203**

1 Some nouns can be counted. Others cannot. Look at the chart. Add more examples.

| **Countable nouns** are things we can count. The word can be singular or plural. Examples: one hat / two hats one candle / six candles 1. _____ 2. _____ | **Uncountable nouns** are things we cannot count. The word cannot be plural. Examples: water cheese coffee trousers rice music 1. _____ 2. _____ |

2 Circle the singular count nouns and underline the plural count nouns and non-count nouns. Then complete the rules with *a*, *an*, or *no article*.

I had cereal, milk, an orange, and tea for breakfast. For lunch, I had a sandwich, juice, and cookies. For dinner, I had chicken, rice, and an apple.

Rules:
- We use _____ and _____ before singular countable nouns.
- We use _____ before plural count nouns and uncountable nouns.

cereal
玉米片

3 Circle *some* and *any* in each sentence. Then complete the rules with *some* and *any*.

A: I'm having some cereal. Is there any milk?
B: No, there isn't any milk. There's some juice.
A: Are there any cookies?
B: No, there aren't any cookies, but there are some croissants.

Rules:
- We use _____ in affirmative sentences with uncountable nouns and plural countable nouns.
- We use _____ in negative sentences and questions with uncountable nouns and plural countable nouns.

affirmative
肯定的

negative
否定的

4 Circle the correct answers to complete the conversation. No article = Ø.

A: On the Day of the Dead, we make a / Ø bread for the dead. It's called *pan de muerto* in Spanish. To make *pan de muerto* you need some / any milk, some / a sugar, and a / an stick of butter.
B: Do you need some / any flour or some / any eggs or some / any oil?
A: You need some / any flour and a / an egg, but you don't need some / any oil. Also, you need a / Ø tablespoon of water.

a tablespoon of
一勺……

Talk about it!

5 Work with a partner. Explain how to make a holiday food. Your partner asks questions to understand better. Use articles and *some/any* before the nouns.

Tell the class about your partner's food. As a class, vote on the food that sounds the best.

WORKBOOK
PAGE 72-73

Unit 10

READING

Festival of the month

the Running of the Bulls Festival
奔牛节

1 Before reading *The Travel Times* is an international magazine. Each month they have a story called "Festival of the month". Look at the pictures and guess the answers to the questions.

1. Where is the festival?
2. What do people do at the festival?
3. Why do they have the festival?

2 Reading Read the article to see if your guesses to exercise 1 were correct.
10_04

the Strolling of the Heifers
母牛散步节

> **HELP reading**
>
> **Understand footnotes**
> When you are reading, look for small numbers in the text. These small numbers are called footnotes. Look at the bottom of the page for more information or definitions of the words.

请注意脚注的位置和作用

approximately
大概；大约

3 Reading Read the article again. Check (✓) the correct box for each statement.
10_04

	Running bulls	Strolling heifers
1. It's over 600 years old.	✓	
2. It's in Spain.		
3. It teaches people about family farms.		
4. It's dangerous.		
5. It's in Vermont.		
6. It lasts for nine days.		
7. There's a parade.		
8. It celebrates female cows.		
9. People come to the festival from around the world.		
10. The first one was in 2002.		

FESTIVAL OF THE MONTH

Running or strolling?

Most people know about the Running of the Bulls Festival that takes place in Pamplona, Spain. During this nine-day festival, people run next to and in front
5 of six bulls through the streets of the old town. It's a tradition that has taken place for more than 600 years. Today, people come from all over the world to experience this dangerous, but exciting, festival.

10 This month's featured festival, however, is not the Running of the Bulls. Instead, it's the Strolling[1] of the Heifers.[2] The what? You ask. That's right—not running, but strolling. And not bulls, but heifers.
15 And rather than Pamplona, Spain, the festival takes place in Brattleboro, Vermont—a town of approximately 12,000 in the United States. The first Strolling of the Heifers Festival was in 2002. It was
20 started as a way to have fun and teach people about the local family farms. The festival takes place for one weekend every June in downtown Brattleboro.

The festival begins with a parade. At the
25 front of the parade are, you guessed it—the heifers. Owners walk alongside the heifers. Then behind them, there are farmers, cows, clowns, floats,[3] and much more. After the parade, there is music,
30 dancing, and food at another location in Brattleboro. There is also a bread-baking contest, an art exhibit, and a film festival.

---

[1] walking slowly
[2] young female cows
[3] large vehicles that are decorated for a parade

Unit 10

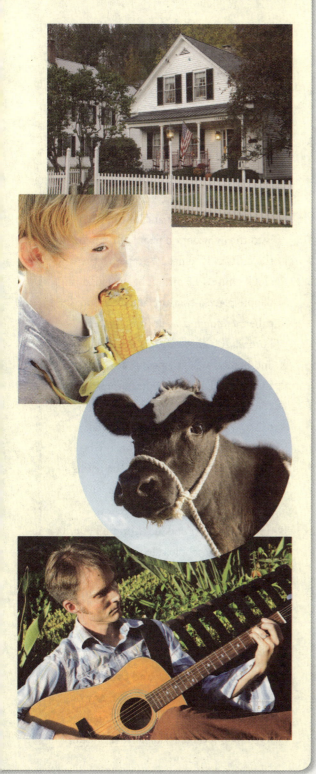

The Travel Times

4 After reading Write the underlined words from the article next to the definitions.

1. from the same city or neighborhood   _local_
2. young female cows   _____
3. a competition   _____
4. not safe   _____
5. next to   _____
6. walking slowly   _____

Talk about it!

5 Work in a group. Create your own festival. Include the information below.

- Where and when does the festival happen?
- What does it celebrate?
- What do people do at the festival?
- What do people wear to the festival?
- What kinds of foods are at the festival?

Tell the class about your festival.

PROJECT

Work in a group. Research information about festivals around the world. Choose one festival. Make a poster with the most important information about it.

Give a presentation to the class about the festival. Re-create and role-play as many of the events as possible.

Unit 10

CULTURE

New Year's around the world

1 Before reading Look at the pictures associated with New Year's celebrations around the world. Do you celebrate New Year's with any of these customs?

A

C

D

B

E

do comedy
表演喜剧

2 Reading 10_05 Read the article. Write the country names below each picture in exercise 1.

3 Reading 10_05 Read the article again. Then read the sentences below. Circle *True* or *False*.

Times Square
时代广场

1. People all over the world celebrate the New Year the same way. — True (False)

2. People in Thailand eat grapes at midnight. — True False

black–eyed peas
豇豆
collard greens
绿叶甘蓝
in fact
事实上
the year ahead
来年

3. In Japan, entertainers compete on TV. — True False

4. In Venezuela, people wear all yellow clothes for good luck. — True False

5. Many people in the United States stay home and watch a party on TV. — True False

6. Ham is a type of vegetable. — True False

Not everybody celebrates the New Year at the same time or in the same way. People in different countries use different calendars and have different customs, such as eating special food or watching fireworks. Some customs are traditional. Some are very surprising or amusing. In Thailand, the custom is to throw water on people. In Spain, the custom is to eat 12 grapes as the clock chimes 12 midnight. In Japan, people place a traditional decoration, called a *kadomatsu*, in front of their homes. The *kadomatsu* is made of pine and bamboo. Many people also watch a show on TV where entertainers compete in teams, usually a red team (women who are wearing red clothes) and a white team (men who are wearing white clothes). The teams sing songs, do comedy, and dance. In Venezuela, people wear yellow underwear for good luck. In the United States, most people celebrate New Year's Eve with parties and fireworks. There is a famous celebration at Times Square in New York. Many people stay home and watch the party on TV. On New Year's Day, some people eat ham, black-eyed peas, and collard greens for good luck. In fact, many of these New Year's customs are intended to bring good luck for the year ahead.

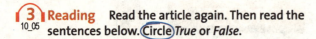

120

Unit 10

4 After reading Circle the correct definitions for the underlined words and phrases in the article.

1. way
   a. manner b. place
2. such as
   a. a lot of b. for example
3. amusing
   a. surprising b. funny
4. as
   a. at the same time b. because
5. In fact
   a. But b. It is true that
6. the year ahead
   a. the next year b. the last year

at the same time
与此同时

Talk about it!

5 Work with a partner. Ask and answer these questions.

1. Which holidays or festivals do you celebrate?
2. Which one is your favorite? Why?
3. Which one is your least favorite? Why?
4. Which holiday customs do you know that are associated with good luck?

PRONUNCIATION

Stress in long words

1 There are different patterns for word stress in long words. Listen and repeat.
10_06

festival (●●●)   amusing (●●●)   celebration (●●●●)

2 Listen and write the words in the correct column. Listen again and practice saying the words.
10_07

| ~~celebrate~~ | decoration | electronic | independence | surprising | potato |
| decorate | delicious | holiday | popular | sandwiches | vegetable |

●●●	●●●	●●●●
celebrate		

Unit 10

CONVERSATION

Accepting and refusing food

1 Look at the picture. Who are the people? What are they doing?

2 Listen to the conversation. Then practice with a group.

seconds
添加的食物

- **Host:** Would anybody like seconds? James, more turkey?
- **James:** Yes, please! I'd love some more.
- **Host:** Great! Here you go, James. Terry, would you like seconds?

stuffed
饱了

- **Terry:** I'm stuffed, but thank you.
- **Host:** OK. How about you, Maria? Seconds?

a little bit
一点儿

- **Maria:** Just a little bit more. Thank you.
- **Host:** OK. Here you go, Maria. Bob? More turkey?

absolutely
必须地

- **Bob:** Absolutely! It's delicious!
- **Host:** Thank you! Here you go, Bob. How about you, Dinah? Would you like more turkey?
- **Dinah:** I'm good. You're a great cook!
- **Host:** OK. And how about you, Tom?

compliment
称赞

- **Tom:** I don't have any more room, but thank you.
- **Host:** No problem.

ENGLISH express

The host/hostess is the person giving the party. He/she usually offers people seconds (more food).

Host: Would you like seconds? = Would you like more food?

请注意用餐时"再添食物"如何表达

CONVERSATION STRATEGY

Refuse politely

When the host offers more food, it's OK to refuse. However, you should say "thank you" and/or compliment the host.

请注意如何礼貌地拒绝主人为你添加食物

3 Write the words in red in the chart.

Accepting food (saying "yes")	Refusing food (saying "no")
I'd love some more.	

Talk about it!

4 Work in a group. Role-play a dinner party. First decide on the host/hostess. Then decide on the food. The host/hostess offers everyone more food. Accept or refuse the food.

Tell me more!

Visit the Takeaway English Online Learning Center at http://olcs.mcgraw-hill-education.com/takeaway/

 Check out the *Takeaway TV* video.

 Improve your English with the online activities.

Unit 10

WRITING

Writing a description of a festival

A B C

1 Before writing Read a description of a festival. Circle the picture that best matches the description.

The Lantern Festival is a Chinese festival. People also call it the Yuan Xiao Festival or the Shang Yuan Festival. People celebrate it during the first month in the lunar year in the Chinese calendar. It is usually in January or February. During the Lantern Festival, children go out at night to temples carrying lanterns. The lanterns look like rabbits. The children solve riddles on the lanterns. They have to guess the answers to funny questions. The other important part of the festival is the food. People eat small dumplings made of sticky rice called Yuan Xiao. The inside of the dumplings are sometimes sweet and sometimes salty. People usually wear normal clothes to the Lantern Festival, but many people wear only new clothes. This festival officially ends the Chinese New Year. I like this festival because it's fun and the lanterns are pretty.

the Lantern Festival
元宵节
the lunar year
农历年
lantern
花灯
solve riddles
猜谜语
sticky rice
糯米

HELP writing

Include details
When you're writing, write two details for each idea or question. This makes your description clearer and more interesting.

请注意写作时如何运用细节表现主题

2 Writing model Read the description again. Find two details for each question and write them in the chart.

Question	Detail 1	Detail 2
1. What's the name of the festival?	the Lantern Festival	the Yuan Xiao or Shang Yuan Festival
2. When do people celebrate it?		
3. What do people do?		
4. What do people wear?		
5. What do people eat?		

3 Planning your writing Now answer the questions about a celebration in your culture.

Question	Detail 1	Detail 2
1. What's the name of the festival?		
2. When do people celebrate it?		
3. What do people do?		
4. What do people wear?		
5. What do people eat?		

4 Writing Now write a description of an important festival (or celebration) in your culture. Use the information in exercise 3 to help you.

WORKBOOK PAGE 74-75

Unit 10

TEST

Test-taking strategy

Read for vocabulary   Some tests have a reading passage followed by vocabulary questions. Some test items ask for a *synonym*—a word with the same meaning. Some ask for an *antonym*—a word with the opposite meaning.

Use these steps to help you read for vocabulary understanding.

1. If you don't know the meaning of a word, look at the context. The context is the words and sentences around a word.
2. Look at the answer choices. Try each answer choice in the test item.
3. Which words are you sure do *not* work? Eliminate these answers.
4. Try your final answer choice again. Does it make sense?

Example
Read the paragraph and answer the vocabulary questions.

Halloween is a popular holiday in the United States. It is celebrated on October 31st. For this holiday, children wear costumes and go from door to door saying, "trick or treat." If the children receive a treat, like candy or fruit, they go to the next door. If they don't receive a treat they might play a trick, like putting toilet paper around a tree. Another Halloween tradition is making Jack O' Lanterns. Children carve or cut scary faces into pumpkins with a knife and then put a candle inside. But don't be scared—it's Halloween!

1. A *treat* is _____ ?
   - ~~A.~~ something stupid   A *treat* is not something stupid.
   - ~~B.~~ something scary   A *treat* is not something scary.
   - **C.** something sweet   This is the correct answer. The context shows that *treat* means something sweet like candy.

PRACTICE

Choose the correct answer. Mark the letter on the Answer Sheet.

1. A synonym for *cut* is ___.
   - A. costume
   - B. carve
   - C. candle

2. *Jack O' Lantern* means ___.
   - A. trick or treat
   - B. door to door
   - C. carved pumpkin

3. Putting toilet paper around a tree is an example of a ___.
   - A. trick
   - B. costume
   - C. treat

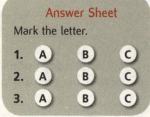

Answer Sheet
Mark the letter.

1. Ⓐ Ⓑ Ⓒ
2. Ⓐ Ⓑ Ⓒ
3. Ⓐ Ⓑ Ⓒ

UNIT SUMMARY

Nouns
apple
balloon
bread
cake
candle
celebration
cemetery
cereal
cheese
chicken
contest
cookie
costume
cowbell
custom
evil spirit
fasting
feast
festival
fireworks
float
flower
food
gift
grave
hat
heifer
holiday
host
hostess
juice
mask
milk
moon
noise
orange
parade
patron saint
potato
prayer
sandwich
seconds
turkey
vegetable
village
way

Adjectives
amusing
dangerous
local
loud
quiet
special
traditional

Verbs
bring
celebrate
decorate
drink
eat
give
honor
stroll
wear

Adverb
alongside

Conjunction
as

Expressions
in fact
loved one
such as
the year ahead

Accept and refuse food
Absolutely!
I don't have any more room.
I'd love some more.
I'm good.
I'm stuffed, but thank you.
Just a little bit more.

Review 2

VOCABULARY

1 Circle the word in each group that is different.

1.	a play	a ballet	(a baseball game)	a concert
2.	windy	temperature	cloudy	foggy
3.	last night	four days ago	yesterday	tonight
4.	box office	fitness center	front desk	guest room
5.	costume	candles	hat	mask
6.	stadium	airport	bus stop	subway station

2 Complete the conversation with the words from the box.

| box office | crowded | fireworks | ~~parade~~ | rain |
| costumes | exhibit | gallery | play | sunny |

Ken: What do you want to do this weekend?

Gina: I don't know. Let's look in the newspaper to see what's going on.

Ken: Good idea. Let's see... The Strawberry Festival is on Saturday in Troy. They have a (1) ____parade____ on Main Street at 1 p.m. People wear (2) _____. At night there are (3) _____ .

Gina: That sounds like fun, but I went a few years ago, and it was really (4) _____. There were too many people there. The weather was good, but it was too hot and (5) _____ . It made me feel tired.

Ken: Yeah, that's true. Anyway, I think it's going to (6) _____ on Saturday. I don't want to get wet. Maybe we should do something inside.

Gina: What about going to see some art?

Ken: That's a good idea. There's an (7) _____ of paintings by a local artist at a (8) _____ downtown.

Gina: That sounds like fun!

Ken: Also, there's a (9) _____ at the Orville Theater. Let's go to that too!

Gina: Sounds great! I'll call the (10) _____ to buy some tickets.

Review 2

GRAMMAR

1 **Circle the correct words to complete the sentences.**

1. My friends and I are going / go to the movies tonight.
2. The movie is playing on / at the Greenville Movie Theater.
3. The Greenville Movie Theater is on / in Jackson Street on / in Greenville.
4. I don't have a / an car, so my sister is driving / drive me to the movie theater.
5. I am meeting / meet my friends outside of the movie theater.
6. The movie is starting / starts at 7:25 in / at the evening.
7. A / An ticket for the movie costs $10.
8. I usually buy some / any candy at the snack bar.

2 **Complete the description of the movie theater using the present continuous.**

Eight movies ____are playing____ (1. play) at the movie theater today. Many people _____ (2. wait) in line at the box office. One woman _____ (3. buy) tickets now. She _____ (4. pay) with a credit card. Some children _____ (5. play) video games at the video arcade. I _____ (6. wait) in line at the snack bar. I _____ (7. buy) popcorn. My friends and I _____ (8. see) a movie called *Trek to Beyond*.

3 **Now it's the next day. Complete the description using the simple past.**

Yesterday ____was____ (1. be) a busy day at the movie theater. My friends and I _____ (2. go) to see a movie called *Trek to Beyond*. It _____ (3. be) good. I _____ (4. buy) popcorn and we _____ (5. eat) it while we _____ (6. watch) the movie. After the movie we _____ (7. play) video games in the arcade. I _____ (8. be) tired when I _____ (9. get) home.

Review 2

LISTENING

1 Before listening Look at the photos and make guesses about Bill and Jan's vacation. Talk about your ideas with a partner.

2 Listening Listen to Bill's conversation with his friend Andy. Check your guesses for exercise 1.

3 Listening Listen to the conversation again. Check (✓) the things Bill and Jan did on their vacation.

- ☐ They went to the beach.
- ☐ They went to see a concert.
- ☐ They played video games in the hotel lobby.
- ☐ They ate at many restaurants.
- ☐ They bought new clothes.
- ☐ They went to a festival.
- ☐ They saw a parade.
- ☐ They saw fireworks.
- ☐ They wore costumes.
- ☐ They bought masks.
- ☐ They took a train.
- ☐ They rode buses.
- ☐ They rented a car.
- ☐ They went to the zoo.
- ☐ They went to a soccer game.
- ☐ They took pictures.

4 After listening Read the sentences. Circle *True* or *False*.

1. Bill and Jan had a terrible time on their vacation.   True   False
2. It was sunny every day.   True   False
3. Bill and Jan probably stayed with a friend.   True   False
4. They ate Mexican food while they were there.   True   False
5. Andy knew what Carnival was.   True   False
6. There were a lot of people at the festival.   True   False
7. Bill and Jan drove a car on Saturday and Sunday.   True   False

Talk about it!

5 Work with a partner. Describe a vacation you took. Talk about things like: where you went, who you went with, how you got there, where you stayed, what the weather was like, what you did, and what you ate.

Review 2

CONVERSATION

1 Look at the picture. Where are the women? What are they talking about? Talk about it with a partner.

2 Complete the conversation with the words in the box. Then listen to check your answers.

| great | I'm stuffed | Let's | terrible |
| how about | just a little | so-so | Would you like to |

Anna: This restaurant is great!

Kerry: Yes, I love it! **(1)** _____ try my salad? It's delicious!

Anna: Sure, thanks! But **(2)** _____.

Kerry: Here you go.

Anna: Thanks. So how was your vacation to Miami?

Kerry: Actually, it was only **(3)** _____.

Anna: Really? Why?

Kerry: The weather was **(4)** _____. It was cold and rainy the whole time.

Anna: Oh, no! That's too bad! How was the hotel?

Kerry: The hotel was **(5)** _____! The rooms and the lobby were big. Also there was an indoor swimming pool.

Anna: Well, that's good! Say, **(6)** _____ ordering dessert?

Kerry: Thanks, but **(7)** _____. **(8)** _____ get coffee instead.

Anna: Great idea!

3 Practice the conversation with a partner.

Talk about it!

4 Work with a partner. Do a role play. Imagine you are in a restaurant having a meal. Talk about a vacation you went on recently. Describe the hotel, the food, and the weather. Then make a plan for a future vacation together.

11 ▶ It's a great job!

In this unit you...
- describe and discuss jobs
- make excuses

Grammar
- review: questions in the simple present
- adverbs of frequency

START

ENGLISH express

Advantages are good things.
Disadvantages are bad things.

请注意区别 advantages 和 disadvantages

Jobs

1 Greet your teacher. Then discuss these questions.

1. What does your teacher do in a typical day?
2. What are the advantages and disadvantages of the job?

advantages and disadvantages
利弊；优点和缺点
job titles
职业名称

2 Write the job titles next to the pictures. Then listen to check your answers.

1 police officer

2

3

4

5

5

6

7

8

astronaut
scientist
nurse
server
financial analyst
graphic designer
~~police officer~~
taxi driver

financial analyst
财务/金融分析师
graphic designer
平面设计师

3 Give the job names for each description.

1. jobs that involve transportation   **police officer, taxi driver, astronaut**
2. jobs that involve working with customers or clients
3. jobs that require a college degree or special schooling
4. jobs that involve handling money
5. jobs that involve using computers

college degree
大学学位
special schooling
特殊教育

Talk about it!

4 Work with a partner. Ask and answer questions about your family and friends' jobs.

A: What does your mother do?
B: She's a financial analyst. What about yours?

A: She's a nurse. What about your brother?
B: He's a student.

Unit 11

LISTENING

About my job

1 Before listening These words are from an interview with a woman who describes her job. Look at the words. What do you think her job is? What do you think she does on a typical day?

START DEMANDING TALK PEOPLE NEW YORK MORNING FINANCIAL MARKETS web EMAIL INDIA JOB WORK 6:00 MEET phone MEETINGS WORLD EARLY WELL-PAYING SCOTLAND INTERESTING

HELP listening

Listen for key words
Think of words you know that are related to the topic of the listening. For this exercise, think about words related to different jobs. For example: businesswoman = computer, finances, meetings.

请注意在听时联想相关的关键词

ENGLISH express

We use adverbs of frequency to talk about how often something happens. These adverbs go after the verb *be* and usually before other verbs.

100% always
usually
often
sometimes
hardly ever
0% never

I am never late for work.
Teachers usually work in schools.

ALSO GO TO
Grammar Takeaway
PAGE 204

请注意频度副词在句中的位置及其意义的差别

financial markets
金融市场

2 Listening Listen to the interview and check your answers to exercise 1.
11_03

3 Listening Listen again. Check (✓) how often the woman does each thing.
11_03

	always	usually	often	sometimes	hardly ever	never
1. starts work at 7:30 a.m.						
2. starts work at 6:00 a.m.						
3. has phone meetings						
4. meets in person						
5. has meetings in India						

in person
亲身; 亲自

4 After listening Read the statements. Circle *True* or *False*.

1. The woman has meetings every morning.   True   (False)
2. She works with people in Scotland.   True   False
3. They hardly ever use email to communicate.   True   False
4. She doesn't like meeting in person.   True   False
5. She likes her job.   True   False

Talk about it!

5 Work with a partner. Choose a job that you know about. Make a schedule of a typical day for someone with that job. Would you want that job? Why or why not? Talk about it.

make a schedule
制定计划

WORKBOOK PAGE 83

Unit 11

VOCABULARY

Job descriptions

job descriptions
工作描述

1 Where do you see job descriptions? What things do people describe?

2 Match the words with the examples. Then listen to check.

1. _h_ dangerous
2. ____ well-paying
3. ____ boring
4. ____ demanding
5. ____ low-paying
6. ____ unusual
7. ____ interesting
8. ____ rewarding

a. "The money isn't very good."
b. "I do the same thing all the time. It isn't very interesting."
c. "Not many people do my job."
d. "The money is great."
e. "I have a lot of responsibility in my job and I work very long hours."
f. "It's a great job because I have the opportunity to do lots of different things."
g. "When you do the job well, you have a great feeling of satisfaction."
h. "I have to be very careful or I could get hurt."

have the opportunity to do
有机会做……
have a feeling of satisfaction
有满足感

3 Write descriptions for the jobs below. Then add two more jobs and descriptions.

job	description
1. doctor	well-paying, demanding, interesting, rewarding
2. teacher	
3. student	
4. police officer	
5.	
6.	

4 Which description would you most like your job to fit? Which would you least like it to have? Number these descriptions from 1 (I'd like it the most) to 8 (I'd like it the least).

____ dangerous   ____ boring   ____ interesting   ____ demanding
____ well-paying   ____ unusual   ____ low-paying   ____ rewarding

Talk about it!

5 Now work with a partner. Compare your lists. Talk about what you rated the same and what you have different. Then talk about jobs that would have those characteristics.

A: I have *rewarding* as number 1 and *well-paying* as number 2. How about you?
B: I have *interesting* as number 1 and *dangerous* as number 2.
A: Really? I have *dangerous* as number 8! Why do you have it as number 2?
B: Because...

Unit 11

GRAMMAR

Review: questions in the simple present

ALSO GO TO
Grammar Takeaway
PAGE **204**

1 Complete the information questions with the correct question words.

| How | ~~What~~ | When | Where | Why |

information questions	answers
1. <u>What</u> do you do?	I'm a financial analyst.
2. _____ do you work?	In New York.
3. _____ do you meet with people from all over the world?	We have phone meetings.
4. _____ do you start work?	Usually at 7:30 a.m.
5. _____ do you start work so early?	Because I work with financial markets all over the world.

ENGLISH express

Yes / No questions don't use a question word. However, they have the same word order as information questions.

A: Do you like your job?
B: Yes, I do.

请注意一般疑问句的语序

2 Look at the sentences in exercise 1. Then put these sentence parts in the correct order to form questions in the simple present.

verb in the infinitive:	rest of sentence:	~~question word:~~	subject:	auxiliary verb:
start	so early?	~~Why~~	you	do

first	second	third	fourth	fifth
question word: Why				

verb in the infinitive
动词不定式
auxiliary verb
助动词

3 Put the words in order to make questions. Then match the questions to the answers.

1. <u>b</u> does / start / she / what time / work / ?
   <u>What time does she start work?</u>
2. _____ a uniform / do / why / wear / you / ?
   _____
3. _____ go / you / where / to school / do / ?
   _____
4. _____ his job / does / like / he / ?
   _____

a. At the local university.
b. At 8:00 in the morning.
c. Yes, he does.
d. Because it's required.

put...in order
排序；整理

Talk about it!

4 Work with a partner. Play "What's my job?" Student A chooses a job, but doesn't tell student B. Student B asks questions and guesses the job.

A: What time do you start work?
B: At about 7:30 a.m.

A: Where do you work?
B: At a school.

A: Are you a teacher?
B: Yes, I am.

133

Unit 11

READING

An out-of-this-world job

1 Before reading Look at the pictures in the magazine article. What kind of magazine is it? What do you think the article is about? Talk about your guesses with a partner.

2 Before reading What do you think are the differences between daily life on Earth and daily life in space? With a partner, make a list.

on Earth
在地球上
in space
在太空中
make a list
列清单

3 Reading 11_05 Read the article. Look for the things on your list.

> **HELP reading**
> Guess the meaning of new words
> When you see a new word, try to figure out if it's a *noun*, *verb*, or *adjective*. This can help you guess the word's meaning.
>
> 请注意阅读时通过词性猜测词义

figure out
想出；理解
assemble parts
组装零件

4 After reading Guess the meaning of the underlined words. Are they nouns, verbs, or adjectives? Compare your answers with a partner.

compare with
与……比较

laptop computer
手提电脑
send emails
发送邮件
space station
空间站

5 After reading Read the statements. Circle *True* or *False*.

1.	Space station crews usually stay in space for over a year.	True	**False**
2.	Astronauts can't speak to their friends when they are in space.	True	False
3.	Astronauts spend a lot of time cooking.	True	False
4.	At a space station, the sun rises many times in a day.	True	False
5.	Astronauts use straps to stay in their beds.	True	False
6.	Astronauts usually relax after lunch.	True	False

mix with
(使)与……混合

LIFE IN SPACE

For most people, traveling in space is a dream. However, for more and more people, working in space on a space station is a reality. A space station is a structure designed for astronauts, or people who live and work in outer space. Life on a space station is NOT easy! In space, there are no hot showers and no pizza delivery. Let's look at some different aspects of life in space.

WORK
Astronauts usually work for about 16 hours a day in space. For work, they do experiments, <u>assemble</u> parts of the space station, and <u>repair</u> satellites. Space station <u>crews</u> are often in space for six to nine months, but sometimes they stay in space for over a year!

FREE TIME
Astronauts have books, MP3 players, and games—just like people on Earth! They use their laptop computers to send emails to family, friends, and <u>colleagues</u>. They can also talk to people back on Earth using technology through their computers and the Internet.

FOOD AND EATING
Astronauts hardly ever need to make their food. It often comes in packets and is ready to eat. Some food can be <u>heated</u> or mixed with

134

water. They always use bags and straws for liquid foods like soups, so that the food doesn't fly around the space station.

HEALTH

Zero gravity and changes in daily routine (the sun comes up every 90 minutes) can cause physical problems for astronauts. To be physically in shape, astronauts exercise for a few hours every day.

SLEEPING

Sleeping can be a problem with no gravity. Astronauts use straps to stay in their beds. Their sleeping bags are often attached to the walls!

A TYPICAL DAY

1. Have breakfast and get ready for the day.
2. Get blood tests for health checks.
3. Do space station maintenance and experiments.
4. Do exercises.
5. Have lunch.
6. Do more exercises.
7. Finish experiments and check station systems.
8. Have dinner and crew meeting to plan the next day.
9. Have free time for emails, phone calls, and personal washing.
10. Go to bed.

Unit 11

CONVERSATION STRATEGY

Ask follow-up questions to make conversations more interesting. For example:
Why?
What else?
What about you?

请注意进一步提问使对话更有趣的方法

Talk about it!

6 Work with a partner. Make a list of the advantages and disadvantages of being an astronaut. Would you like to be an astronaut? Why or why not? Talk about it with your partner.

zero gravity
失重；零重力
come up
出现；发生

PROJECT

Work in a group. Do research on the Internet to make a list of 10 unusual jobs. Then choose two jobs. Make a poster or electronic presentation with the most important information about each one. Answer these questions for each job:

• What do people with the job do?
• What is a typical day like for the job?
• What makes the job unusual?
• How do people get the job? Is there special training?

Present your information to the class. The class votes on (**1**) the most unusual job and (**2**) the job most students would like to have.

attach to
系上；附上

make electronic presentation
用电脑做陈述

do maintenance
保养；维护

vote on
就……表决

personal washing
个人洗漱

Unit 11

SONG

Uncle Bertie's nephew

1 Before listening Who are the people in your family? What are their jobs?

2 Before listening Match the family words to the definitions.

1. _b_ aunt
2. ____ cousin
3. ____ nephew
4. ____ niece
5. ____ uncle

a. your mother or father's brother
b. your mother or father's sister
c. your brother or sister's daughter
d. your brother or sister's son
e. your uncle or aunt's son or daughter

3 Listening 11_06 Read the verses to the song *Uncle Bertie's nephew*. Guess the order of the verses. Number the verses from 1 to 5. Then listen to check your guesses.

4 After listening Circle the best answer. Then check your answers with a partner.

1. The singer of the song is ____ .
   A. Uncle Bertie
   B. Uncle Bertie's nephew
   C. Uncle Bertie's brother
2. The singer ____ .
   A. doesn't have a job
   B. has a difficult job
   C. has an easy job
3. The singer ____ .
   A. has money and is happy
   B. has money and is unhappy
   C. doesn't have much money

5 After listening Write the underlined words and expressions in the song next to the definitions.

1. a person who works driving a car _____
2. in fashion _____
3. expensive clothes _____
4. allows, makes possible _____
5. the sound you make when something is funny _____

lie in bed
躺在床上

UNCLE BERTIE'S NEPHEW

Chorus
Every day, I wake up by myself.
Every day, I get up by myself.
Every day, every day, oh I miss
you every day that you're away.

☐ I go to work at twelve, twelve-thirty.
My <u>chauffeur</u> drives me to the door.
I like my job with Uncle Bertie.
He <u>lets</u> me watch TV all day,
up on the fourteenth floor.

☐ After work I meet my friends at Marty's.
My nights are <u>laughter</u>, fun, and song.
We go to all the <u>trendy</u> parties.
We dance all night until it's light,
but still there's something wrong.

☐ I wake up every day at seven.
I lie in bed for four more hours.
I get up at about eleven.
I brush my teeth, I shave my face,
and then I take a shower.

☐ I have my breakfast at the table.
I like my coffee black and strong.
I put on my <u>designer labels</u>,
I comb my hair, I shine my shoes,
but still there's something wrong.

☐ I have my lunch with cousin Mabel.
It's expensive and it's three hours long.
We always have our favorite table,
some caviar, a big cigar,
but still there's something wrong.

Unit 11

Talk about it!

6 In your opinion, what are the most important things in life? Number the things from 1 (most important) to 6 (least important).

_____ to like your job   _____ to be happy
_____ to be good at work   _____ to be healthy
_____ to be in love   _____ to be rich

Now work with a partner. Compare your lists. Talk about what's different and why.

in one's opinion
某人认为；
某人的意见是……

be good at
擅长……

PRONUNCIATION

Intonation in questions

1 Intonation is the way a person's voice goes up and down when talking. Listen to the intonation in the questions and complete the rules below.

yes / no questions	information questions
Do you like your job?	What do you do at work?
Do you work close to home?	What company do you work for?
Are you a scientist?	When do you go to class?

- With _____ questions the intonation falls (↓) at the end of the question.
- With _____ questions the intonation rises (↑) at the end of the question.

2 Work with a partner. Make a list of questions about jobs. Mark the intonation. Then ask and answer them using the correct intonation.

up and down
起伏地

Unit 11

CONVERSATION

Making excuses

1 When do you make excuses? Why do you make them?

2 Complete the conversations with expressions from the box. Then listen to check your answers.

Be polite
Use words like please, excuse me, sorry, and thank you to be more polite when you make excuses.

请注意如何礼貌地表达歉意或托词

in a hurry
匆忙

| I don't have time | I have a lot of homework to do |
| I'm busy | I'm in a hurry   I'm not hungry right now |

Conversation 1
A: Excuse me.
B: Yes?
A: Can I ask you some questions, please?
B: I'm sorry, but _I don't have time_ .
A: OK. Thanks anyway.

Conversation 2
A: Excuse me. Would you like to try our pizza?
B: No, thanks. _____ .
A: Do you want some coffee?
B: I'm sorry, but _____ .
A: OK. Sorry to bother you.

Conversation 3
A: Hey, Brian!
B: Hi, Alison.
A: Do you want to go to the movies?
B: I'm sorry, but _____ .
A: OK. Maybe another time.

Conversation 4
A: Hey, Jen! Can you help me with my homework?
B: I'm sorry, but _____ .
A: OK. I'll ask someone else.

3 Practice the conversations in exercise 2 with a partner.

Talk about it!

4 Work with a partner. Take turns asking questions. Politely say no by making an excuse.

A: Would you like to go out to eat tonight?
B: I'm sorry, but I have to do homework.
A: OK. Maybe another time.

Tell me more!

Visit the Takeaway English Online Learning Center at http://olcs.mcgraw-hill-education.com/takeaway/

 Check out the *Takeaway TV* video.

 Improve your English with the online activities.

Unit 11

WRITING

Writing a job description

HELP writing
Write a topic sentence
When you're writing, write a topic sentence for each paragraph. The topic sentence should give the main idea of the paragraph.
请注意写作时使用主题句

1 Writing model Read the job description. Check (✔) the name of the job that you think it describes. Then underline the topic sentence in each paragraph.

☐ an engineer ☐ a taxi driver ☐ a language teacher ☐ a server

Typical responsibilities and schedule
People in this job have two main responsibilities. They plan lessons and teach several classes of students. Most people usually work Monday through Friday, and sometimes Saturday. Some people teach in the morning or evening. Other people teach from 9 a.m. to 5 p.m.

Advantages and disadvantages
There are advantages and disadvantages to the job. One advantage is that people in this job live in many different countries. In addition, they work with lots of different people and make friends all over the world. Also, they feel good because they are helping people. One disadvantage is that they often travel to different parts of the city each day, and they don't make a lot of money. Also, they spend a lot of time away from home, and they often miss their family and friends.

Education and training
People with this job need special training in order to be hired by a school. They usually get a certificate or a Master's degree from a university. While they are in school they learn about the language and how to teach it. They often do an internship in a classroom with a more experienced teacher to get more experience.

in addition
另外；此外

get a certificate
获得证书
Master's degree
硕士学位
do an internship
实习

graphic organizer
结构图；表格

2 Before writing Now complete the graphic organizer using more information about the job in exercise 1.

Responsibilities	1. plan lessons 2.
Schedule	1. usually Monday through Friday 2.
Advantages	1. travel to many different countries 2.
Disadvantages	1. don't make a lot of money 2.
Education and training	1. learn about the language 2.

3 Planning your writing Now choose a job you are interested in. Complete a graphic organizer like the one in exercise 2. If necessary, do research on the Internet.

4 Writing Write a description of your job. Use the information in exercise 3 to help you.

Unit 11

TEST

Test-taking strategy

Reading for the main idea   Some tests have readings where you must identify the main idea of a paragraph or paragraphs. The main idea is the most important or the *biggest* idea in a reading. Ask yourself: *In general, what is this reading about?* Don't worry about specific information.

Use these steps to help you read for the main idea.

1. Read any title or headline to help identify the main idea.
2. The main idea is often stated in the first or second sentence.
3. After reading the paragraph, try to summarize it in one sentence.
4. Look for repeated words, phrases, or ideas in the reading.

> *Example*
> **Read the paragraph and answer the question.**
> Being a police officer isn't always easy. The job can be very rewarding and interesting, but it can also be dangerous. Like many jobs, there are both advantages and disadvantages with this kind of work. If you like doing something different every day and working with people, and you don't mind long hours, this job might be for you. On the other hand, the pay is not great and the work can be very demanding.
> 1. What is the main idea of this paragraph?
>   A. Police work is dangerous and demanding.
>   B. There are good and bad things about police work.
>   C. Being a police officer is more difficult than most jobs.
>
>   ~~A.~~ This answer only focuses on the disadvantages.
>   B. This is the correct answer. The reading talks about advantages and disadvantages.
>   ~~C.~~ This answer only focuses on the disadvantages.

PRACTICE

Read the paragraph and answer the question. Mark the letter on the Answer Sheet.

My sister is a financial analyst. She travels all over the world and earns lots of money. She loves being in London one week and Shanghai the next. She doesn't have much of a personal life, but she says that will come later, when she's older. My mother doesn't understand. She thinks my sister should get married and have a family. Personally, I'm with my sister.

1. What does the author think about his sister's job?
   A The advantages are greater than the disadvantages.
   B His sister doesn't have time for a personal life.
   C His mother is unhappy with the situation.

Answer Sheet
Mark the letter.
1.

Unit 11

UNIT SUMMARY

Nouns
astronaut
chauffeur
colleague
engineer
financial analyst
graphic designer
language teacher
nurse
police officer
scientist
server
taxi driver

Verbs
make (money)
meet (people)
repair
start (work)
have (meetings /phone meetings)
travel
work (with people)

Adjectives—Describing jobs
boring
dangerous
demanding
interesting
low-paying
rewarding
unusual
well-paying

Adverbs of frequency
always
hardly ever
never
often
sometimes
usually

Make excuses
Excuse me
Sorry
Thank you

12 ▶ Great vacations

In this unit you...
- talk about types of vacations
- discuss vacation activities
- make and respond to suggestions

Grammar
- *go* + gerund

START

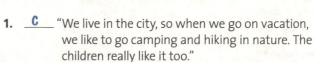

go on vacation
度假

Where do you go on vacation?

1 Look at the pictures. Who are the people? Where do you think they are? What are they doing? How do you think they feel?

2 Match the descriptions to the pictures. Then listen and check your answers.
12_01

go camping
野营
go hiking
远足; 徒步旅行

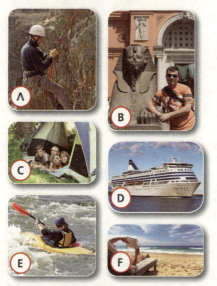

go rock climbing
攀岩
go on a cruise
乘船巡游

go kayaking
划独木舟

1. __C__ "We live in the city, so when we go on vacation, we like to go camping and hiking in nature. The children really like it too."
2. _____ "When we go on vacation, we like to relax and do nothing. So we usually go to the beach. We swim and sunbathe."
3. _____ "I love the mountains. I always go hiking and rock climbing."
4. _____ "Last year we went on a cruise. It was wonderful because they had everything you could want right on the boat—food, entertainment, and even sports."
5. _____ "I love exploring new cities and towns. I spend hours at museums and drinking coffee in the cafés."
6. _____ "Last summer we went on an adventure vacation. We went kayaking."

3 Look at the vacations in exercise 2. Number them from 1 (my favorite) to 6 (my least favorite).

Talk about it!

4 Work with a partner. Talk about your lists from exercise 3. Say why your number 1 is your favorite vacation and why number 6 is your least favorite.

Unit 12

LISTENING

Favorite vacations

1 Before listening A news reporter is interviewing Samantha. Look at the pictures. What do you think Samantha likes to do on vacation?

2 Listening (12_02) Listen and check your guesses for exercise 1.

3 Listening (12_02) Listen to the conversation again. Write *P* for activities Samantha did in Paris, *CR* for activities she is going to do in Costa Rica, or *X* for neither.

1. _CR_ go snorkeling
2. ____ go shopping
3. ____ go to museums
4. ____ go dancing
5. ____ go rock climbing
6. ____ go hiking
7. ____ sunbathe
8. ____ go sightseeing
9. ____ go bicycling
10. ____ go rafting
11. ____ take a river cruise
12. ____ go windsurfing

HELP listening

Listen for time and place
In a conversation, listen for the time and place of events. This information helps you understand the rest of the conversation.

请注意听对话中的时间和地点信息

Costa Rica
哥斯达黎加
go snorkeling
浮潜
go rafting
漂流
take a river cruise
乘游船
go sightseeing
观光
go windsurfing
风帆冲浪

4 After listening Circle the correct words to complete the sentences.

1. Samantha **likes** / doesn't like vacations out in nature.
2. Samantha likes / doesn't like adventure vacations.
3. Samantha likes / doesn't like vacations in cities.
4. Samantha's trip to Paris was two years ago / is next month.
5. Samantha's trip to Costa Rica was two years ago / is next month.

ENGLISH express

Like can be a verb.
I like to go sightseeing.
Like can also be a preposition.
What was it like?

请注意 like 的词性及用法

Talk about it!

5 Work with a partner. Tell your partner about your favorite vacation. When and where did you go? Who did you go with? What did you do?

Unit 12

VOCABULARY

Vacation activities

1 Number these vacation activities from 1 (the activity you like most) to 8 (the activity you like least). Talk about your answers with a partner.

- [ ] go swimming
- [ ] eat at restaurants
- [ ] go shopping
- [ ] go to the beach
- [ ] play tennis
- [ ] go to museums
- [ ] go bike riding
- [ ] go dancing

2 Write the names of these vacation activities under the pictures. Then listen and check.

take a tour
旅行

go hiking	go ice climbing	go snorkeling
~~go horseback riding~~	go sightseeing	go windsurfing
go rafting	go skiing	take a tour

go horseback riding _____ _____ _____

_____ _____ _____ _____ _____

3 Name the activities from exercises 1 and 2 that you can do in the places mentioned below.

1. inside _go to museums_
2. outside _____
3. in the water _____
4. when it's hot _____
5. when it's cold _____

Talk about it!

4 Work with a partner. Talk about your favorite activities to do while you are on vacation.

A: When I'm on vacation, I like to go rock climbing and camping.
B: Really? I don't like adventure vacations. I like to go sightseeing and shopping.

Unit 12

GRAMMAR

ALSO GO TO
Grammar Takeaway
PAGE 205

Go + gerund

1 Read the sentences. Circle the verb *go* in each sentence. Underline the word after *go* in each sentence. Then complete the rule.

present	past	future
I usually go sightseeing when I'm on vacation.	He went sightseeing last summer.	I'm going hiking in the mountains next summer.
She always goes shopping when she's on vacation!	We went shopping when we were in Paris.	We're going snorkeling in the ocean tomorrow.
We don't go rock climbing because it's dangerous.	I didn't go dancing last night.	She isn't going horseback riding on her next vacation.

go horseback riding
骑马

We use _____ + gerund to talk about leisure activities. A gerund is a verb that's used like a noun. Gerunds end in _____. In these sentences _____ is the verb and it agrees with the subject.

2 Complete the sentences with the correct tense and form of *go* + gerund. Then listen
12_04 and check your answers.

1. Erik _went snorkeling_ in Bermuda last year.
2. We _____ tomorrow.
3. We _____ every summer.

4. Tom _____ every winter.
5. Dan _____ on his next vacation.
6. I _____ in New York last weekend!

Talk about it!

3 Work with a partner. Ask and answer the questions. Use the correct verb tense.

1. What activities do you like to do when you go on vacation?
2. What activities do you not like to do when you go on vacation?
3. What activities did you do on your last vacation?

WORKBOOK
PAGE 92-93

Unit 12

READING

A travel blog

1 Before reading Look at the pictures from the travel blog. Where do you think the people writing the blog are? What do you think they are doing?

ENGLISH express
To have a good / great time means to enjoy something.
I had a great time on vacation.
Did you have a good time skiing?
请注意"玩得开心"的表达方式

2 Reading Read the blog to check your guesses to exercise 1.

the blog entry
博客条目

3 After reading Match each sentence to the blog entry. Check (✔) the correct box.

	Bonjour!	A difficult day
1. The weather is very hot.	☐	☐
2. They like the art.	☐	☐
3. She wrote the blog in a café.	☐	☐
4. They aren't having a good vacation.	☐	☐

4 After reading Write the underlined adjectives in the travel blogs next to the definitions.

1. very good
   fantastic
2. too many people in a place
   _____
3. not quiet
   _____
4. costs a lot of money
   _____
5. quiet and relaxing
   _____
6. not interesting
   _____
7. with a lot of tourists and stores for tourists
   _____

alice and jenny's travel blog

We are two Canadians traveling around the world. These are our stories and pictures.

August 25th

bonjour!

Bonjour, everyone! That means "hello" in French! Well, we finally made it to Europe, and our first stop is Paris! We're having a good time here. It's a really interesting place, never _boring_. There's a lot to see and do. Yesterday morning we went to an art gallery. It was really _crowded_; there were so many people! After that we went and had lunch at a restaurant. It was very good, but _expensive_. Then we walked around the old part of the city. It was so quiet and _peaceful_. I'm writing this blog entry in a café in the most beautiful city square. We're taking lots of photos.

Love,

Alice and Jenny

Unit 12

5 After reading Match the antonyms (opposites). Do they describe positive or negative things? Write N for negative or P for positive.

1. _d_ boring _N_
2. ___ crowded ___
3. ___ expensive ___
4. ___ fantastic ___
5. ___ hot ___
6. ___ noisy ___
7. ___ touristy ___

a. cheap ___
b. cold ___
c. horrible ___
d. interesting _P_
e. not crowded ___
f. not touristy ___
g. peaceful ___

> **HELP reading**
> Build vocabulary through antonyms
> *Antonyms* are two words that mean the opposite. Find antonyms to words you know to learn more vocabulary.
>
> 请注意通过反义词扩大词汇量

Talk about it!

6 Make a list of your top 5 places to go on vacation. Write adjectives to describe each place on your list. Then talk with a partner. Decide on the place you both want to go. Tell the class what place you chose and explain why.

Top 5 places for vacation
1. Brazil: exciting, crowded
2. Paris: expensive, touristy...

decide on
决定; 下决心

August 30
a difficult day

Hello, everyone! Hope everything back home is going well! We're in Cairo right now. The hotel is a long way from downtown, and it's on a very *noisy* street. It's impossible to sleep at night. We've visited a lot of monuments. The pyramids were *fantastic*! We saw the Sphinx yesterday, but it was smaller than we expected. It was really *touristy*, with a lot of people selling souvenirs and things. It's also incredibly hot. Jenny feels a little sick today, and she's staying in bed. I hope she feels better when we go to Luxor.
Love,
Alice and Jenny

PROJECT

Work in a group of three. Choose three activities that you all like to do on vacation. Do research on the Internet to find the best one or two places in the world to do your activities. Prepare a poster or presentation with information to present to the class. Be sure to answer the following questions for each activity:

1. What is the activity?
2. Where are the best places to do this activity?
3. Describe each place. What makes it good for this activity?
4. What time of year is best to go there?
5. How much does it cost to do this activity in each place?
6. Are there any dangers? If so, what?

the Sphinx
狮身人面像

go to Luxor
去卢克索(埃及)

Unit 12

CULTURE

Holidays and vacation days

1 Before reading What's your favorite holiday? Do people go to school or work on this day?

> **culture matters**
> In British English, a **holiday** means a vacation.
> I'm going on **holiday** to Mexico.
>
> 请注意"假期"的不同表达方式

2 Reading Read the information about holidays and vacation days.

Memorial Day (美国) 阵亡将士纪念日
Independence Day 独立日
Columbus Day 哥伦布发现美洲纪念日
Veterans Day 退伍军人节

In American English, a **holiday** is an official day off from work or school. These days are sometimes called national holidays or public holidays. There are 10 national holidays in the United States. They are New Year's Day, Martin Luther King Jr. Day, Presidents' Day, Memorial Day, Independence Day, Labor Day, Columbus Day, Veterans Day, Thanksgiving Day, and Christmas Day. In the United States, people who work for the government get days off from work on the national holidays. However, the government doesn't require private companies and schools to give these days off. In fact, most companies do not give their employees all of the national holidays.

A **vacation day** is also a day off from work. However, vacation days are different for each workplace and each person. Many companies in the United States give their employees ten vacation days per year when they first start their job. Employees then get more days after five or ten years. However, companies are not required by law to give vacation days.

3 After reading Work with a partner. Answer the questions.

1. What are the national holidays in your country?
2. Does the government require all schools and companies to give the national holidays off?
3. Do people get vacation days in your country?
4. How many vacation days do people usually get?

give the national holidays off 国庆放假

paid vacation days 带薪休假的天数

4 Listening Now listen to a talk show about paid vacation days around the world. Complete the chart.

| ~~Japan~~ | South Korea | Finland | Mexico |
| Brazil | the United States | Austria | |

country	minimum legal vacation time
1.	35 days
2.	35 days
3.	30 days
4. Japan	18 days
5.	10 days
6.	7 days
7.	no legal minimum

148

Unit 12

5 After listening Read the sentences. Circle *True* or *False*.

1. Brenda works for the U.S. government. True **False**
2. Most countries in the world have laws about how many vacation days True False
   companies give their employees.
3. Companies in the U.S. don't give their employees any vacation days. True False
4. The radio announcer probably doesn't get 35 vacation days in a year. True False

Talk about it!

6 Work with a partner. Ask and answer the questions.

1. How many vacation days do people usually get in your country?
2. What do people usually do on their vacation days? Where do they usually go?
3. What do people usually do on national holidays in your country?
4. Do you think it's important to have days off? Why?
5. Do you think it's better for the government or the private company to decide how many days off employees get? Why?

   A: I think it's better for the government to make a law about how many days off people have.

   B: Really? Why?

   A: Because companies...

have days off
休假; 放假

PRONUNCIATION

The /ŋ/ sound

1 The letters *ng* at the end of a word, such as in the *-ing* ending, do not usually
12_08 have a /g/ sound. However, in the middle of a word, there is usually a /g/ sound. Listen and repeat.

| camping | hiking | English | singer |

2 Now work with a partner and practice pronouncing these words.
12_09 Then listen and check.

| sightseeing | climbing | single | windsurfing |
| England | skiing | rafting | angry |

149

Unit 12

CONVERSATION

Making and responding to suggestions

1. Do you usually make your own vacation plans? If not, do you make suggestions? Does the other person listen to your suggestions? Why or why not?

2. Read the conversation. Then write the words in red in the chart below.
(12_10)

Doug: Let's go on vacation next summer!
Carol: Sure. Where do you want to go?
Doug: Hmm.... What about Thailand?
Carol: I don't know. I love Thailand, but I went there last summer. What about going somewhere new?
Doug: Sounds good to me. Where do you want to go?
Carol: I know! Why don't we go on a hiking trip in Peru?
Doug: A hiking trip? I'd rather not. Maybe something more relaxing.
Carol: Well then, how about Mexico? We can sunbathe on the beach and also go sightseeing.
Doug: That sounds perfect! Let's go!

> **CONVERSATION STRATEGY**
>
> **Make suggestions**
> You can make suggestions with **What about** in two ways:
>   **What about** + noun / noun phrase
>   **What about** + verb-ing
> What about _a trip to Peru_?
> What about _going_ somewhere new?
>
> 请注意 what about 的搭配

make suggestions
提建议

a hiking trip
徒步旅行

making suggestions	agreeing (saying "yes")	disagreeing (saying "no")
Let's		

Talk about it!

3. Work in a group of three or four. Make plans for a vacation next summer. Use the conversation in exercise 2 to help you.

4. Tell the class about your group's vacation. Decide which group has the most exciting vacation plans.

Group A: We're going to Australia and New Zealand. First, we're going snorkeling at the Great Barrier Reef...

Tell me more!

Visit the Takeaway English Online Learning Center at http://olcs.mcgraw-hill-education.com/takeaway/

 Check out the *Takeaway TV* video.

 Improve your English with the online activities.

Unit 12

WRITING

Writing a travel blog

1 Before writing When you travel, how do you communicate with your friends and family back home?

HELP writing
Use adjectives
Use adjectives in your writing to make it more interesting. Adjectives help your reader "see" what you are writing about.

请注意写作中充分发挥形容词的修饰作用

communicate with 与……交流/沟通

2 Writing model Read Nancy's travel blog. Where is she? Is she having a good time? Underline the adjectives in her blog.

---

http://www.travel/newyork

Travel Blog!

New York, New York!
June 26

Hello, everyone!

I'm having a <u>great</u> time in New York. The weather is fantastic—sunny, but not too hot. The hotel is perfect. It's in the center of the city and not too expensive. Yesterday we went to the Metropolitan Museum of Art. It was a little crowded. Right now I'm sitting in a small café next to Central Park. There are a lot of people here walking around with their families. There are some artists drawing pictures and some dancers dancing in the street. It's great!

Talk to you all soon!

Nancy

the Metropolitan Museum of Art
大都会美术馆
Central Park
中央公园

---

3 Planning your writing Now complete the chart with information about a vacation.

Where are you?	
Who are you with?	
What's the weather like?	
What activities did you do?	
What are you doing now?	

4 Writing Now write a blog entry for your vacation. Use the information in exercises 2 and 3 to help you.

WORKBOOK PAGE 94-95

Unit 12

TEST

Test-taking strategy

Summarizing   Summarizing is writing down or saying the main points of what you read or hear. A good summary includes only the main ideas. It is the general idea without all the details.

Use these steps to help you summarize.

1. Don't write down or repeat everything—only the main ideas.
2. Write down or repeat only important details.
3. Write down or repeat key words and phrases to identify Who, What, When, Where, Why, and How.
4. Write down or say only enough to give the general idea.
5. Take clear notes while you are reading or listening.

Example
You read this information.

We love to go on vacation. We go for two weeks every summer and every winter. We go to a lot of different places, but always someplace where we can do outdoor activities. We go to the beach to swim and sunbathe. We go to the mountains to hike and rock climb. We especially love camping in the forest. Last year we went camping next to a beautiful river.

You see this test question.

1. Read again. What is the best summary of the first three sentences?
   - A. We go to a lot of different places.   This is a detail.
   - B. We vacation every summer.   This is a detail.
   - C. We vacation for two weeks.   This is a detail.
   - D. We love to vacation outdoors.   This is the correct answer.

PRACTICE

Answer Sheet
Mark the letter.
1. A B C D
2. A B C D

Choose the correct answer. Mark the letter on the Answer Sheet.

1. Read. What is the best summary of the paragraph?
   - A The beach is great for swimming and sunbathing.
   - B The beach, mountains, and forest are great places to vacation.
   - C You can go rock climbing in the mountains.
   - D We love to camp in the forest.

2. Read. What is the best summary of the last three sentences?
   - A The city is not a good place to vacation.
   - B You can go kayaking in the forest.
   - C There are too many people and cars in the city.
   - D We love to camp next to a river.

Unit 12

UNIT SUMMARY

Nouns
beach
holiday
museum

Verbs—
Vacation activities
hiking
go camping
go bicycling
go dancing
go kayaking
go rafting
go shopping
go sightseeing
go snorkeling
go to the beach
go to museums
go windsurfing
relax
rock climbing
sunbathe
swim
take a river cruise

Adjectives
boring
cheap
cold
crowded
expensive
fantastic
great
hot
horrible
interesting
noisy
peaceful
perfect
touristy

Make suggestions
How about...
What about...

Respond to suggestions
I don't know.
I'd rather not...
Sounds good to me!
That sounds perfect!

Expressions
Let's go!

13 ▶ Cities around the world

In this unit you...
- describe cities
- compare cities
- agree and disagree

Grammar
- comparatives and superlatives

START

What's the city like?

1 Look at the picture. Describe what you see and feel.

2 Read the list of words that describe cities. Match the words to the definitions. Then listen and check.
<small>13_01</small>

1. __d__ population
2. _____ climate
3. _____ capital
4. _____ public transportation
5. _____ location
6. _____ nightlife
7. _____ cost of living

a. the weather; for example, warm and mild
b. entertainment and things to do at night; for example, restaurants, clubs, and theaters
c. where something is in the world; we sometimes use directions to talk about this
d. the number of people that live in an area
e. how much money it costs to live in an area, including the price for housing, food, and entertainment
f. the government center of a state or country
g. vehicles for everybody to use; for example buses, trains, subways, airplanes, and taxis

public transportation
公共交通

cost of living
生活费用

Talk about it!

3 Work with a partner. Use the information in the chart to talk about the cities. Then add one more city to the chart.

A: Where's San Francisco?
B: It's on the west coast of the United States.
A: Really? And what's it like?
B: Well, the climate...

ENGLISH express
We sometimes use **directions** to talk about **location**.

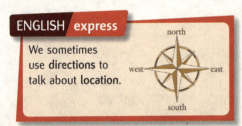

请注意方位词的英文表达方式

World cities	location	climate	population	nightlife	public transportation	cost of living
San Francisco	United States: west coast	mild, sometimes foggy	750,000	a lot of restaurants	good	expensive
Tokyo	central Japan: east coast	hot summers and mild winters	12,500,000	a lot of restaurants and clubs	excellent	very expensive
Mexico City	central Mexico	mild	18,300,000	a lot of restaurants and clubs	good	not expensive

Unit 13

LISTENING

Comparing cities

1 Before listening Look at the pictures. What do you know about Seoul and Sydney?

Seoul

Sydney

2 Listening Listen to Andy talking to his new friend Chul. Circle the correct word for each sentence.
13_02

1. Andy is from Seoul / ~~Sydney~~.
2. Andy is living in Seoul / Sydney.
3. Andy is working at / studying at the university.

HELP listening

Preview the tasks
Before you listen, read the questions. This will help you listen with a focus.

请注意听录音前读题

3 Listening Listen to the rest of the conversation. What do Andy and Chul discuss?
13_03

4 After listening Read the sentences. Circle *True* or *False*.

1. Seoul and Sydney are very different.	~~True~~	False
2. The summers are hotter in Sydney.	True	False
3. Sydney is smaller.	True	False
4. Seoul is more crowded.	True	False
5. Public transportation is better in Sydney.	True	False
6. It's more expensive to eat out in Seoul.	True	False

eat out
在外面吃饭

Talk about it!

5 Work with a partner. Ask and answer the questions.

1. Would you rather live in Seoul or Sydney? Why?
2. Is it important for you to live in a modern city? Why or why not?
3. How do Seoul and Sydney compare to your city?

would rather
宁愿; 宁可

compare to
与……相比

Unit 13

VOCABULARY

Tell me about the city

1 What's important to you in a city? Number these items from 1 to 5 (1 = most important).

☐ cost of living ☐ climate ☐ public transportation
☐ nightlife ☐ things / places in the city

2 13_04 Look at the list of words about cities. Put the words in three groups. Use a dictionary if necessary. Then listen and check. Then add more words you know to each group.

| ~~busy~~ | clean | ~~coast~~ | crowded | dangerous | dirty | downtown | ~~foggy~~ |
| harbor | humid | mild | noisy | safe | skyscraper | suburbs | tropical |

describing climate	describing cities	things / places in a city
foggy	busy	coast

3 Complete the paragraph about Panama City with words from exercise 2.

the Republic of Panama 巴拿马共和国 (中美洲)

the Pacific Ocean 太平洋

Panama City is the capital of the Republic of Panama in Central America. It has a population of approximately 1.2 million, so it's a little (1) _____ . Panama City is located on the (2) _____ of the Pacific Ocean, at the entrance of the Panama Canal. It has a (3) _____ climate, so most of the year it's very hot and (4) _____ . There are many (5) _____ in downtown Panama City, and also

high-rise apartments 高层公寓

high-rise apartments in the (6) _____ .

Talk about it!

4 Think of a city in the world. Describe it using words from this unit. Your partner guesses the city.

A: This city is big and crowded. It has some skyscrapers downtown, but it also has many old buildings and temples. The climate is tropical, so it's hot and humid all year. It's in southeast Asia in Thailand.

B: Is it Bangkok?

A: Yes!

GRAMMAR

Comparatives and superlatives

ALSO GO TO
Grammar Takeaway
PAGE 206

1 Read these city descriptions. Underline the adjective in each sentence. Then complete the rules below by circling the correct words.

comparatives	superlatives
Sydney is smaller than Seoul.	Sydney is the biggest city in Australia.
Seoul is more crowded than Sydney.	In Asia, Tokyo is the most expensive city to live in.
The cost of living is less expensive in Sydney.	In South America, Lima is the least expensive city to live in.

- Comparative sentences compare 2 / 3 or more things. For short words, add -er than / more than. For long words, add -er than / more than.
- Superlative sentences compare 2 / 3 or more things. For short words, use the + -est / the + most. For long words, use the + -est / the + most.

2 Look at the information about three cities in the United States. Complete the sentences with the comparative or superlative form of the adjective in parentheses.

city	population	air quality (10=clean / 1=dirty)	average temperature (summer / winter)	crime rate (per 1000 people)
New York	8,391,000	6.8	87°F / 27°F (31°C / -3°C)	7
Los Angeles	3,831,200	3.2	77°F / 50°F (25°C / 10°C)	8
Miami	386,681	7.5	91°F / 63°F (33°C / 17°C)	16

air quality
空气质量
average temperature
平均气温
crime rate
犯罪率

1. In New York the air is __cleaner than__ in Los Angeles. (clean)
2. Los Angeles is _____ New York. (dangerous)
3. Miami is _____ Los Angeles. (warm)
4. New York is _____ city. (cold)
5. Los Angeles is _____ Miami. (safe)
6. Miami is _____ city. (dangerous)
7. Los Angeles is _____ New York. (dirty)
8. New York is _____ city. (dangerous)

ENGLISH express

Good and bad have irregular forms:
good – better – the best
bad – worse – the worst

Seoul's public transportation is better than Sydney's public transportation.
Sydney is the worst city for driving.

请注意 good 和 bad 的比较级和最高级形式

Talk about it!

3 Work with a partner. Choose three cities in your country and compare them.

A: How about Puebla, Guadalajara, and Monterrey?
B: OK. Guadalajara is the largest of the three cities.
A: Yes, and Puebla is the coldest.
B: I think it's the highest, too.
A: Yes, I think you're right. What else?

Puebla, Mexico

Puebla
普埃布拉
(墨西哥中部)
Guadalajara
瓜达拉哈拉市
(墨西哥西部)
Monterrey
蒙特雷市
(墨西哥东北部)

WORKBOOK
PAGE 99–100

Unit 13

READING

A world-class city

1 Before reading What do you know about Sydney, Australia? Read the sentences and circle your guesses.

1. Sydney is / isn't the capital of Australia.
2. Sydney's immigrants (the people who came to live there) are mostly from Europe / from all over the world.
3. The weather in Sydney is usually hot / cold.
4. The 2000 / 2004 Summer Olympic Games were in Sydney.

2 Reading Now read the magazine article and check your guesses to exercise 1.

3 After Reading Read these statements. Circle *True* or *False*.

1. Sydney is a state capital, but not the national capital. — **True** / False
2. Sydney is the oldest city in Australia. — True / False
3. Sydney is smaller than Canberra. — True / False
4. Less than four million people live in Sydney. — True / False
5. Sydney is on the coast. — True / False
6. Sydney has a warm climate for most of the year. — True / False
7. The lifestyle in Sydney is influenced by California and Europe. — True / False
8. People in Sydney usually wear formal clothes. — True / False

HELP reading

Preview section titles
Read the section titles before you read the entire article. They tell you what each section is about.

请注意借助章节标题了解文章大意

state capital
州首府; 州政府

national capital
国家首都

multicultural city
多元文化城市

Sydney—the perfect city!

Sydney is Australia's most famous city. Although many people think it's the capital of Australia, it's only the capital of the state of New South Wales. The capital of Australia is Canberra. Sydney is, however, the biggest and oldest city in the country.

Growth of a multicultural city

In little more than two hundred years, Sydney has grown to become the most multicultural city in Australia. The first group of immigrants came to Australia from Europe. Then, in the 1970s, most of Australia's immigrants came from Asia. Today, the population of Sydney is more than four million, and the culture of the city

Unit 13

4 After reading Work with a partner. Compare Sydney to the city you live in. How are they the same? How are they different? Complete the chart with your ideas.

things that are the same	things that are different
They're both big cities.	Sydney is more modern.

is a combination of the cultures of the people who live there. When you go to a restaurant in Sydney, you can find cuisine from around the world, including Thai, Japanese, Korean, Chinese, Greek, Italian, and Mexican foods.

Life in Sydney

The climate, with almost eight months of good weather, makes Sydney the perfect city for outdoor life. What's more, the city has more than 30 beaches along the 37 miles (60 kilometers) of its coast. In Sydney harbor, one of the world's most spectacular bays, you can find the Sydney Opera House, Australia's most well-known building. Passing by the Opera House is a constant parade of small boats, yachts, ferries, and enormous cruise ships.

In Sydney, a California lifestyle has been combined with European influences in its cafés, movie theaters, theaters, and concert halls. Shorts and sandals are the most popular clothes to wear, and beer and barbecues are everywhere.

Today and beyond

Sydney has come a long way in a short time. In the year 2000, the city hosted the Summer Olympic Games. This put Sydney even more in the spotlight. Sydney is a world-class city that's looking toward the future.

Talk about it!

5 Work in groups. Talk about your charts from exercise 4.

> **A:** Sydney and Caracas are both big cities.
> **B:** Yes, and I think Sydney is more modern. Is that right?
> **C:** Yes, I think so.
> **A:** Also Sydney…

CONVERSATION STRATEGY

Use I think so when you think something is correct, but you are not 100% certain. The negative form is I don't think so.

请注意 I think so 所表达的意思及其否定形式

PROJECT

Work in a group. Choose another important city in the world. Research information about the city, and write a magazine article that answers the questions below. Also include photos.

1. What is the history of the city?
2. What is the current population?
3. What's the climate like?
4. What are the food and lifestyle like?
5. What are the most important sights and activities in the city?
6. What are the most important events in the city's history?

what's more
而且; 此外

Sydney harbor
悉尼港
the Sydney Opera House
悉尼歌剧院
pass by
经过; 过去
cruise ship
大型游船; 豪华游船
combine with
与……结合

in the spotlight
使显著
world-class city
世界一流城市
look toward
为……做好准备

Unit 13

CONVERSATION STRATEGY
Use I'm not sure to say "I don't know".

SONG

All around the world

请注意"我不知道"的不同表达方式

1 Before listening Match the cities to the countries. Two cities are in the same country. Then look at the photos on the page. Can you find any of these cities?

1. _b_ Bogota   a. Canada
2. ____ Delhi   b. Colombia
3. ____ Istanbul   c. India
4. ____ Karachi   d. Japan
5. ____ Montreal   e. Mali
6. ____ Mumbai   f. Pakistan
7. ____ Seoul   g. South Korea
8. ____ Timbuktu   h. Turkey
9. ____ Tokyo

2 Before listening What do you know about each of the cities in exercise 1? Talk about it with a partner.

A: I know Tokyo is a very modern city.
B: That's true. I think they also have traditional things like old temples. What's Timbuktu like?
A: I'm not sure. Do you know?
B: No, I'm not sure either!

3 Listening (13_06) Listen and complete the song with the city names from exercise 1.

All around the world

Chorus 1

(1) _____ is smaller than (2) _____,
Which isn't quite as big as (3) _____.
And (4) _____ is enormous,
And (5) _____ even bigger,
But (6) _____ is the biggest of them all.

I met a girl in (7) _____.
She looked like you,
But she was just a little taller.
And then a girl in (8) _____,
Beneath the stars,
With eyes like yours but hers were smaller.

Chorus 2

I just don't know where I can find
A girl to take you off my mind.
I need the biggest city in the whole wide world,
And maybe there I'll find that girl.

Chorus 1

There was a girl in (9) _____.
She was beautiful,
But not as beautiful as you are.
I've met girls all around the world
With lips that smile and hair that curls.
But none of them compares with you, dear.

Chorus 2
Chorus 1

Unit 13

4 Listening Listen again. Answer the question. Check (✓) your answer.
13_06

Who is *you* in the song?

- [ ] the singer's girlfriend
- [ ] the singer's mother
- [ ] the singer's ex-girlfriend

5 After listening Match the underlined words and expressions in the song to the definitions.

1. very big — *enormous*
2. under, below — _____
3. is smaller than — _____
4. possibly — _____
5. had the same appearance as — _____
6. make me forget — _____

Talk about it!

6 Work with a partner. Talk about the questions.

1. Do you like to visit different cities and countries?
2. Do you want to live in a different city or country? Why? Why not?
3. Do you have any friends or family in different countries?
4. Do people from your country go to other countries to work? Where do they go?

PRONUNCIATION

Sentence stress

1 In English, we stress the most important words in a sentence. These are the words that carry the
13_07 meaning. Listen and repeat.

<u>Tokyo</u> is more <u>modern</u> than <u>Mexico City</u>.
<u>New York</u> is the most <u>exciting</u> city in the <u>world</u>!

2 Listen and underline the words that are stressed.
13_08

1. The country is more relaxing than the city.
2. The country is safer than the city.
3. The city is more interesting than the country.
4. The city is louder than the country.
5. The country is cleaner than the city.

Unit 13

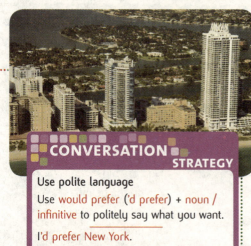

CONVERSATION

Agreeing and disagreeing

1 Which city would you prefer to live in: Los Angeles, Miami, or New York? Explain.

2 Listen to a conversation between two friends.
13_09
1. Which city does Jack prefer? _____
2. Which city does Liza prefer? _____

3 Complete the conversation with expressions from
13_09 the box. Then listen again to check your answers.

I don't know about that.	I know what you mean.	That's true, but...
I see what you mean, but...	I totally agree.	That's so true!

CONVERSATION STRATEGY

Use polite language
Use **would prefer** (**'d prefer**) + noun / infinitive to politely say what you want.
I'd prefer New York.
Jason **would prefer to live** in Seattle.

请注意礼貌用词 prefer 的用法

prefer to
较喜欢; 宁愿

Jack: Which city would you prefer to live in: Los Angeles, Miami, or New York?

Liza: Well, New York is the biggest city. And it's probably the most interesting.

Jack: (1) _That's true, but..._ the air is cleaner in Miami, and it's also the warmest city. I really like warm weather.

Liza: (2) _____ I don't like cold weather. But Miami is also the most dangerous!

Jack: (3) _____ I don't want to be unsafe...

Liza: And what about all those hurricanes?

plan ahead
提前计划

Jack: (4) _____ I think people can plan ahead for the hurricanes. So it's not a big problem.

Liza: (5) _____ There are a lot of problems with the hurricanes every year.

Jack: Yeah, but anyway, I still think I'd prefer Miami. It has a good lifestyle.

Liza: (6) _____ Overall, it's probably a nice place to live.

Talk about it!

4 Work with a partner. Choose three cities you know. Which of the cities would you prefer to live in? Talk about it with your partner. Use the expressions in exercise 2 to agree and disagree.

Tell me more!

Visit the Takeaway English Online Learning Center at http://olcs.mcgraw-hill-education.com/takeaway/

 Check out the *Takeaway TV* video.

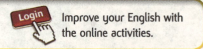 Improve your English with the online activities.

Unit 13

WRITING

Writing a comparison essay about two cities

1 Before writing What do you know about Dublin (Ireland) and Singapore? Read the sentences and circle your guesses.

1. Dublin is bigger / smaller than Singapore.
2. Dublin is more / less humid than Singapore.
3. Dublin is more / less modern than Singapore.

> **HELP writing**
> Write a concluding sentence
> When you write, end each paragraph with a concluding sentence. This sentence should summarize the main idea of the paragraph.
>
> 请注意在段落结束时使用结束句

2 Writing model Read the model and check your guesses to exercise 1. Then read it again. Underline the comparatives and superlatives. Circle the concluding sentence.

A comparison of two cities: Dublin and Singapore

Dublin and Singapore are both cities, but they are very different. Singapore is an island nation and also a city. It is the smallest country in southeast Asia. Dublin is the largest city in the Republic of Ireland and it's also the capital. It's on the southeast coast, on the River Liffey. Singapore is very close to the equator and is hotter and more humid than Dublin. The climate in Dublin is milder. Singapore is much bigger than Dublin. It has a population of 5,075,000, compared to approximately 1,046,000 in Dublin. Also, Singapore is more modern and the public transportation is better. However, Dublin is a very pretty city. It has many beautiful old buildings and parks. These two cities are very different, but it is impossible to say which one is the best.

Dublin

Singapore

island nation
岛国
the Republic of Ireland
爱尔兰共和国
the River Liffey
利菲河(爱尔兰)

3 Planning your writing Choose a city to compare to your city. Complete the chart.

	city 1:	city 2:
location		
weather		
population		
adjectives that describe it		

4 Writing Now write a comparison of the two cities. Use the information in exercises 2 and 3 to help you.

Unit 13

TEST

Test-taking strategy

Describing a picture Many tests ask students to describe a picture. The student may be asked to describe the picture orally (by speaking) or by writing about it.

Use these steps to help you describe a picture.

1. Avoid single word answers or lists. Use full sentences. On some tests you will be given vocabulary to use.
2. Avoid complicated explanations or grammar.
3. Answer the questions: *Who? What? When? Where? Why?* and *How?*
4. Imagine you are describing the picture to someone who can't see it.
5. Make your description interesting with color and detail. Use adjectives!
6. Practice describing different pictures with a partner before the test.

Hispanic family
西班牙家庭
grilled meat
烤肉

palm tree
棕榈树

Example picture

Example description

There is a Hispanic family eating a delicious meal outside. There is grilled meat, fruit, vegetables, and juice on the table. It looks like grandparents, parents and children. I think it's in a tropical country because there are palm trees and the climate looks warm.

It is during the day so it could be lunch. They are all wearing colorful clothes, and they look very happy. I think it might be a barbecue.

PRACTICE

Describe this picture. Write as many descriptive sentences as you can think of.

UNIT SUMMARY

Nouns
capital
climate
cost of living
location
nightlife
population
transportation

Nouns—places in the city
coast
downtown
harbor
skyscraper
suburb

Adjectives—describing cities
big
clean
crowded
dangerous
dirty
enormous
exciting
harbor
modern
noisy
safe
small

Adjectives—climate
foggy
hot
humid
tropical

Agreeing expressions
I know what you mean.
I totally agree.
That's true!

Disagreeing expressions
I don't know about that.
I know what you mean, but...

Polite disagreeing expressions
I'd prefer...
I would prefer to...

14 ▶ Wildlife

In this unit you...
- talk about endangered animals
- describe animal actions
- use measurements

Grammar
- *can* and *can't* for ability and permission

START

ENGLISH express
Animals that are endangered have a very low population. They might become extinct (no more living in the world).

请注意"动物濒临灭绝"的不同表达法

endangered animal
濒危动物
become extinct
灭绝；绝种

Endangered animals

1 What's your favorite animal? Why? Have you ever seen an endangered animal? Where?

2 Write the names of the endangered animals under the pictures. Then listen and check.
14_01

Black Rhinoceros
黑犀牛

| Spotted Tree Frog | ~~Bengal Tiger~~ | Black Rhinoceros | Giant Panda |

Bengal Tiger
孟加拉虎

1. _Bengal tiger_   2. _____   3. _____   4. _____

3 Listen to information about the four endangered animals. Complete the chart with the words from the box. Then listen again and check.
14_02

| India | ~~1,500~~ | Australia | Black Rhinoceros | 3,600 | China | 3,000 |

animal	place	population
Bengal Tiger		1,500
Giant Panda		
Spotted Tree Frog		4,000
	Africa	

Talk about it!

4 Work with a partner. Make a list of the animal names that you know in English. Put a star (*) next to the ones that are endangered. Use the Internet if necessary.

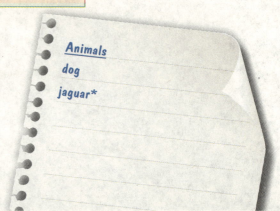

Unit 14

ENGLISH express
We say *male* and *female* when we talk about animals. With people, a *male* is a man or a boy. A *female* is a woman or a girl.

请注意 male 和 female 的用法

LISTENING

An endangered bird

1 Before listening Label the picture of the birds with the words in the box.

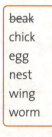
- ~~beak~~
- chick
- egg
- nest
- wing
- worm

1. beak
2. _____
3. _____
4. _____
5. _____
6. _____

2 Listening Listen to part of an interview about the kakapo, an endangered bird. Circle *True* or *False*.

14_03

1. The kakapo is a kind of parrot.   True   False
2. The kakapo doesn't have wings.   True   False
3. The kakapo can't fly.   True   False
4. The kakapo lives up in the trees in New Zealand.   True   False

3 Listening Listen to the rest of the interview. Circle the correct answers.

14_04

1. Right now, the kakapo population is _____.
   A 7   B 60   C 67
2. The chicks are _____.
   A on the islands   B in the wild   C with scientists
3. The islands are safe because there are no _____.
   A rats or cats   B people   C birds
4. People can help by _____.
   A visiting the islands   B sending money   C not visiting the islands

HELP listening

Listen for specific information

When you listen for specific information, make sure you know exactly what you're listening for and what task you have to complete. Read all of the questions *before* you listen.

请注意带着问题听具体信息

Talk about it!

4 Work with a partner. Talk about the questions.

1. What are common birds in your country? What do they look like? Where do they live? What do they eat?
2. What endangered birds live in your country?

WORKBOOK PAGE 104

Unit 14

VOCABULARY

Animal actions

1 Animals can do many things. Match the actions to the animals.

1. _____ swim   a. bird
2. _____ fly   b. lion
3. _____ run fast   c. fish

2 Write the actions next to the pictures. Then listen and check.
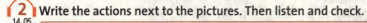

| climb | hear | hibernate | hide | hunt | jump | lay eggs | see |

1. _see_
2. _____
3. _____
4. _____
5. _____
6. _____
7. _____
8. _____

3 Write the actions from exercise 2 in the sentences.

1. Many animals _____ other animals. Then they eat them.
2. We use our eyes to _____ .
3. Kangaroos live in Australia. They _____ to get around.
4. Most animals _____ when they're scared. This way, other animals and people can't see them.
5. We use our ears to _____ .
6. Some animals _____ , or sleep, in winter.
7. Dogs can't _____ trees, but cats can.
8. Birds _____ in nests. Then they sit on the eggs until they hatch.

this way
这样；
用这种办法

Talk about it!

4 Work with a partner. Describe an animal and its actions. Your partner guesses the animal.

A: This animal is very big. It hunts for food, and it hibernates in the winter.
B: Is it a bear?
A: Yes!

Unit 14

GRAMMAR

Can and can't for ability and permission

ALSO GO TO
Grammar Takeaway
PAGE **207**

1 Read the sentences. <u>Underline</u> *can* or *can't* in each sentence. Circle the verb.

1. Kakapos can (lay) two sets of eggs in one year.
2. Maria can't swim today. She's sick.
3. **A:** Can I come in?
   B: Yes, you can.
4. Kakapos can't fly, but they can climb trees.

ENGLISH express

Can't is the contraction for *cannot*. We usually use *can't* in conversation.

请注意 can 的否定形式及用法

2 Look at the chart. We use *can* and *can't* + verb in base form to talk about ability or permission.

	affirmative	negative	question	answer
ability	He can hear us. Tigers can swim.	It can't fly. Dogs can't climb.	Can you swim? Can kakapos fly?	Yes, I can. No, they can't.
permission	You can sit here.	You can't sit here.	Can I sit here?	Yes, you can.

3 Complete each sentence with *can* or *can't* plus the verb in parentheses. Also
14_06 write *A* for Ability or *P* for Permission. Then listen and check your answers.

1. __A__   Penguins __can't fly__, but they __can swim__. (fly / swim)
2. _____   My dog _____ in the house, but it _____ on the sofa. (**come / sit**)
3. _____   Bats _____, but they _____. (**see / hear**)
4. _____   People visiting the zoo _____ the baby rhinoceros, but they _____ it. (**see / touch**)
5. _____   The ostrich _____, but it _____ fast. (**fly / run**)
6. _____   Tigers _____, but they _____. (**jump / fly**)
7. _____   **A:** _____ bats _____? (**fly**)
           B: Yes, they _____.
8. _____   **A:** _____ Tom _____ to the movies? (**go**)
           B: No, he _____. He's doing homework tonight.

penguin

bat
baby rhinoceros
小犀牛

ostrich

Talk about it!

4 Tell a partner about what you can and can't do. Say three things that are true and one thing that is not true. Your partner guesses the one that's not true.

A: I can use a computer. I can play tennis. I can't cook. I can't speak English.
B: You *can* cook. You make great tacos!
A: Yes! That's right!

make tacos
做玉米饼

Unit 14

READING

Animal facts

1 Before reading What do you know about tigers? Complete the sentences.

1. Tigers live...
2. They eat...
3. They can...

HELP reading

Skim for the general idea
You can skim (read quickly) to get the general idea of a text. It's not always necessary to read and understand every word. In this exercise you need general information. Read the text quickly. Look for words that help you complete the task.

请注意如何快速略读抓住文章大意

encyclopedia article
百科全书中的文章

2 Reading Read the encyclopedia article and answer the questions.
14_07

1. What animal is it about? _____
2. Where does it live today? _____
3. Is this animal endangered? _____

Siberian Tiger
西伯利亚虎

light color
浅色

wild boar
野猪(雄性)

thanks to
由于；因为

conservation and protection program
保护项目

http://www.encyclodopedia-thesiberiantiger.com

encyclopedia

The Siberian Tiger

The **Siberian tiger** (*Panthera tigris altaica*) is a rare kind of tiger. It is one of the largest tigers in the world. It is also endangered.

Male Siberian tigers are usually 9 to 11 feet (2.7 to 3.3 meters) long, from head to tail. There are some reports, however, of males being more than 11.5 feet (3.5 meters) long. Males usually weigh 440 to 660 pounds (200 to 300 kilograms). Females are normally smaller than males. They are usually 8 to 9.5 feet (2.4 to 2.9 meters) long from head to tail, and weigh between 220 and 440 pounds (100 and 200 kilograms).

Siberian tigers live in very cold habitats. They have thick fur and large feet for walking in snow. They are usually of a light orange and brown color. Siberian tigers can hunt very well. They eat other wild animals, such as wild boars, deer, and even black bears.

In the early 1900s, Siberian tigers lived in north eastern China, the Korean peninsula, north eastern Mongolia, and south eastern Russia. Today there are almost no Siberian tigers in South Korea, and only a small number of them living in Russia. In the 1940s there were approximately 50 tigers in Russia. Thanks to conservation and protection programs, the present population in the wild is estimated to be about 500, mostly in China and Russia.

Unit 14

3 After reading Complete the chart with the facts.

scientific name		
colors		
weight	male:	female:
length	male:	female:
present population		

Talk about it!

4 Work with a partner. Look at the information about the three different endangered species. You can give money to help one animal. Talk about which one you want to help and why.

Animal Aid

Investing in the future and our natural heritage
With a small donation, you can help save animals in danger.

- The Siberian tiger (mostly in China and Russia)—approximate population of 500
- The Giant Panda (China)—approximate population of 1,200
- The kakapo (New Zealand)—approximate population of 60

Act now before it's too late!

invest in
投资；购买
in danger
处于危险中

A: I think we should help the kakapo because there aren't many of them.
B: That's true, but in my opinion...

PROJECT

Work with a partner. Choose another endangered animal to research. Write an encyclopedia article that answers the following questions:

1. Where does this animal live?
2. How many are there in the world?
3. What does it look like?
4. What can it do?
5. What does it eat?
6. What conservation efforts are going on to help the animal?

conservation efforts
为保护付出的努力

Unit 14

CULTURE

Wildlife conservation vacations

1 Before reading Look at the subtitles and pictures in the brochure. Guess the answers to these questions.

1. What do you think wildlife conservation vacations are?
2. Who goes on these vacations?
3. What do the people do when they're there?

2 Reading Read the first part of the wildlife conservation brochure. Circle *True* or *False*.
14_08

1. These vacations are in different places. False
2. College students and working adults can go on these vacations. True False
3. Children can go on these vacations. True False
4. You can work with animals on these vacations. True False
5. Accommodations (where you sleep) are included in the price. True False

in good health
身体健康

3 Reading Read the rest of brochure. Which vacation does each sentence talk about? Write *CR* for Costa Rica, *M* for Mexico, or *T* for Thailand.
14_09

1. __T__ Stay for 4 weeks.
2. _____ Work with jaguars, birds, and turtles.
3. _____ Live in tents on the beach.
4. _____ Cook and work in the camp.
5. _____ Live in air-conditioned bungalow apartments.
6. _____ Work with elephants.
7. _____ Stay for 10 weeks.
8. _____ Visit the city and the beach.

air-conditioned bungalow apartments
有空调的别墅公寓

Talk about it!

4 Work with a partner. Talk about these questions.

1. Which conservation vacation would you like to go on? Explain why.
2. What can you learn on these vacations? Make a list.
3. What conservation projects are there in your country?

WILDLIFE CONSERVATION VACATIONS

Do you want to have an exciting adventure vacation? Do you want to help animals and ecosystems that are in danger? If you want a different type of vacation, these trips are perfect for you.

Who are these vacations for?

We organize conservation vacations for people of all ages and professions. You work in a team on one of many projects. These projects include research and work with endangered animals around the world. You also work with local communities.

What are the requirements? You need to...

- be at least 18 years of age
- be in good health
- have a valid passport
- pay for food, extras, etc.
- pay for your plane ticket, accommodations, and travel costs.

Unit 14

Country: COSTA RICA
Weeks: 5
Cost: $2,550
Description: Explore the beautiful rainforests of Costa Rica and work on a variety of forest and marine conservation projects.
Activities: These include working with mammals (mostly jaguars), birds, and marine turtles. You will record information and also work with children in the local community.
Accommodations: Accommodations are simple but comfortable at the Cromos Biological Research Station in the forest near the coast. You will help in the camp, doing cooking and other camp work.

Country: MEXICO
Weeks: 10
Cost: $3,500
Description: This is a coral reef research and community education program. In this program you can explore and study one of the largest coral reef systems in the world.
Activities: You will stay on a beautiful beach on the Caribbean Sea and study the animals and plants of the coast and the waters. You will spend most days snorkeling and scuba-diving on the reef. Also, you can visit the Mayan ruins and learn some Spanish.
Accommodations: Tent accommodations are provided in a beautiful beach location.

Country: THAILAND
Weeks: 4
Cost: $1,500
Description: This project is in an established elephant camp near the city of Pattaya. Currently there are 18 elephants living in the camp. In the past, these elephants worked in the forests, but they are no longer needed there. They are in danger of being abandoned or taken to the cities, where they live in bad conditions.
Activities: During this vacation you will work with the elephants and take care of them.
Accommodations: Accommodations are bungalow apartments near the camp. The camp is near the city and also the beautiful beach of Jomtien. You can visit both of these in your free time. Rooms have air-conditioning, hot water, and TV.

a variety of
各种各样的……
coral reef system
珊瑚礁系统

the Caribbean Sea
加勒比海

scuba-diving
配戴水肺的潜水；
轻便潜水
Mayan ruins
玛雅遗址
Biological Research Station
生物研究站

PRONUNCIATION

The sounds /aɪ/ *five* and /ɪ/ *it*

1 The vowel *i* has different sounds in English. It can have the long sound /aɪ/ as in *five*, or the short sound /ɪ/ as in *it*. Put the words into two groups according to the *i* sound.

| animal | dig | hibernate | kind | ostrich | tiger |
| climb | fish | hide | Mexico | swim | wild |

/aɪ/ *five*	/ɪ/ *it*
	animal

2 Now listen and check your answers to exercise 1.

Unit 14

the metric system
十进制; 公制

Caribbean islands
加勒比群岛
the Imperial System
英制系统

shortened version
缩写形式

CONVERSATION

Using measurements

1 Read the information about measurements in the world. Which system does your country use?

2 🎧 14_12 Listen to two conversations. Where do you think each one takes place, in the U.S. or in another country?

3 🎧 14_12 Complete the conversations with expressions from the box. Then listen to check your answers.

in length	in weight	long
~~tall~~	weigh	weighs

1. **Dr. Smith:** How tall are you, Maria?
   Maria: I'm five feet six inches (**1**) _tall_ .
   Dr. Smith: How much do you weigh?
   Maria: I (**2**) _____ 125 pounds.

2. **Bill:** How much does the kakapo weigh?
   Mr. Kim: It (**3**) _____ about 3.5 kilos.
   Bill: How long is the kakapo?
   Mr. Kim: It's usually 30 centimeters (**4**) _____ .
   Bill: And what about the koala? How much does it weigh?
   Mr. Kim: A male koala is usually 12 kilos (**5**) _____ .
   Bill: And what is the length of the koala?
   Mr. Kim: The male koala is usually about 78 centimeters (**6**) _____ .

culture matters

Most countries in the world use the metric system. Common units of measure are the meter, centimeter, and kilogram. The United States and some Caribbean islands use the Imperial System of measurement. Common units of measure are the foot, the inch, the yard, and the pound.

请注意常用的度量单位
(不同的国家和地区使用不同的度量方法)

CONVERSATION STRATEGY

Use shortened words

In conversation, we use shortened versions of long words. For example, say **kilos** instead of kilograms.

请注意在口语中常使用缩略语

Talk about it!

4 Work with a partner. Say the weight or height of something. Your partner guesses the question you are answering.

A: 185 centimeters tall.
B: How tall are you?
A: No!
B: How tall is your dad?

A: Yes!
B: OK, my turn... 3.4 kilos in weight.
A: How much did you weigh as a baby?
B: Yes!

Tell me more!

Visit the Takeaway English Online Learning Center at http://olcs.mcgraw-hill-education.com/takeaway/

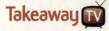 Check out the *Takeaway TV* video.   Improve your English with the online activities.

Unit 14

WRITING

Writing an essay about an endangered animal

HELP writing
Make a plan with details
Before you write, plan out the key details of your writing.
请注意在写作前谋划好关键细节

plan out
策划；筹划

grizzly bear
灰熊(分布于北美)

1 Before writing Match the animal names to the pictures.

1. polar bear   2. koala   3. grizzly bear   4. panda bear

A. ☐   B. ☐   C. ☐   D. ☐

2 Writing model Read the model essay. Label the key details of the writing.

| what people can do to help | ~~name and description of animal~~ | current population |
| where they live | why they're in danger | |

The Koala: an animal in danger

Koalas are small animals with gray fur. They usually weigh between 11 and 40 pounds (5 and 18 kilos). Koalas are very cute. They are a symbol of Australia, the only country they live in. Although the koala is not officially endangered (the population is estimated to be between 40,000 and 80,000), there is a danger that koalas will be extinct in 15 or 20 years. This is because its habitat is being destroyed, and also because of accidents with cars and attacks from dogs. People who want to help can give money to different organizations that are working to protect koalas, such as the Koala Protection Society and the Australian Koala Foundation.

1. _name and description_
2. _____
3. _____
4. _____
5. _____

because of
因为；由于

the Koala Protection Society
考拉保护协会
the Australian Koala Foundation
澳大利亚考拉基金会

3 Planning your writing Now choose an animal to write about. Plan the key details of your report in the chart below. Use the Internet as necessary.

name and description	
where they live and population	
why they're in danger	
what people can do to help	

4 Writing Now write an essay about your animal. Use the information in exercises 2 and 3 to help you.

Unit 14

TEST

Test-taking strategy

make inferences
推论；推断

Making inferences (drawing conclusions) An inference is something you figure out that you didn't already know or learn. You can use information or clues that you do have to infer, or figure out, new information or facts.

Use these steps to help you make inferences.

make sure (that)
确信

1. Make sure that you clearly understand the information provided.
2. Use information that you already know to help you.

read between the lines
领会言外之意

3. Read between the lines: what conclusions can you draw from all the information you have?

make sense
有意义；有道理

4. Does your inference or conclusion make sense? Can you argue why it is true?

ENGLISH express

Use *probably* when something is likely. You are not 100% sure.
It will *probably* rain today.

请注意 probably 的词义及其在句中的位置

Example
Based on the information, answer the questions. Mark the letter on the Answer Sheet.

Bats are not birds, but they can fly. Bats can't see very well, but they can hear very well.

Ostriches can't fly, but they can run fast. They lay the largest eggs of any bird. Penguins are birds, but they can't fly. They can, however, swim very well.

1. Which one of these animals is a mammal?

   ~~A.~~ penguin — Penguins and ostriches are both birds so one is probably not a mammal.
   B. bat — This is the correct answer. A bat is not a bird so it's probably a mammal.
   ~~C.~~ ostrich — Ostriches and penguins are both birds so one is probably not a mammal.

PRACTICE

Read the paragraph and answer the questions. Mark the letter on the Answer Sheet.

1. What is the largest animal discussed?
   A bat
   B ostrich
   C penguin

2. Which animal is a very good hunter at night?
   A bat
   B ostrich
   C penguin

3. Which animal loves to eat fish?
   A bat
   B ostrich
   C penguin

Answer Sheet
Mark the letter.
1. A B C
2. A B C
3. A B C

WORKBOOK PAGE 110

Unit 14

UNIT SUMMARY

Nouns—animals
bear
bird
frog
ostrich
owl
penguin
rabbit
squirrel
tiger

Nouns—endangered animals
Bengal Tiger
Black Rhinocero
Giant Panda
Grizzly Bear
Koala
Polar Bear
Siberian Tiger
Spotted Tree Frog

Verbs—animal actions
climb
dig
eat
fish
fly
hear
hibernate
hide
hunt
jump
lay eggs
run
see
swim

Units of measure
centimeter
foot
inch
kilogram
meter
pound
yard

Expressions—using measurements
(number) + inches + long
(number) + meters + long
(number) + feet + long
(number) + yard + long

(number) + pounds + weight
(number) + kilograms + weight

15 ▸ All about sports

> **In this unit you...**
> • discuss sports
> • describe sports actions
> • talk about rules
>
> **Grammar**
> • *must* and *have to*

START

What sports do you play or do?

1 Look at the picture above. Where are the people? What are they doing? How do you think they feel?

2 Write the names of the sports under the pictures. Then listen and check.
15_01

| gymnastics |
| ping-pong |
| taekwondo |
| volleyball |
| hockey |
| ~~rugby~~ |
| track |
| yoga |

taekwondo
跆拳道

 1. _rugby_
 2. _____
 3. _____
 4. _____
 5. _____
 6. _____
   7. _____
 8. _____

3 Write the sports from exercises 1 and 2. Then add more sports you know.

1. played / done in a building:
   yoga,
2. played / done outside:
3. played / done alone:
4. played / done with a team:

> **ENGLISH express**
>
> We use **play** for sports that involve a ball. We use **do** for most other sports.
>
> I **play** soccer.
> She **does** gymnastics.
>
> 请注意 play 和 do 与体育项目的搭配

Talk about it!

4 Number these sports from 1 (your favorite) to 7 (your least favorite). Then talk with a partner about your answers.

	baseball	basketball	gymnastics	ping-pong	soccer	taekwondo	skiing
play/do							
watch							

A: My favorite sport to play is ping-pong. What do you have as number 1?
B: I have soccer as number 1 for my favorite sport to play. I have basketball as number 1 for my favorite sport to watch.

Unit 15

LISTENING

My favorite sport

1 Before listening You will hear three interviews. The people are talking about their favorite sports. Look at the words they use. Talk about any new words as a class. Predict (guess) each person's favorite sport. Write it next to the name.

HELP listening

Make predictions
Before you listen, make predictions (guesses) about what you will hear. Then listen for information to confirm your predictions.

请注意对听力内容进行预测

1. Samantha _____ 2. Masumi _____ 3. Doug _____

SCARED GO FAST EXCITING TRAIL BEAUTIFUL VACATION MOUNTAINS WINTER SNOW

BALANCE COORDINATION WHITE CLOTHES PROTECT MYSELF PUNCHES RULES DISCIPLINE KICKS BLACK BELT

WONDERFUL COORDINATION ICE WIN TEAM PUCK SCHOOL GRASS SMALL BALL

2 Listening Listen to the three interviews. Check your predictions in exercise 1. Then answer these questions. Check (✔) the correct boxes.
15_02

	Samantha	Masumi	Doug
1. Who does a sport that isn't very popular?			✔
2. Who doesn't do the sport often?			
3. Who plays on a team?			
4. Who started doing the sport 8 years ago?			
5. Who has to travel to do the sport?			
6. Who has to wear special white clothes?			

3 After listening Answer the questions about you.

1. What are your favorite sports to play / do? (If you don't play / do any sports, what's your favorite sport to watch?) _____
2. What do you like about the sports? _____

Talk about it!

4 Work with a partner. Talk about your answers to exercise 3.

A: What are your favorite sports?
B: One of my favorite sports is badminton.
A: What do you like about it?
B: It's hard but fun to play. And it's good exercise. What about you?
A: I like to play soccer. It's...

Unit 15

VOCABULARY

Sports actions

take turns
轮流
act out
把……表演出来

1 Work in a group. Take turns acting out different sports. The group guesses the sport.

2 Write the sports action words under the pictures. Then listen and check.

bounce   hit   kick   lose   score   ~~throw~~   tie   win

1. throw
2. _____
3. _____
4. _____
5. _____
6. _____
7. _____
8. _____

3 Write the sports action words from exercise 2 to make phrases.

1. _hit, throw_ the baseball
2. _____ the game
3. _____ a point
4. _____ with another team
5. _____ the soccer ball
6. _____ a goal

Talk about it!

4 Work with a partner. Describe a sport and its actions. Your partner guesses the sport.

run up and down
a court
在球场上跑来跑去
bounce the ball
拍球

A: You play this sport with a team. Players run up and down a court. They bounce the ball. Then they throw the ball into a basket.
B: Is it basketball?
A: Yes!

Unit 15

GRAMMAR

Must and **have to**

ALSO GO TO
Grammar Takeaway
PAGE **208**

1 Read the sentences. <u>Underline</u> *must / must not* and *have to / don't have to* in each sentence. Check the box to say if it's obligation (necessity), no obligation (choice), or prohibition (not allowed). Then complete the rule.

	obligation	no obligation	prohibition
1. You <u>don't have to</u> go fast if you're scared. You can choose an easier trail and go slower.		✓	
2. There are no mountains where I live, so I have to go during my vacation.			
3. Students must wear special white clothes.			
4. We must not hit each other in the head.			
5. You don't have to play it on ice. You can play it on grass too.			

We use ___*must*___ and _____ to talk about obligation. We use _____ to talk about prohibition. We use _____ to talk about having no obligation.

2 Complete each sentence with *must, must not, have / has to,* or *don't / doesn't have to* plus the word in parentheses.

1. Basketball players __must not run__ with the ball. They must bounce it all the time. (**run**)
2. Gymnasts also _____ how to dance. This is required of everyone. (**learn**)
3. Tennis players _____ the ball if it's out of the lines. It's their choice. (**hit**)
4. Athletes _____ junk food. It's important that they have a healthy diet. (**eat**)
5. Baseball players _____ good at hitting the ball, so they have to practice every day. (**be**)

out of the lines
越界
have a healthy diet
健康饮食

Talk about it!

3 Work with a partner. Choose two sports. Write the rules of the game. Use *must, must not, have / has to* or *don't / doesn't have to*.

4 Now read the rules to the class. The class guesses the sport.

A/B: In this sport, teams must have 11 players. Players on the field have to kick the ball or hit it with their head. They must not throw the ball.

Class: It's soccer!

A/B: Yes!

Soccer rules:
1. Teams must have 11 players.
2. Players on the field have to kick the ball or hit it with their head.

Unit 15

READING

A great sporting moment

1 Before reading Look at the titles of the two newspaper articles. Guess the answers to these questions.

1. What sport are the articles about?
2. Who are the teams?
3. Why is the game important?
4. Who won?

HELP reading

Scan for key words
When you have a set of specific questions, you can scan the text for those details. Look for key words that help you find the answers.

请注意查读的技巧

2 Reading Read the articles and check your guesses to exercise 1.

First U.S.–Cuba game in 40 years

The Baltimore Orioles are now the first U.S. baseball team to visit Cuba in 40 years. The Orioles played the Cuban national team yesterday and won the game 3–2. But it wasn't an easy victory. The Orioles were up 2–0 after the second inning, but the score was 2–2 when the final inning started. The two teams played in front of 50,000 people at the *Estadio Latinoamericano* in Havana. Fidel Castro was there. Baseball is extremely popular in Cuba, and Castro is Cuba's number 1 baseball fan. He played baseball for the University of Havana when he was a student.

Orioles lose to Cubans in return game

The Cubans took revenge last night for the game they lost in Havana two months ago. The Baltimore Orioles beat the Cubans 3–2 in Cuba, but in yesterday's return game at the Camden Yards stadium, the Cubans beat the Orioles 12–6. Rain stopped the game for 56 minutes in the first inning. When the game started again, the Orioles could not stop the Cubans. This was the first ever game between a Cuban and an American team in the United States, and the Cuban fans at the stadium celebrated the victory with music and dancing.

the Baltimore Orioles 巴尔的摩金莺队
take revenge 报仇
the Cuban national team 古巴国家队
return game 回访比赛
the Camden Yards stadium 金莺公园球场
the second inning 第二局
the Estadio Latinoamericano 拉丁美洲棒球场
Fidel Castro 菲德尔·卡斯特罗（古巴领导人）

3 Reading Read the articles again. Circle the correct words to complete each sentence.

1. The Baltimore Orioles are from Cuba / **the United States**.
2. The first game was in Cuba / the United States.
3. Fidel Castro was / wasn't at the game.
4. The Baltimore Orioles / Cuban national team won the first game.
5. The final score of the first game was 2–0 / 3–2.
6. The second game was played at the Camden Yards stadium / Estadio Latinoamericano.
7. The Baltimore Orioles / Cuban national team won the second game.
8. The final score of the second game was 3–2 / 12–6.

Unit 15

4 After reading Circle *True* or *False*.

1. The last game between Cuba and a U.S. team was 40 years ago.   **True**   False
2. The Baltimore Orioles won the first game in the final inning.   True   False
3. Fidel Castro doesn't know a lot about baseball.   True   False
4. The second game was two months after the first game.   True   False
5. It rained during the second game.   True   False
6. There were no Cuban fans at the second game.   True   False

Talk about it!

5 Work with a partner. Talk about great sporting moments.

A: One great sporting moment was when Michael Phelps swam at the 2008 Olympics in Beijing.

B: That was really exciting! I remember that too. Another great sporting moment was when Spain won the FIFA World Cup championship in 2010.

the FIFA World Cup championship
世界杯足球赛冠军

PROJECT

Work in a group and choose a sport. One person will be a sports announcer. The others will be players. Prepare a role-play of a few minutes in a game / match / competition. Present your role-play to the class. The "sports announcer" describes what is happening.

183

Unit 15

SONG

The game of life

1 Before listening Read the questions below. Circle the best answers for you. Then talk about your answers with a partner. How are you the same? How are you different?

1. When you have to make a difficult decision, how do you do it?
   a. I usually talk it over with _____.
   b. I usually write down my ideas.
   c. I don't usually talk to anyone. I just think about it alone.
   d. other: _____

2. When you have to make a difficult decision, how long does it take you?
   a. I'm fast—usually a few hours or less.
   b. It usually takes a few days.
   c. I'm slow—it can take me weeks or more.
   d. other: _____

talk over with 与……协商; 洽谈

carry on 继续; 坚持下去

in the lyrics 歌词中

2 Listening 15_05 Listen to the song. Write the missing words in the lyrics. You may use the words more than once.

| can't | dark | game | have to | lose |
| rules | side | ~~win~~ | winner | |

3 After listening What is the main idea of the song? Circle the best answer.

1. Sports are good for you.
2. Baseball is difficult.
3. It is important to be a good loser.
4. You have to make your own decisions in life.

4 After listening Write the expressions in red in the song next to their meanings.

1. _____ = your last chance
2. _____ = to come up against something that is difficult and unexpected
3. _____ = to do something very well
4. _____ = clear and simple

come up against 碰到; 遭遇

The Game of Life

Sometimes you have to play
Though you think you'll never
(1) __win__ .
You have to carry on
When you want to give in.
You can choose,
You don't have to (2) _____ .

Sometimes you have to stand up
When they tell you that you
(3) _____ .
Sometimes you have to be strong
When they tell you that
  you aren't.
You can choose,
You don't have to (4) _____ .

Chorus

In the (5) _____ of life
There are no (6) _____
  in black and white.
The road you take,
You decide.

It's difficult to see much
When everything seems
  (7) _____ .
And life throws a curve ball,
You (8) _____ bat it out of
  the park.
You can choose,
You don't have to (9) _____ .

Chorus

If you want to be a
  (10) _____ ,
But the other (11) _____
  is strong.
And you're two down in
  the ninth,
You have to carry on.
You can choose
You don't have to (12) _____ .

Chorus

You have to fight
For the things you believe
  are right.
The change you make
Comes from inside.

Talk about it!

5 Work with a partner. Talk about the questions.

1. Why are sports important? Do you think they're just for physical exercise or do you think they also teach people how to deal with problems and how to work with other people? Explain your answer.

2. What do you think about sports video games? Are they the same as doing the sport? Why or why not? Do you think people exercise less because of video games?

culture matters

A curve ball is a ball that seems to be going one way and then changes direction, making it difficult to hit.
In baseball, each team plays nine innings. The game ends when the team loses three players in the ninth inning.

请注意了解棒球的相关知识

curve ball
弧线球；曲球

PRONUNCIATION

Have to / has to

1 We pronounce *have to* like hafta, and *has to* like hasta.
15_06

In writing	In speaking
I *have to* go.	I *hafta* go.
She *has to* go.	She *hasta* go.

2 Listen to the sentences. Circle *have to* or *has to*.
15_07

1. (have to)   has to
2. have to   has to
3. have to   has to
4. have to   has to
5. have to   has to
6. have to   has to

fight for
为……而战

Unit 15

CONVERSATION

Talking about rules

1 Imagine you want to join a sports club. Write four questions to ask about the club rules.

2 Complete the conversation with expressions from the box. Then listen to check your answers.
15_08

> **CONVERSATION STRATEGY**
> **Gain time**
> Use um and ah to pause in a conversation and give you time to think.
>
> 请注意交流时恰当使用语气词

| allowed | am I allowed | is it possible | not allowed | possible | prohibited |

Receptionist: Welcome to the sports club! Do you have any questions?
Linda: Um... Yes, I do. (1) __Is it possible__ to bring a friend with me?
Receptionist: As a guest?
Linda: Yes.
Receptionist: Guests are (2) _____, but you have to buy a one-day pass. A pass is $8.00 for the day.
Linda: Wow! That's expensive. Is it cheaper for children?
Receptionist: Actually, children under the age of 12 are not allowed in the gym.
Linda: Ah... I see. And (3) _____ to bring my own food to the gym?
Receptionist: It's (4) _____ to bring your own drinks into the gym. Food, however, is only allowed in the snack bar, and you have to buy it there.
Linda: Does that include in the changing rooms?
Receptionist: Yes, that's right. Eating in the changing rooms is (5) _____ either. And smoking is (6) _____ anywhere in the gym.
Linda: Well, that's no problem. I don't smoke!

a one-day pass
一天的通票

in the gym
在体育馆/健身房

changing room
更衣室

Talk about it!

3 Work with a partner. Imagine one of you works in a sports club. The other is joining and has questions about the rules. Role play the conversation. Use the words and phrases from exercise 2.

Tell me more!

Visit the Takeaway English Online Learning Center at http://olcs.mcgraw-hill-education.com/takeaway/

 Check out the *Takeaway TV* video.

 Improve your English with the online activities.

Unit 15

WRITING

Writing a description of a sport

1 Writing model Complete the description of a sport with words from the box. What is the sport?

| court | ~~game~~ | point | run | throw | tie |

This is a (1) __game__ that started in the U.S.A. The game is played on a (2) _____ between two teams of five players. Players can (3) _____ or pass the ball to other players, but they have to bounce the ball when they (4) _____ with it. Players must not kick the ball. To score a (5) _____, players have to "make a basket" (throw the ball into the other team's basket). The winner is the team that scores the most points. If the two teams (6) _____ the game, they play five minutes of overtime to decide the winner.

make a basket
投篮

play five minutes of overtime
打5分钟的加时赛

2 Before writing Complete the word map with information from the model.

HELP writing

Make a word map
Before you write, make a word map with the most important words and ideas.

请注意使用词汇图开拓写作思维

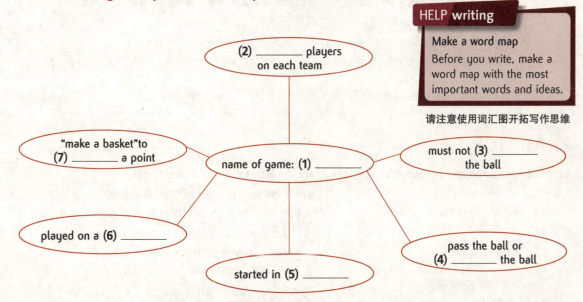

3 Planning your writing Now choose a sport to write about. On a piece of paper, make a word map like the one in exercise 2. Write the details of your description. Use the Internet as needed.

4 Writing Now write a description of your sport. Use the information in exercise 3 to help you.

Unit 15

TEST

Test-taking strategy

Reading for detail Some tests have readings where you must read very carefully in order to find specific information. The specific information, or detail, supports the main idea of the reading.

Use these steps to help you read for detail.

1. Understand the difference between the main idea and supporting detail.
2. Know what information you are looking for. Read the questions carefully.
3. Pay close attention to each word, fact, or number as you read—stay focused!
4. Highlight or underline important information as you read.
5. If you can't highlight or underline, take notes.

pay attention to 注意；专心于

fitness club 健身俱乐部
rules and regulations 规章制度

> **Example**
> Read the paragraph and answer the questions. Mark the letter on the Answer Sheet.
>
> I love my new fitness club, but there are a lot of rules and regulations. I pay $29 dollars a month, but I can only go on Mondays, Wednesdays, and Fridays. Tuesdays, Thursdays, and Saturdays are for women. The club is closed on Sunday. Also, if I want to bring a guest it is free the first time and $7 each time after that. Any food or drink is prohibited in the club except for water. Plastic bottles are allowed, but glass is not. Oh yeah, you have to bring your own towel and if you forget they charge you $5 to borrow one. There really are a lot of rules!
>
> 1. When can men use the club?
>   - ~~A.~~ Tuesdays, Thursdays, and Saturdays.   These are the days for women.
>   - ~~B.~~ They can't use the club on Sundays.   This information is true, but doesn't answer the question.
>   - C. Mondays, Wednesdays, and Fridays.   This is the correct answer.

PRACTICE

Read the paragraph and answer the questions. Mark the letter on the Answer Sheet.

1. What is allowed in the club?
    - A glass water bottles
    - B food
    - C your own towel

2. How much do guests pay?
    - A $7 every visit
    - B $7 the second visit and every time after that
    - C $7 the first visit and $5 after that

3. What is the main idea of the paragraph?
    - A He likes the club, but there are some disadvantages.
    - B There are a lot of rules and regulations.
    - C Men can only go three days a week, and not on Sunday.

Answer Sheet
Mark the letter.
1. A B C
2. A B C
3. A B C

WORKBOOK PAGE 117

UNIT SUMMARY

Unit 15

Noun
game
player
rules
winner

**Nouns—
sports**
baseball
basketball
gymnastics
hockey
ping-pong
rugby
skiing
soccer
taekwondo
track
volleyball
yoga

**Verbs—
sports actions**
bounce
hit
kick
lose
play
score
tie
throw
win

**Adjectives—
describing sports**
fun
hard

**Expressions—
talking about rules**
It's allowed.
It's not allowed
It's possible.
It's prohibited.

Review 3

VOCABULARY

Put the words and phrases in the five groups. Then write more words that you know in each group.

~~astronaut~~	demanding	hibernate	nest	ping-pong	snorkeling	tiger
bounce	engineer	hockey	noisy	sightseeing	suburb	win
crowded	go rafting	low-paying	panda	skyscraper	take a tour	

jobs	vacations	cities	wildlife	sports
astronaut				

GRAMMAR

Circle the correct answers to complete the conversation.

Jack: Hey, Lisa! How was your trip to Australia?

Lisa: It was amazing! It was (**1**) **the best** / the goodest vacation of my life!

Jack: That's great! (**2**) What / When did you do?

Lisa: Well, we spent some time in the city and some time at the beach.

Jack: Really? What did you do in the city?

Lisa: Let's see… We went (**3**) sightsee / sightseeing, and we went to some museums.

Jack: And what did you do on the beach?

Lisa: Well, we (**4**) went / going snorkeling.

Jack: Really? How was it?

Lisa: It was amazing! I think it was (**5**) better / gooder than snorkeling in the Caribbean.

Jack: Were the beaches as beautiful as the beaches in the Caribbean?

Lisa: No, the beaches in Australia were (**6**) beautifuler / more beautiful. Also you (**7**) don't have to / must not wear a life jacket like in the Caribbean because it's easy to swim in the water. You (**8**) can / must if you want to, but it's not necessary.

Jack: Well, you (**9**) have to / must not wear a life jacket if you (**10**) can't / can swim.

Lisa: Well yes…. Then you have to wear one!

Review 3

LISTENING

Listen to three short conversations. What is each person talking about? Circle the correct answer. Then listen again and check your answers.

Conversation 1	**A**	work	**B**	a sport	**C**	a vacation	**D**	an animal
Conversation 2	**A**	a city	**B**	a sport	**C**	a vacation	**D**	an animal
Conversation 3	**A**	a city	**B**	a sport	**C**	work	**D**	an animal

READING

Read Sam's travel blog. Circle *True* or *False*.

1. Sam is in the jungle.
   True   **False**
2. Sam didn't like being in the jungle.
   True   False
3. Jorge and Antonio speak English.
   True   False
4. Jorge and Antonio were noisy at night.
   True   False
5. Sam liked the jungle better than the river trip.
   True   False
6. Sam is traveling with another person.
   True   False

Talk about it!

Work with a partner. Play the "20 Questions" game. Choose a word from Units 1–5. Your partner asks you questions to guess the word. You can only say *yes* or *no*.

A: Is it a sport (job, animal, noun, verb, activity, person, etc.)?
B: No, it isn't.
A: Is it an animal?
B: Yes, it is.
A: OK! Can it…

Sam's Blog

Hello everyone!

We're back in the city again after three days in the jungle. It was amazing there—very exotic with a lot of interesting plants and animals. It wasn't boring at all! The jungle can be very noisy at night; it was incredible. We stayed in a small cabin with two Mexican tourists, Jorge and Antonio. They were really friendly and we had a good time together. Their English was better than my Spanish! I think the jungle was the best part of our trip, better than our boat trip up the river last week. I have to go now. We're staying in a hostel and it's my turn to cook—but I can't cook well! I'm looking forward to seeing everyone back home soon!

Best wishes to all!

Sam

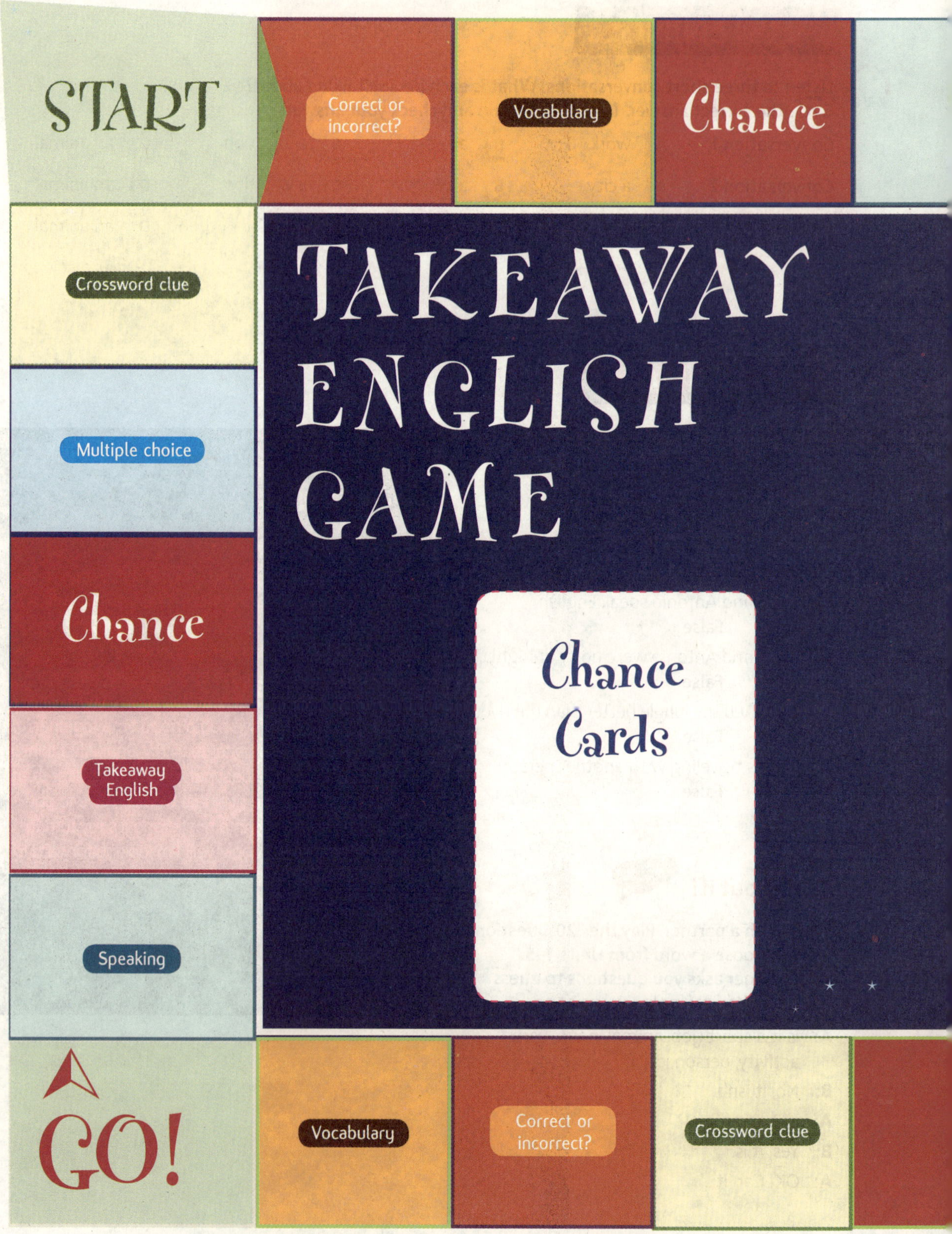

Review 3

TAKEAWAY ENGLISH GAME

START

- Correct or incorrect?
- Vocabulary
- Chance

- Crossword clue
- Multiple choice
- Chance
- Takeaway English
- Speaking

GO!

- Vocabulary
- Correct or incorrect?
- Crossword clue

Chance Cards

Review 3

| Speaking | Takeaway English | Multiple choice | Spell it | GO! |

PLAY THE TAKEAWAY ENGLISH BOARD GAME.

YOU WILL NEED

- A DIE
- SOME SMALL COINS OR COUNTERS
- THE CHANCE CARDS
- 2 or 3 players or teams
- 1 question reader (with "Question and Answer" page)

HOW TO PLAY

Throw the die and move your counter.
The question reader asks you a question.
Answer the question.
If you land on a Chance square, pick a Chance card.
If you land on a Go! square, take another turn.

SCORE

1 point for a correct answer (unless doubled by a Chance card).

TO WIN THE GAME

The first player or team to get 20 points wins the game.

After each game, a different person is the question reader.

| Crossword clue | Correct or incorrect? | Chance | Vocabulary | Speaking |

| Spell it | Chance | Multiple choice | Takeaway English | GO! |

WORKBOOK PAGE 118-122

GRAMMAR TAKEAWAY 1

Grammar Takeaway

Verbs

Verbs describe...
- actions: I walk to school. (verb: *walk*)
- states: I am Korean. (verb: *be*)

The verb *be*

Use *be* for personal information. Use *not* to negate the verb *be*.

affirmative	negative
I am (I'm) from Seoul.	I am not (I'm not) from Sydney.
You are (You're) from Seoul.	You are not (You aren't) from Sydney.
He is (He's) from Seoul.	He is not (He isn't) from Sydney.
She is (She's) from Seoul.	She is not (She isn't) from Sydney.
It is (It's) from Seoul.	It is not (It isn't) from Sydney.
We are (We're) from Seoul.	We are not (We aren't) from Sydney.
You are (You're) from Seoul.	You are not (You aren't) from Sydney.
They are (They're) from Seoul.	They are not (They aren't) from Sydney.

Other verbs

Some verbs add *s* with *he*, *she*, and *it*. Use *do/does + not* for the negative.

affirmative	negative
I / You / We / They work.	I / You / We / They don't work.
He / She / It works.	He / She / It doesn't work.

Some verbs add *es* with *he*, *she*, and *it*.

I guess / she guesses   I teach / he teaches

Verbs that end in *y*, change the *y* to *i*, and then add *es*.

I study / he studies

GRAMMAR TAKEAWAY 2

ALSO GO TO:
Unit 2 Grammar
PAGE 17

Grammar Takeaway

Yes/no questions with be

am / are / is + subject

Are you American?   Is she a teacher?

short answers

questions	affirmative	negative
Are you Korean?	Yes, I am.	No, I'm not.
Is he / she / it Japanese?	Yes, he / she / it is.	No, he / she / it isn't.
Are we from China?	Yes, we are.	No, we aren't.
Are they doctors?	Yes, they are.	No, they aren't.

Information questions with be

We use Who, What, When, Where, Why, and How at the start of questions when we want information.

question word + am / are / is + subject

What's your name?   Where are they from?

A: Who are you?
B: I'm the teacher.

A: What's your job?
B: I'm a hotel manager.

A: When's your birthday?
B: It's April 2nd.

A: Where are you from?
B: I am from Thailand.

A: Why are you here?
B: To learn English.

A: How is your name spelled?
B: N-i-c-h-o-l-a-s.

Contractions

who is = who's
what is = what's

when is = when's
where is = where's

why is = why's
how is = how's

GRAMMAR TAKEAWAY 3

Grammar Takeaway

ALSO GO TO: Unit 3 Grammar PAGE 29

Simple present

We use the simple present to talk about:

- **habits and routines**
  I get up at 8:00 a.m.
- **factual information**
  Tokyo is in Japan.
  New York has a famous park.
- **likes and dislikes**
  I like cats, but I don't like dogs.
- **personal information**
  I am from Mexico.
  Max doesn't play soccer, but he swims.

Affirmative and negative statements

affirmative	negative
I / You / We / They leave at 7:00 a.m.	I / You / We / They don't leave at 7:00 a.m.
He / She / It leaves at 7:00 a.m.	He / She / It doesn't leave at 7:00 a.m.

Yes/no questions and short answers

questions	short answers
Do I / you / we / they leave at 7:00 a.m.?	Yes, I / you / we / they do. No, I / you / we / they don't / do not.
Does he / she / it leave at 7:00 a.m.?	Yes, he / she / it does. No, he / she it doesn't / does not.

Information questions

questions	answers
When do you eat lunch?	I eat lunch at noon.
What does she do after work?	She goes shopping.

Spelling changes of the third-person singular

- most verbs: add *s* — live / lives, work / works, get / gets
- verbs ending in *ss, sh, ch, x*: add *es* — miss / misses, finish / finishes, watch / watches, fix / fixes
- verbs ending in consonant + *y*: change *y* to *ies* — fly / flies, try / tries, study / studies
- irregular third person spellings: *have, go, do* — have / has, go / goes, do / does

GRAMMAR TAKEAWAY 4

ALSO GO TO:
Unit 4 Grammar
PAGE 41

Grammar Takeaway

There is and There are

We use *there is* and *there are*: to say that something exists.
to say where something is.

In sentences with *there is* and *there are*, the verb *be* agrees with the object.

affirmative	negative
There's an ATM near here.	There isn't an ATM near here.
There are two ATMs near here.	There aren't any ATMs near here.

questions	answers	
Is there an ATM near here?	Yes, there is.	No, there isn't.
Are there any ATMs near here?	Yes, there are.	No, there aren't.

We use *some* with plural nouns in affirmative statements.
There are some expensive restaurants on this street.

We use *any* with plural nouns in questions and negative statements.
Are there any cafés on Elm Street?   No, there aren't any cafés on Elm Street.

Prepositions of location

We use prepositions of location to explain where something is.

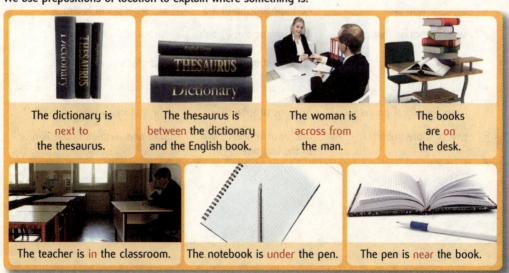

The dictionary is next to the thesaurus.

The thesaurus is between the dictionary and the English book.

The woman is across from the man.

The books are on the desk.

The teacher is in the classroom.

The notebook is under the pen.

The pen is near the book.

197

GRAMMAR TAKEAWAY 5

ALSO GO TO:
Unit 5 Grammar
PAGE 53

Grammar Takeaway

Possessive adjectives

My, *your*, *his*, *her*, *its*, *our*, and *their* are possessive adjectives.
They tell who or what someone or something belongs to.
Possessive adjectives can never stand alone. They must be used with a noun.

subject pronouns	possessive adjectives
I have a family.	That's my family.
You have a sister.	Is that your sister?
He has a wife.	That's his wife.
She has a son.	That's her son.
It is my fish.	Its name is Nemo.
We have a grandmother.	That's our grandmother.
They have a grandfather.	This is their grandfather.

Possessive nouns

We use possessive nouns to talk about things or people that belong to other things or people.

- singular nouns — Add apostrophe (') + s. — My sister's son is shy.
- singular nouns that end in s — Add apostrophe (') only. — Nicholas' hair is brown.
  OR
  Add apostrophe (') + s. — Nicholas's hair is brown.
- plural nouns — Add apostrophe (') only. — The teachers' computers are fast.
- irregular plural nouns — Add apostrophe (') + s. — The children's father is Bill.
- two or more subjects — Add apostrophe (') + s to the last one. — Jake and Nicole's house is nice.

GRAMMAR TAKEAWAY 6

ALSO GO TO:
Unit 6 Grammar
PAGE 69

Grammar Takeaway

Simple past

We use the simple past to talk about actions that happened at a specific time in the past.

simple past of *be*		
affirmative	I / He / She / It was at home.	You / We / They were at home.
negative	I / He / She / It wasn't at home.	You / We / They weren't at home.
question and answer	Was she at the party?	Were they at the party?
	Yes, she was. / No, she wasn't.	Yes, they were. / No, they weren't.

simple past of regular verbs	
affirmative	I / You / He / She / It / We / They finished at 12:00.
negative	I / You / He / She / It / We / They didn't finish at 12:00.
question and answers	Did you finish the book? Yes, I did. / No, I didn't.

Simple past spelling rules for regular verbs

- Add *ed* to the infinitive of most verbs.   play / played
- When the infinitive ends in *e*, add *d*.   like / liked
- When the infinitive ends in *y*, change the *y* to *i*, and then add *ed*.   study / studied

Simple past of irregular verbs

Many verbs have irregular past forms. Sentence formation follows the same rules as regular verbs.

affirmative	I / You / He / She / It / We / They went home.	
negative	I / You / He / She / It / We / They didn't go home.	
question and answer	Did you go home?	Yes, I did. / No, I didn't.

Some irregular past forms *(For a complete list, see page 140.)*

break	broke	get	got	put	put	think	thought
buy	bought	go	went	read	read	wake	woke
do	did	have	had	see	saw	win	won
drive	drove	make	made	take	took	write	wrote
eat	ate	meet	met				

199

GRAMMAR TAKEAWAY 7

ALSO GO TO:
Unit 7 Grammar
PAGE 81

Grammar Takeaway

Present continuous

We use the present continuous:
- to talk about actions happening now

    I'm writing an email. (now)
    I'm studying Chinese. (at this moment)

- for events arranged in the future

    We're meeting Ivan tonight.

affirmative	negative
I am sleeping.	I am not sleeping.
He / She / It is sleeping.	He / She / It is not sleeping.
You / We / They are sleeping.	You / We / They are not sleeping.

questions	answers	
Am I sleeping?	Yes, I am.	No, I am not.
Is he / she / it sleeping?	Yes, he / she / it is.	No, he / she / it is not.
Are you / we / they sleeping?	Yes, you / we / they are.	No, you / we / they are not.

Spelling rules

- Add *ing* to most verbs.
- When the verb ends in *e*, drop the *e* and add *ing*.
- When the verb ends in consonant + vowel + consonant, double the last letter, and add *ing*.
- Do not double *w*, *x*, or *y*.

wear / wearing   study / studying

write / writing   take / taking

sit / sitting   chat / chatting

play / playing

Contractions

I am working. = I'm working.

He / She / It is working. = He's / She's working.

They are working. = They're working.

You are working. = You're working.

We are working. = We're working.

He is not working = He's not working. OR He isn't working.

Is he working? Yes, he is. (NOT: ~~Yes, he's.~~) / No, he isn't.

GRAMMAR TAKEAWAY 8

ALSO GO TO:
Unit 8 Grammar
PAGE 93

Grammar Takeaway

Present continuous for the future

We use the present continuous to talk about arrangements.

> Arrangements are planned events, usually with other people.
>
> I'm having dinner with Jocelyn tonight.
> We're going shopping next Saturday.

Simple present for the future

We use the simple present to talk about scheduled events.

> Scheduled events are part of a schedule or timetable.
> They include travel times and business meetings.
>
> My train arrives next Friday at 3:25 p.m.
> The concert starts at 7:00 p.m. tomorrow.
>
> We only use a few verbs this way.
> For example: *arrive, leave, start, finish, begin, end, open, close*

Future time expressions

We usually use future time expressions to indicate the future.

Common future time expressions	
tonight	the day after tomorrow
tomorrow	next Tuesday / week / month / year

GRAMMAR TAKEAWAY 9

ALSO GO TO:
Unit 9 Grammar
PAGE 105

Grammar Takeaway

Prepositions *in*, *on*, and *at*

at

	We use *at* before:
• a time	The game starts at 7:00 p.m.
• a place	The game is at the O'Neill Stadium.
• an address	The stadium is located at 79 West Street.

in

	We use *in* before:
• a month	My birthday is in May.
• a time of day	The ballet is in the evening.
• a city	She lives in San Francisco.
• a state	San Francisco is in California.
• a country	California is in the United States.

on

	We use *on* before:
• a day	The concert is on Thursday.
• a date	School starts on September 3rd.
• a street	I live on Davis Street.

GRAMMAR TAKEAWAY 10

ALSO GO TO:
Unit 10 Grammar
PAGE 117

Grammar Takeaway

Articles with countable and uncountable nouns

Countable nouns are things we can count. They have a singular form and a plural form.

Examples:
- one hat / two hats
- one potato / six potatoes
- one balloon / thirty balloons

We use *a* and *an* before singular countable nouns.

Examples:
- They light a candle every day.
- I ate an egg for breakfast.

Uncountable nouns are things we cannot count. They are singular.

Examples:
- water   juice   cheese
- rain   rice   money

We use *no article* before plural countable nouns and uncountable nouns.

Examples:
- Eggs are good for you.
- I made soup for dinner.

Some words are countable and uncountable, but with a change in meaning.

Compare:
- There's some coffee in the coffeepot.
- Your hair is very long.
- Would you like a coffee?
- There's a hair in my sushi.

We can describe quantities of uncountable nouns using another (countable) noun.

two bottles of water   three cups of coffee   two packets of rice

Some and *any* with uncountable and plural nouns

We use *some* in affirmative sentences with uncountable and plural nouns.
We use *any* in negative sentences and questions with uncountable and plural nouns.

affirmative	negative	questions
There is some popcorn in the box.	I don't have any popcorn.	Do you have any popcorn?
There are some masks on the table.	There aren't any masks.	Are there any masks?

203

GRAMMAR TAKEAWAY 11

ALSO GO TO:
Unit 11 Grammar
PAGE 133

Grammar Takeaway

Questions in the simple present

Yes / no questions with be	verb subject the rest Is she Mexican? A: Is she Mexican? B: Yes, she is. OR B: No, she isn't.
Information questions with be	question word verb subject the rest Where are you from? A: Where are you from? B: I'm from Korea.
Yes / no questions with other verbs	auxiliary verb subject infinitive the rest Do you like your job? A: Do you like your job? B: Yes, I do. OR B: No, I don't.
Information questions with other verbs	question word auxiliary verb subject infinitive the rest How do you get to work? A: How do you get to work? B: I take the train.

Adverbs of frequency

Adverbs of frequency tell us how often something happens.

0% ── 100%

| never | hardly ever / rarely | sometimes | often | usually / normally | always |

Adverbs of frequency usually go <u>before</u> the verb in a sentence.
    We often go to the opera. NOT: ~~We go often to the opera.~~

Adverbs of frequency go <u>after</u> the verb *be*.
    He is always happy. NOT: ~~He always is happy.~~

Normally, *usually*, and *sometimes* can also go at the beginning or the end of a sentence.
    Normally he's happy to help.   He's normally happy to help.   He's happy to help normally.

Always, *never*, and *rarely* cannot go at the beginning of a sentence.
    ~~Always~~ I always walk to work.   ~~Never~~ I never watch TV.   ~~Rarely~~ I rarely visit them.

In a question, the adverb of frequency goes <u>after</u> the subject.
    Do you always walk to work?
    Are you normally so happy?
    Why does class never start on time?

GRAMMAR TAKEAWAY 12

ALSO GO TO:
Unit 12 Grammar
PAGE 145

Grammar Takeaway

Go + gerund

In the construction, *go* + gerund:
  Go is the verb. It agrees with the subject and time.
  The gerund is a verb that's used like a noun. The gerund ends in *ing*.

simple present	
affirmative	I / You / We / They go shopping on Saturdays. She / He goes shopping on Saturdays.
negative	I / You / We / They don't go rafting because it's dangerous. She / He doesn't go rafting because it's dangerous.
question	Do I / you / we / they go camping in the winter? Does she / he go camping in the winter?

simple present	
affirmative	I / You / She / He / We / They went shopping when we were in Paris.
negative	I / You / He / She / We / They didn't go dancing last night.
question	Did I / you / he / she / we / they go horseback riding yesterday?

future	
affirmative	I am going hiking in the mountains next month. He / She is going hiking in the mountains next month. You / We / They are going hiking in the mountains next month.
negative	I'm not going snorkeling in Thailand. He / She isn't going snorkeling in Thailand. You / We / They aren't going snorkeling in Thailand.
question	Am I going kayaking tomorrow? Is he / she going kayaking tomorrow? Are you / we / they going kayaking tomorrow?

Gerund formation

Add *ing* to most verbs: raft*ing*, ski*ing*, rid*ing*, bicycl*ing*

When the verb ends in consonant + *e*, drop the *e* and add *ing*.

When the verb ends in consonant + vowel + consonant, double the last letter, and add *ing*. Do not double *w*, *x*, or *y*.

Do not double the consonant for verbs with two syllables that end in consonant + vowel + consonant if the stress is *not* on the last syllable.

GRAMMAR TAKEAWAY 13

ALSO GO TO:
Unit 13 Grammar
PAGE 157

Grammar Takeaway

Comparatives and superlatives

	comparatives *Comparative sentences compare two things.*	superlatives *Superlative sentences compare three or more things.*
Short words 1-syllable adjectives or 2-syllable adjectives that end in *y*	New York is bigger than Los Angeles. Los Angeles is dirtier than New York.	New York is the biggest city in the United States. Los Angeles is one of the dirtiest cities in the United States.
Long words adjectives with 2 or more syllables	The plane is more expensive than the bus. The bus is less expensive than the train. Downtown is more crowded than the suburbs.	The plane is the most expensive form of transportation. The bus is the least expensive. Tokyo is one of the most crowded cities in the world.

Irregular comparatives and superlatives

adjective	comparative	superlative
good	better	best
bad	worse	worst
far	farther	farthest

Spelling rules for comparatives and superlatives

1-syllable adjectives	add *-er* or *-est* small – smaller – smallest
1-syllable adjectives that end in *e*	add *-r* or *-st* nice – nicer – nicest
1-syllable adjectives that end in vowel + consonant	double the consonant and add *-er* or *-est* big – bigger – biggest
2-syllable adjectives that end in *y*	change the *y* to *i* and add *er* or *est* dirty – dirtier – dirtiest

Grammar Takeaway

ALSO GO TO:
Unit 14 Grammar
PAGE 169

Can and *can't* for ability and permission

We use *can* and *can't* with the verb in base form to talk about ability and permission.
The negative form is written as one word: *cannot*. The contraction is *can't*.

can / can't for ability

affirmative	I / You / They can swim. I / You / They took lessons last year. He / She can drive. He / She took lessons last year.		
negative	I / You / They can't swim. I / You / They don't know how. He / She can't drive. He / She doesn't know how.		
questions and answers	Can you / they swim? Can he / she / it swim?	Yes, I / they can. Yes, he / she / it can.	No, I / they can't. No, he / she / it can't.

can / can't for permission

affirmative	I / You / They can eat this apple. There are more in the refrigerator. He / She can eat this apple. There are more in the refrigerator.		
negative	I can't eat this apple. It's Meg's apple. He / She can't eat this apple. It's Meg's apple.		
questions and answers	Can you / they eat this apple? Can he / she eat this apple?	Yes, I / they can. Yes, he / she / it can.	No, I / they can't. No, he / she can't.

GRAMMAR TAKEAWAY 15

ALSO GO TO
Unit 15 Grammar
PAGE 181

Grammar Takeaway

Must and have to / has to

We use *must* and *have to* to talk about obligation (something that's a necessity).
Have to is more common.

| must / have to / has to | I / She / They must wear special white clothes.
I / You / We / They have to go to practice today.
He / She has to go to practice tomorrow. |

Must not

We use *must not* to talk about prohibition (something that's not allowed).

| must not | I / You / He / She / We / They must not hit the ball too hard.
Soccer players must not throw the ball. |

Don't have to / doesn't have to

We use *don't have to / doesn't have to* to talk about lack of obligation (something that's a choice).

| don't have to / doesn't have to | I / You / We / They don't have to throw the ball.
He / She doesn't have to hit the ball. |

Questions and Answers

Questions with *have to / has to* ask about obligation or lack of obligation.
Questions with *must not* are not common.

| have to | Do you have to go to practice today?
Yes, I do. / No, I don't. |
| has to | Does he have to go to practice today?
Yes, he does. / No, he doesn't. |

IRREGULAR VERBS

Base form	Simple past
be	was / were
bring	brought
buy	bought
come	came
do	did
drink	drank
drive	drove
eat	ate
fall	fell
get	got
give	gave
go	went
hang	hung
have	had
hear	heard
know	knew
lie	lay
leave	left
make	made
meet	met
read	read
ride	rode
rise	rose
run	ran
say	said
see	saw
sell	sold
sing	sang
sit	sat
sleep	slept
speak	spoke
swim	swam
take	took
teach	taught
think	thought
wake up	woke up
wear	wore
write	wrote

KEY TO PHONETIC SYMBOLS

Vowels

Symbol	Sample word
/æ/	hat
/eɪ/	name
/ɑː/	father
/ɔː/	mall
/e/	get
/iː/	he
/ə/	about
/ɒ/	cross
/ɜː/	nurse
/ɪ/	gift
/aɪ/	line
/əʊ/	old
/uː/	do
/ʊ/	book
/ɔɪ/	boy
/aʊ/	town
/ʌ/	mother
/ɪə/	here
/eə/	pair
/ʊə/	tour

Consonants

Symbol	Sample word
/b/	bike
/d/	day
/dʒ/	just, age
/f/	fine
/g/	give
/h/	happy
/k/	car
/l/	let
/m/	make
/n/	no
/ŋ/	sing
/p/	pick
/r/	run
/s/	son
/ʃ/	shoe
/t/	ten
/tʃ/	watch
/θ/	thousand
/ð/	this
/v/	very
/w/	wife
/j/	yes
/z/	zero
/ʒ/	television

VOCABULARY

Vocabulary

NOTE:
The following list includes productive vocabulary in *Takeaway English 1*.

A

a billion people 10亿人
a feast 大餐
a hiking trip 徒步旅行
a little bit 一点儿
a one-day pass 一天的通票
a single parent 单身父亲/母亲
a tablespoon of 一勺……
a variety of 各种各样的……
absolutely / 'æbsəluːtlɪ / adv. 必须地
accept an invitation 接受邀请
across from 在……对面
act out 把……表演出来
actually / 'æktjʊəlɪ / adv. 实际上；事实上
advantages and disadvantages 利弊；优点和缺点
affirmative / ə'fɜːmətɪv / adj. 肯定的
air quality 空气质量
air-conditioned bungalow apartments 有空调的别墅公寓
airplane / 'eəpleɪn / n. 飞机
airport / 'eəpɔːt / n. 机场
Al Muntaha 顶层餐厅
alarm clock 闹钟
all over the world 全世界
alone / ə'ləʊn / adj. 独自的；孤独的
alongside / əlɒŋ'saɪd / prep. 在……旁边
amazing / ə'meɪzɪŋ / adj. 令人惊讶的
American / ə'merɪkən / adj. 美国人；美国的
American English 美式英语
amusing / ə'mjuːzɪŋ / adj. 有趣的
appearance / ə'pɪər(ə)ns / n. 外观
apprentice carpenter 木工学徒
approximately / ə'prɒksɪmətlɪ / adv. 大概；大约
April / 'eɪprəl / n. 四月
apron / 'eɪpr(ə)n / n. 围裙
Arabian Gulf 阿拉伯湾
arcade / ɑː'keɪd / n. (内设投角子电子游戏机等的)游乐场
Argentina / ˌɑːdʒən'tiːnə / n. 阿根廷(位于拉丁美洲)
arrive / ə'raɪv / v. 到达

art / ɑːt / n. 艺术；美术
as a routine 作为常规
Asia / 'eɪʒə / n. 亚洲
assemble parts 组装零件
astronaut / 'æstrənɔːt / n. 宇航员
at a café 在咖啡馆里
at night 在夜里
at the beach 在海滩上
at the door 在门口
at the gallery 在美术馆
at the same time 与此同时
ATM 自动取款机
attach to 系上；附上
August / 'ɔːgʌst / n. 八月
aunt / ɑːnt / n. 姑妈；阿姨
Australia / ɒ'streɪlɪə / n. 澳大利亚
Australian band 澳大利亚乐队
auxiliary verb 助动词
avenue / 'æv(ə)njuː / n. 大街
average temperature 平均气温
awful / 'ɔːfʊl / adj. 糟糕的；极坏的

B

baby rhinoceros 小犀牛
bacon / 'beɪk(ə)n / n. 培根
ballet / 'bæleɪ / n. 芭蕾舞
balloon / bə'luːn / n. 气球
baseball / 'beɪsbɔːl / n. 棒球
baseball game 棒球比赛
basketball / 'bɑːskɪtbɔːl / n. 篮球
be associated with 与……相关联
be good at 擅长……
be located in 座落于
be popular with... 受……欢迎
be related to 与……相关
beach / biːtʃ / n. 海滩
beauty salon 美容院
because of 因为；由于

211

VOCABULARY

become extinct 灭绝; 绝种
Bengal Tiger 孟加拉虎
best man 男傧相
Biological Research Station 生物研究站
birthday / 'bɜːθdeɪ / n. 生日
Black Rhinocero 黑犀牛
black-eyed peas 豇豆
blog / blɒg / n. 博客
bookstore / 'bʊkstɔː / n. 书店
boot / buːt / n. 靴子
bored / bɔːd / adj. 无聊的; 无趣的
boring / 'bɔːrɪŋ / adj. 无聊的; 枯燥的
bounce / baʊns / v. 弹跳
bounce the ball 拍球
box office 售票处
Brazil / brəˈzɪl / n. 巴西（拉丁美洲国家）
Brazilian / brəˈzɪlɪən / adj. 巴西人; 巴西的
break down 出故障
bride / braɪd / n. 新娘
bridesmaid / 'braɪdzmeɪd / n. 女傧相
Brisbane / 'brɪzbən / n. 布里斯班（澳大利亚东部城市）
British / 'brɪtɪʃ / adj. 英国的
British English 英式英语
brother-in-law n. 姐夫; 妹夫
brunch / brʌn(t)ʃ / n. 早午餐
buffet / 'bʊfeɪ / n. 自助餐
bus stop 公交车站
business center 商务中心
by car (bus, train) 坐汽车（公交车, 火车）

C

café / 'kæfeɪ / n. 咖啡馆
cafeteria / kæfɪ'tɪərɪə / n. 食堂; 自助餐厅
calendar / 'kælɪndə / n. 日历
call home 打电话回家
call in "sick" 打电话请病假
Canada / 'kænədə / n. 加拿大（北美洲国家）
candle / 'kænd(ə)l / n. 蜡烛
candy / 'kændɪ / n. 糖果
capital / 'kæpɪt(ə)l / n. 首都; 省会
Caribbean islands 加勒比群岛
carry on 继续; 坚持下去
cash / kæʃ / n. 现金
Casual Friday 星期五便装日
celebrate / 'selɪbreɪt / v. 庆祝

celebrated / 'selɪbreɪtɪd / adj. 著名的
celebration / selɪ'breɪʃ(ə)n / n. 庆祝; 庆典
celebrity / sɪ'lebrɪtɪ / n. 名人; 名声
cell phone 手机
Celsius (C) / 'selsɪəs / n. 摄氏度
cemetery / 'semɪtrɪ / n. 墓地; 公墓
center / 'sentə / n. 中心; 中央
centimeter / 'sentɪmiːtə / n. 厘米
Central Park 中央公园
cereal / 'sɪərɪəl / n. 玉米片
ceremony / 'serɪmənɪ / n. 典礼; 仪式
changing room 更衣室
chat / tʃæt / v. 聊天; 闲谈
chat with sb. 与某人聊天
chauffeur / 'ʃəʊfə / n. 司机
check email 查阅邮件
cheese / tʃiːz / n. 奶酪
China / 'tʃaɪnə / n. 中国
Chinese / ˌtʃaɪ'niːz / adj. 中国人; 中国的
clap your hands 拍拍手
climate / 'klaɪmət / n. 气候
closing night 闭幕夜
clothing store 服装店
coast / kəʊst / n. 海岸
coffee / 'kɒfɪ / n. 咖啡
collard greens 绿叶甘蓝
colleague / 'kɒliːg / n. 同事
college degree 大学学位
Columbus Day 哥伦布发现美洲纪念日
combine with 与……结合
come up against 碰到; 遭遇
come up 出现; 发生
communicate with 与……交流/沟通
compare to 与……相比
compare with 与……比较
compliment / 'kɒmplɪm(ə)nt / v. 称赞
computer programmer 电脑程序设计师
computer science 计算机科学
concert / 'kɒnsət / n. 演唱会; 音乐会
concert hall 音乐厅
conference / 'kɒnf(ə)r(ə)ns / n. 会议
conservation and protection program 保护项目
conservation efforts 为保护付出的努力
contest / 'kɒntest / n. 比赛
convenience store 便利店

VOCABULARY

cook / kʊk / n. 厨师 v. 烹调
cook dinner 做晚餐
coral reef system 珊瑚礁系统
cost of living 生活费用
Costa Rica 哥斯达黎加
costume / 'kɒstjuːm / n. 戏装
country / 'kʌntri / n. 国家
cousin / 'kʌz(ə)n / n. 堂/表兄弟姐妹
cowbell / 'kaʊbel / n. 牛铃
credit card 信用卡
crime rate 犯罪率
Croatia / krəʊ'eɪʃə / n. 克罗地亚
croissant / krwɑːsɒŋ / n. 羊角面包
crowded / 'kraʊdɪd / adj. 拥挤的
cruise ship 大型游船;豪华游船
curve ball 弧线球;曲球
custom / 'kʌstəm / n. 习俗

D

daily / 'deɪli / adj. 日常的
daily routines 日常生活
daily updates 每日更新
dangerous / 'deɪn(d)ʒ(ə)rəs / adj. 危险的
date / deɪt / n. 日期
date of birth 出生日期
December / dɪ'sembə / n. 十二月
decide on 决定;下决心
decorate / 'dekəreɪt / v. 装饰
delicious / dɪ'lɪʃəs / adj. 美味的;可口的
demanding / dɪ'mɑːndɪŋ / adj. 要求高的
department store 百货商店
distinguish / dɪ'stɪŋgwɪʃ / v. 区分
Diwali / dɪ'wɑːli / n. (印度)排灯节
do an internship 实习
do comedy 表演喜剧
do homework 做作业
do maintenance 保养;维护
dollar / 'dɒlə / n. 美元
downtown / 'daʊntaʊn / n. 市区;市中心
dress code 着装要求
Dubai / 'djuːbaɪ / n. 迪拜

E

earrings / 'ɪərɪŋz / n. 耳环
easygoing / 'iːzɪˌgəʊɪŋ / adj. 脾气随和的

eat out 在外面吃饭
eighteenth / eɪ'tiːnθ / 第十八
eighth / eɪtθ / 第八
electronics store 电子产品商店;家电城
elementary school 小学
eleventh / ɪ'lev(ə)nθ / 第十一
email address 电子邮件地址
emergency exit 紧急出口
employee / emplɔɪ'iː / n. 雇员;职员
encyclopedia article 百科全书中的文章
endangered animal 濒危动物
engineer / endʒɪ'nɪə / n. 工程师
England / 'ɪŋglənd / n. 英国;英格兰
enormous / ɪ'nɔːməs / adj. 庞大的;大量的
entertainment / entə'teɪnm(ə)nt / n. 娱乐
entertainment events 娱乐活动
enthusiastic / ɪnˌθjuːzɪ'æstɪk / adj. 热情的;狂热的
entrance / 'entr(ə)ns / n. 入口
envelope / 'envələʊp / n. 信封
e-pal / ɪ'pæl / n. 网友
e-reader 电子阅读器
Europe / 'jʊərəp / n. 欧洲
event / ɪ'vent / n. 事件
evil spirit 幽灵;恶魔
excited / ɪk'saɪtɪd / adj. 兴奋的
exciting / ɪk'saɪtɪŋ / adj. 令人激动的
expensive / ɪk'spensɪv / adj. 贵的;价格高的

F

facility / fə'sɪlɪti / n. 设施;设备
factory worker 工厂工人
Fahrenheit (F) / 'færən'haɪt / n. 华氏度
fall in love with sb. 爱上某人
fantastic / fæn'tæstɪk / adj. 极好的;极出色的
fasting / 'fɑːstɪŋ / n. 禁食;斋戒
feast / fiːst / n. 宴会
feature / 'fiːtʃə / v. 以……为特色;由……主演
February / 'febrʊəri / n. 二月
fed / fed / adj. 厌烦的
festival / 'festɪv(ə)l / n. 节日
Fidel Castro 菲德尔·卡斯特罗(古巴领导人)
fifteenth / fɪf'tiːnθ / 第十五
fifth / fɪfθ / 第五
fight for 为……而战
figure out 想出;理解

VOCABULARY

fill out 填写
financial analyst 财务/金融分析师
financial markets 金融市场
fireworks / 'faɪəwɜ:ks / n. 烟火
first / fɜ:st / 第一
first name 名
fish / fɪʃ / v. 捕鱼
fitness center 健身中心
fitness club 健身俱乐部
fix my hair 做头发
float / fləʊt / n. 彩车
Florence / 'flɔrəns / n. 弗罗伦萨
foggy / 'fɒgɪ / adj. 多雾的
food court （商场内）美食区
foot / fʊt / n. 英尺
Ford's Department Store 福特百货商店
fourteenth / fɔ:'ti:nθ / 第十四
fourth / fɔ:θ / 第四
France / frɑ:ns / n. 法国
free / fri: / adj. 免费的
French / fren(t)ʃ / adj. 法国人；法国的
Friday / 'fraɪdeɪ / n. 星期五
front desk 前台
fun / fʌn / adj. 有趣的
future / 'fju:tʃə / n. 未来

G

gallery / 'gæl(ə)rɪ / n. 美术馆；画廊
game / geɪm / n. 比赛
get a certificate 获得证书
get a haircut 剪发
get downtown 到市区
get dressed 穿衣服
get married 结婚
get ready for work 准备去工作
get together 聚会
get up 起床
Giant Panda n. 大熊猫
gift shop 礼品店
give the national holidays off 国庆放假
Global Language School 国际语言学校
go bicycling 骑自行车
go camping 野营
go dancing 去跳舞
go hiking 远足；徒步旅行

go home 回家
go horseback riding 骑马
go kayaking 划独木舟
go off 响起来
go on a cruise 乘船巡游
go on vacation 度假
go rafting 漂流
go rock climbing 攀岩
go shopping 购物
go sightseeing 观光
go skiing 去滑雪
go snorkeling 浮潜；潜水
go to bed 上床
go to Luxor 去卢克索(埃及)
go to the beach 去沙滩
go to the movies 去看电影
go to work 去工作
go windsurfing 风帆冲浪
go to museums 去博物馆
grandchildren / 'græn'tʃɪldrən / n. 孙子/女
grandfather / 'græn(d)fɑ:ðə / n. 祖父
grandmother / 'græn(d)mʌðə / n. 祖母
graphic designer 平面设计师
graphic organizer 结构图；表格
grave / greɪv / n. 墓穴；坟墓
greet someone 与某人打招呼
grilled meat 烤肉
grizzly bear 灰熊(分布于北美)
groom / gru:m / n. 新郎
Guadalajara / ˌgwɑ:dlə'hɑ:rə / n. 瓜达拉哈拉市(墨西哥西部)
guest room 客房
gym / dʒɪm / n. 健身房；体育馆
gymnastics / dʒɪm'næstɪks / n. 体操

H

hang out 闲逛
harbor / 'hɑ:bə / n. 海港（城市）
hard / hɑ:d / adj. 困难的
hardly ever 几乎不……
hardware store 五金店
hardworking / 'hɑ:dˌwɜ:kɪŋ / adj. 努力工作的
have meetings /phone meetings 开会/电话会议
have a feeling of satisfaction 有满足感
have a great time 玩得很高兴
have a healthy diet 健康饮食

VOCABULARY

have an accident 出事故
have classes 上课
have days off 休假；放假
have fun 玩得开心
have math class 上数学课
have the opportunity to do 有机会做……
have the same appearance 长相/外观一样
heifer / 'hefə / n. 小母牛
hibernate / 'haɪbəneɪt / v. 冬眠
hide / haɪd / v. 躲藏
high up 在高处
high-rise apartments 高层公寓
hiking / 'haɪkɪŋ / v. 徒步旅行；远足
Hindu festival 印度教节日
Hispanic family 西班牙家庭
history / 'hɪst(ə)rɪ / n. 历史
hit / hɪt / v. 击；打
hockey / 'hɒkɪ / n. 曲棍球；冰球
holiday / 'hɒlɪdeɪ / n. 节日；假期
honeymoon / 'hʌnɪmuːn / n. 蜜月
honor / 'ɒnə(r) / v. 尊敬；给……荣誉
horrible / 'hɒrəb(ə)l / adj. 可怕的；糟糕的
host / həʊst / n. 主人
hostess / 'həʊstɪs / n. 女主人
hotel facilities 饭店设施
hotel manager 酒店经理
humid / 'hjuːmɪd / adj. 潮湿的；湿润的
hunt / hʌnt / v. 打猎；觅食

I
in a hurry 匆忙
in addition 另外；此外
in advance 提前
in common with 与……有共同之处
in danger 处于危险中
in fact 事实上
in front of 在……前面
in general 总体上来说
in good health 身体健康
in high school 上高中
in line 成一直线；有秩序
in one's opinion 某人认为；某人的意见是……
in order 按顺序；依次
in person 亲身；亲自
in space 在太空中

in the gym 在体育馆/健身房
in the lyrics 歌词中
in the spotlight 使显著
inch / ɪntʃ / n. 英寸
Independence Day 独立日
informal situation 非正式场合
informal way 非正式的方式
inside / ɪn'saɪd / n. 里面；内部
interesting / 'ɪnt(ə)rɪstɪŋ / adj. 有趣的
international / ɪntə'næʃ(ə)n(ə)l / adj. 国际的；世界的
invest in 投资；购买
Iran / ɪ'rɑːn / n. 伊朗
island nation 岛国
Istanbul / ˌɪstæn'buːl / n. 伊斯坦布尔
Italian food 意大利菜

J
January / 'dʒænjʊ(ə)rɪ / n. 一月
Japan / dʒə'pæn / n. 日本
Japanese / ˌdʒæpə'niːz / adj. 日本人；日本的
jewelry store n. 珠宝店
job descriptions 工作描述
job titles 职业名称
July / dʒʊ'laɪ / n. 七月
June / dʒʊn / n. 六月

K
Kauai / 'kauaɪ / n. 考艾岛(美夏威夷群岛之一)
kick / kɪk / v. 踢
kid / kɪd / n. 小孩
kilogram / 'kɪləgræm / n. 千克
Koala / kəʊ'ɑːlə / n. 考拉
Korea / kə'rɪə / n. 韩国；朝鲜
Korean / kə'rɪən / adj. 韩国人；韩国的

L
L.A. 洛杉矶
language teacher 语言教师
lantern / 'læntən / n. 花灯
laptop computer 手提电脑
last name 姓
last night 昨天晚上
lay eggs 产蛋
lazy / 'leɪzɪ / adj. 懒惰的
learn about 学习关于……

VOCABULARY

leisure / ˈleʒə / n. 空闲
lie in bed 躺在床上
lie on the sofa 躺在沙发上
light color 浅色
live music 现场音乐会
lobby / ˈlɒbɪ / n. 大厅；休息室
local / ˈləʊk(ə)l / adj. 当地的
location / lə(ʊ)ˈkeɪʃ(ə)n / n. 地点；位置
look alike 看起来像……
look toward 为……做好准备
look up information 查找资料
lose / luːz / v. 输掉
loud / laʊd / adj. (声音)大的
lounge / laʊn(d)ʒ / n. 休息室
loved one 所爱的人
low-paying 收入低的
lunch break 午休
luxurious / lʌgˈʒʊərɪəs / adj. 奢侈的

M

make (money) v. 挣(钱)
make a basket 投篮
make a list 列清单
make a loud noise 发出很大的响声
make a mental image 想象一幅画面
make a poster 做海报
make electronic presentation 用电脑做陈述
make inference 推论；推断
make invitations 发出邀请
make sense 有意义；有道理
make suggestions 提建议
make sure (that) 确信
make tacos 做玉米饼
mall / mɔːl / n. 商场
March / mɑːtʃ / n. 三月
Master's degree 硕士学位
math / mæθ / n. 数学
May / meɪ / n. 五月
Mayan ruins 玛雅遗址
medicine / ˈmeds(ə)n / n. 医学；药
meet (people) v. 与人见面
meet friends 会友
meet up 偶然遇到；见面
Memorial Day (美国)阵亡将士纪念日
Mexican / ˈmeksɪkən / adj. 墨西哥人；墨西哥的

Mexico / ˈmeksɪkəʊ / n. 墨西哥
Middle Eastern 中东的
miss / mɪs / v. 想念
mix with (使)与……混合
modern / ˈmɒd(ə)n / adj. 现代化的
Monday / ˈmʌndeɪ / n. 星期一
Monterrey / ˌmɔːnterˈreɪ / n. 蒙特雷市(墨西哥东北部)
morning routine 每天早晨的安排
mother-in-law n. 岳母
mountain / ˈmaʊntɪn / n. 高山
movie theater 电影院
multicultural city 多元文化城市
museum / mjuːˈzɪəm / n. 博物馆
music / ˈmjuːzɪk / n. 音乐，乐曲
music concert 音乐会
Muslim countries 穆斯林国家

N

national capital 国家首都
national elections 全国大选
National Holiday 国庆节
necklace / ˈneklɪs / n. 项链
negative / ˈneɡətɪv / adj. 否定的
nephew / ˈnefjuː / n. 侄子；外甥
new releases 新片
New Zealand 新西兰
next to 紧挨着；在……旁边
niece / niːs / n. 侄女；外甥女
nightlife / ˈnaɪtlaɪf / n. 夜生活
nineteenth / naɪnˈtiːnθ / 第十九
ninth / ˈnaɪnθ / 第九
noisy / ˈnɔɪzɪ / adj. 嘈杂的；喧闹的
North America 北美洲
November / nə(ʊ)ˈvembə / n. 十一月

O

Oceania / ˌəʊsɪˈɑːnɪə / n. 大洋洲
October / ɒkˈtəʊbə / n. 十月
on display 展出
on Earth 在地球上
one million 100万
online travel site 在线旅游网站
opening party 开幕派对
opera / ˈɒp(ə)rə / n. 歌剧
ostrich / ˈɒstrɪtʃ / n. 鸵鸟

VOCABULARY

out of the lines 越界
outdoor café 户外咖啡馆
outgoing / ˈaʊtɡəʊɪŋ / adj. 外向的；对人友好的
outside / aʊtˈsaɪd / n. 外部
owl / aʊl / n. 猫头鹰

P

package / ˈpækɪdʒ / n. 包裹
paid vacation days 带薪休假的天数
painting exhibit 画展
pajamas / pəˈdʒɑːməz / n. 睡衣
palm tree 棕榈树
parade / pəˈreɪd / n. 游行；阅兵
paragliding / ˈpærəɡlaɪdɪŋ / n. 滑翔伞运动
parent / ˈpeər(ə)nt / n. 父亲（或母亲）
pass by 经过；过去
patron saint 守护神
pay attention to 注意；专心于
pay with cash 用现金支付
peaceful / ˈpiːsfʊl / adj. 和平的；平静的
penguin / ˈpeŋɡwɪn / n. 企鹅
perfect / ˈpɜːfɪkt / adj. 完美的；极好的
personal information 个人信息
personal washing 个人洗漱
personal/business network 个人/商业网络
personality / pɜːsəˈnælɪtɪ / n. 个性
Peru / pəˈru / n. 秘鲁（拉丁美洲国家）
pharmacy / ˈfɑːməsɪ / n. 药店
physical education 体育
pick up 捡起
picnic / ˈpɪknɪk / n. 野餐
ping-pong / ˈpɪŋpɒŋ / n. 乒乓球
Pirates of the Caribbean 《加勒比海盗》（电影名）
pita bread 皮塔饼；圆面饼
plan ahead 提前计划
plan out 策划；筹划
planet / ˈplænɪt / n. 行星；星球
play / pleɪ / n. 话剧；比赛
play dominoes 玩多米诺骨牌
play five minutes of overtime 打5分钟的加时赛
play golf 打高尔夫
play soccer 踢足球(英式)
play tennis 打网球
play video games 打电子游戏
player / ˈpleɪə / n. 运动员

Polar Bear 北极熊
police officer 警察
poor / pɔː / adj. 贫穷的；可怜的
popcorn / ˈpɒpkɔːn / n. 爆米花
population / pɒpjʊˈleɪʃ(ə)n / n. 人口
post office 邮局
potato / pəˈteɪtəʊ / n. 土豆；马铃薯
pound / paʊnd / n. 英镑
prayer / preə / n. 祈祷
prefer to 较喜欢；宁愿
pretty good 相当不错
programmer / ˈprəʊɡræmə / n. 程序设计员
public holidays 公共假日
public transportation 公共交通
Puebla / ˈpweblɑː / n. 普埃布拉(墨西哥中部)
put...in order 排序；整理

Q

quiet / ˈkwaɪət / adj. 安静的；温顺的

R

Ramadan / ˌræməˈdæn / n. 斋月
read between the lines 领会言外之意
read email 查看电子邮件
Real Madrid 皇家马德里队
reception / rɪˈsepʃ(ə)n / n. 宴会；接待
relax / rɪˈlæks / v. 休息
rent a car 租一辆车
rental car company 租车公司
repair / rɪˈpeə / v. 修理
restaurant / ˈrestrɒnt / n. 餐馆；饭店
restroom / ˈrestruːm / n. 洗手间；休息室
return game 回访比赛
rewarding / rɪˈwɔːdɪŋ / adj. 有益的；值得的
rise / raɪz / v. 上升
rising/falling intonation 升/降调
rock climbing 攀岩
romantic movie 爱情片
routine / ruːˈtiːn / n. 日常工作；例行公事
row / rəʊ / n. 行；排
rugby / ˈrʌɡbɪ / n. 英式橄榄球
rules / ruːlz / n. 规则；条例
rules and regulations 规章制度
run up and down a court 在球场上跑来跑去

217

VOCABULARY

S

sad / sæd / adj. 伤心的；难过的
sales department 销售部
sales manager 销售经理
salesperson / 'seɪlzpɜːs(ə)n / n. 售货员
San Jose 圣约瑟(首都)
sandwich / 'sæn(d)wɪdʒ / n. 三明治
Sao Paolo 圣保罗
Saturday / 'sætədeɪ / n. 星期六
scheduled events 已经计划好的/安排好的活动
science / 'saɪəns / n. 科学
science exhibit 科学展
science fiction books 科幻书籍
scientist / 'saɪəntɪst / n. 科学家
score / skɔː / v. 得分
Scottish / 'skɔtɪʃ / adj. 苏格兰人；苏格兰的
scuba-diving 配戴水肺的潜水；轻便潜水
sculpture exhibit 雕塑展
seat / siːt / n. 座位
second / 'sek(ə)nd / adj. 第二的；次要的
Second Avenue 第二大道
seconds / 'sek(ə)nz / n. 添加的食物
see the sights 欣赏风光
send emails 发送邮件
September / sep'tembə / n. 九月
serious / 'sɪərɪəs / adj. 严肃的；认真的
server / 'sɜːvə / n. 服务员
seventeenth / ˌsevən'tiːnθ / 第十七
seventh / 'sev(ə)nθ / 第七
shoe store 鞋店
shopping centre 购物中心
shopping guide 购物指南
shopping habits 购物习惯
shortened version 缩写形式
Siberian Tiger 西伯利亚虎
similar to 与……相似
sit in the sun 晒太阳
sit on the chair 坐在椅子上
sixteenth / sɪks'tiːnθ / 第十六
sixth / sɪksθ / 第六
ski / skiː / v. 滑雪
skiing / 'skiːɪŋ / n. 滑雪
skyscraper / 'skaɪskreɪpə / n. 摩天大楼
snack bar 小卖部
soccer match 足球比赛

social activity 社交活动
social network sites 社交网站
social studies 社会学科
software engineer 软件工程师
solve riddles 猜谜语
so-so / 'səʊsəʊ / adj. 一般的；平常的
South America 南美洲
space station 空间站
Spain / speɪn / n. 西班牙
Spanish / 'spænɪʃ / adj. 西班牙语；西班牙人；西班牙的
special / 'speʃ(ə)l / adj. 特别的
special schooling 特殊教育
spectacular / spek'tækjʊlə / adj. 壮观的；惊人的
Spotted Tree Frog 斑点树蛙
squirrel / 'skwɪr(ə)l / n. 松鼠
St. Patrick's Day 圣帕特里克日
stadium / 'steɪdɪəm / n. 体育馆
stage / steɪdʒ / n. 舞台
stamp / stæmp / n. 邮票
state / steɪt / n. 州
state capital 州首府；州政府
station / 'steɪʃ(ə)n / n. 车站
stay open 继续营业
sticky rice 糯米
store / stɔː / n. 商店
stroll / strəʊl / v. 散步；闲逛
student profile 学生档案
stuffed / stʌft / adj. 饱了
suburb / 'sʌbɜːb / n. 郊区
subway / 'sʌbweɪ / n. 地铁
subway station 地铁站
such as 比如
suite / swiːt / n. 套房；家具
sunbathe / 'sʌnbeɪð / v. 晒日光浴
Sunday / 'sʌndeɪ / n. 星期日
Sunday brunch 周日早午餐
sunglasses / 'sʌnɡlɑːsɪz / n. 太阳镜
Sunset Film Festival 落日电影节
supermarket / 'suːpəmɑːkɪt / n. 超市
surf the Internet 上网
swimming pool 泳池
Sydney harbor 悉尼港

T

taekwondo / taɪ'kɔndəʊ / n. 跆拳道

VOCABULARY

take a boat ride 乘船游玩
take a river cruise 乘游船
take a shower 淋浴
take a tour 旅行
take a trip 去旅行
take a walk 散步
take revenge 报仇
take turns 轮流
Taksim Square 塔克西姆广场
talk on the phone 煲电话粥
talk over with 与……协商; 洽谈
taxi driver 出租车司机
taxi stand 出租车上下站
tell the difference 分清
temperature / 'temp(ə)rətʃə / n. 温度
Temperature scales 温度计
tenth / tenθ / 第十
terminal / 'tɜːmɪn(ə)l / n. 末端; 终点
terminal building 航站楼
terrible / 'terɪb(ə)l / adj. 很糟的; 可怕的
Thai / taɪ / adj. 泰国人; 泰国的
thanks to 由于; 因为
the Australian Koala Foundation 澳大利亚考拉基金会
the Bahamas 巴哈马群岛
the Baltimore Orioles 巴尔的摩金莺队
the blog entry 博客条目
the Burj Al Arab hotel 伯瓷酒店(帆船酒店)
the Camden Yards stadium 金莺公园球场
the capital city 首都
the Caribbean Sea 加勒比海
the Central Hotel 中央酒店
the Chinese calendar 中国农历
the Cuban national team 古巴国家队
the day before yesterday 前天
the Day of the Dead 亡灵节
the Empire State Building 帝国大厦(美国纽约市)
the Estadio Latinoamericano 拉丁美洲棒球场
the FIFA World Cup championship 世界杯足球赛冠军
the final match 决赛
the first row 第一排
The Hairdresser 《理发师》
the Imperial System 英制系统
the Islamic calendar 伊斯兰日历
the Koala Protection Society 考拉保护协会
the Lantern Festival 元宵节

the Louvre 卢浮宫
the lunar year 农历年
the Marmara Hotel 马尔马拉酒店
the metric system 十进制; 公制
the Metropolitan Museum of Art 大都会美术馆
the Museum of Modern Art 现代艺术博物馆
the Pacific Ocean 太平洋
the Phoenix Art Museum 凤凰艺术博物馆
the Place Vendome 旺多姆广场
the Republic of Ireland 爱尔兰共和国
the Republic of Panama 巴拿马共和国(中美洲)
The Ritz 丽兹酒店
the River Liffey 利菲河(爱尔兰)
the Running of the Bulls Festival 奔牛节
the Scottsdale stadium 斯科茨代尔体育场
the second inning 第二局
the Sphinx 狮身人面像
the Strolling of the Heifers 母牛散步节
the Sydney Opera House 悉尼歌剧院
the United Arab Emirates 阿联酋
the United States 美利坚合众国
the year ahead 来年; 明年
theater / 'θɪətə / n. 剧院; 电影院
third / θɜːd / 第三
thirteenth / θɜː'tiːnθ / 第十三
this morning 当天早上
this way 这样; 用这种办法
three days ago 三天前
throw / θrəʊ / v. 扔
Thursday / 'θɜːzdeɪ / n. 星期四
ticket / 'tɪkɪt / n. 票; 入场券
tie / taɪ / v. 与……打成平局
Times Square 时代广场
toast / təʊst / n. 烤面包
tool / tuːl / n. 工具
touristy / 'tʊərɪstɪ / adj. 适宜游览的
track / træk / n. 跑道
traditional / trə'dɪʃ(ə)n(ə)l / adj. 传统的
train station 火车站
transportation / trænspɔː'teɪʃ(ə)n / n. 交通; 运输
travel agent 旅行社
travel brochure 旅游手册
travel for leisure 休闲旅行
trip / trɪp / n. 旅行
tropical / 'trɒpɪk(ə)l / adj. 热带的

VOCABULARY

Tuesday / 'tjuːzdeɪ / n. 星期二
turkey / 'tɜːkɪ / n. 火鸡
TV show 电视节目
twelfth / twelfθ / 第十二
twentieth / 'twentɪəθ / 第二十
twenty-first / ˌtwentɪ'fɜːst / 第二十一
twenty-second / ˌtwentɪ'sekənd / 第二十二
twenty-third / ˌtwentɪ'θɜːd / 第二十三
twice a month 一个月两次
twice as many as 两倍多
twist / twɪst / v. 扭动
type / taɪp / v. 打字

U
UCLA 加州大学洛杉矶分校
under the stars 在星空下
unusual / ʌn'juːʒʊəl / adj. 非常规的
up and down 起伏地

V
vegetable / 'vedʒtəb(ə)l / n. 蔬菜
Venice / 'venɪs / n. 威尼斯
verb in the infinitive 动词不定式
Veterans Day 退伍军人节
volleyball / 'vɒlɪbɔːl / n. 排球
vote for 投票(选举)
vote on 就……表决

W
wake up 醒来
watch the concert 观看演唱会
water polo 水球运动
wear / weə / v. 穿戴
wear an apron 系围裙
wear jeans 穿牛仔裤
wear sneakers 穿运动鞋
weather / 'weðə / n. 天气
wedding / 'wedɪŋ / n. 婚礼
wedding ceremony 结婚典礼
wedding gown 婚纱
wedding reception 婚宴
Wednesday / 'wenzdeɪ / n. 星期三
well-known / ˌwel'nəʊn / adj. 广为人知的
well-paying / ˌwel'peɪɪŋ / adj. 收入高的
what's more 而且; 此外

while / waɪl / conj. 当……时候
widowed / 'wɪdəʊd / adj. 寡居的
widowed wife 寡妇
wild boar 野猪(雄性)
win / wɪn / v. 赢; 赢得
winner / 'wɪnə / n. 胜利者
world-class city 世界一流城市
would rather 宁愿; 宁可

Y
yard / jɑːd / n. 码 (1码=3英尺)
yesterday afternoon 昨天下午
yoga / 'jəʊgə / n. 瑜珈
yoga class 瑜伽课

Z
zero gravity 失重; 零重力

AUDIOSCRIPT

Unit 1 Let's begin!

Page 3, Exercise 2

Teacher: What's your first name?
Rita: My first name's Rita.
Teacher: How do you spell it?
Rita: R-i-t-a.
Teacher: What's your last name?
Rita: My last name's Valdez.
Teacher: How do you spell it?
Rita: V-a-l-d-e-z.
Teacher: OK, thanks. What's your date of birth?
Rita: It's March 14th, 1992.
Teacher: OK. Let's see… That's 3, 1-4, 1-9-9-2.
Rita: That's right.
Teacher: Great! And what country are you from, Rita?
Rita: I live in the United States.
Teacher: What city?
Rita: Miami.
Teacher: What's your email address?
Rita: It's ritavaldez@smail.gt.
Teacher: How do you spell it?
Rita: r-i-t-a-v-a-l-d-e-z at s-m-a-i-l dot g-t.
Teacher: Thank you.
Rita: You're welcome.

Page 4, Exercise 4

1. February eleventh two thousand seven
2. October seventeenth nineteen eighty-nine
3. July eighth two thousand nine
4. April ninth twenty sixteen
5. December twenty-third twenty twelve

Unit 2 All about me!

Page 15, Exercises 2 and 3

Marc: Hi! Do you work at Tomlin Company?
Debra: Yes, I do. What about you?
Marc: I do too. I'm a new employee.
Debra: Oh, that's great! Welcome to Tomlin Company! I'm Debra Johnson.
Marc: Nice to meet you, Debra. I'm Marc Sanchez.
Debra: Nice to meet you too! What's your job?
Marc: I'm a computer programmer. What about you?
Debra: I'm a manager. I work in the sales department.
Marc: That's great!
Debra: Yes, I like it a lot! Where are you from?
Marc: I'm from New York, but my parents are from Spain. What about you?
Debra: I'm from California. Listen, I have to go now. See you at work!
Marc: Goodbye, Debra. See you later!

Unit 3 Tell me about your day

Page 27, Exercises 3 and 4

Teresa: Oh, Jane… I'm so tired today.
Jane: Yes, Teresa, I can see that. What time do you get up in the morning?
Teresa: Well, I get up early. I get up at six. That's why I'm tired!
Jane: You get up at six! Why?
Teresa: Well, because I need time to get ready. I get up… I take a shower… and I get dressed. Then I eat breakfast.
Jane: So, what time do you leave home?
Teresa: I leave at seven thirty.
Jane: Seven thirty! It takes you an hour and a half to get up and eat breakfast?
Teresa: Well, yes. I take my time. Then I walk to work, and that takes thirty minutes.
Jane: What time do you start work?
Teresa: I start work at eight o'clock. What time do you get up?
Jane: Oh, I get up at seven thirty. In thirty minutes, I can do everything. I leave home at eight, and at eight thirty, I start work.
Teresa: That's great. … Oh, I'm so tired…

Page 33, Pronunciation, Exercise 2

plays   eats
gets   exercises
does   has
watches   goes
works   teaches
brushes   takes

221

AUDIOSCRIPT

Page 36, Practice

1.
Kim: Hi, Paul. Do you have a language class today?
Paul: Oh... Hi, Kim. Yes. I have Spanish class. How about you?
Kim: I have Korean. What time is your class?
Paul: It's at 9 in the morning.

2.
Anita: Hey, Mike. Do you usually get up early on Saturday?
Mike: No, I usually get up late.
Anita: What time do you get up?
Mike: Usually at 10 o'clock.
Anita: That's not late! I get up at noon!

Unit 4 Let's go shopping!

Page 39, Exercise 2

Alicia: Hi, Wanda! How are you?
Wanda: Hi, Alicia! I'm fine. How are you?
Alicia: Fine, thanks. I have a question. Is there a jewelry store near here? I need to buy some earrings.
Wanda: A jewelry store? Let's see... No... But Young's Department Store is on Main Street. It's next to the big bookstore.
Alicia: Oh, right! Thanks. And one more thing... Is there a shoe store near here? I need to buy some new boots too.
Wanda: Yes, there is... Actually, there are two shoe stores.
Alicia: Really? Where are they?
Wanda: Let's see... There's one on Main Street, next to the department store. And there's also the one on Center Street between the hardware store and the electronics store. They have great shoes!
Alicia: Wow! Great! Thanks very much!
Wanda: You're welcome. See you later.

Page 40, Exercise 3

Conversation 1
Man: Two tickets, please.
Woman: For which movie?
Man: Let's see... The Dark Man.
Woman: OK. That's twenty-one dollars, please. Cash or credit?
Man: Cash... Let's see... Here's twenty-five dollars.
Woman: Thank you... and that's four dollars in change.
Man: Thank you!
Woman: Enjoy the movie!

Conversation 2
Woman: Hi! May I help you?
Man: Yes, one coffee, please.
Woman: What size?
Man: Large, please.
Woman: OK. Anything else?
Man: Let's see... how about a sandwich?
Woman: That's five dollars.
Man: OK. Here you are!
Woman: Thank you!

Conversation 3
Man: May I help you?
Woman: Yes, two big envelopes, please.
Man: OK. Here you are. Do you want to buy stamps also?
Woman: Umm... Yes.
Man: OK. How many?
Woman: Fifteen.
Man: OK. That's seven dollars. Cash or credit?
Woman: Credit. Here you go.
Man: Thanks.
Woman: Thank you!

Unit 5 My family

Page 51, Exercises 2 and 3

Lily: This is a nice picture, Amanda.
Amanda: Thanks, Lily! That's a picture of me with my family. We're on vacation in California. That's me hugging my mom, Barbara. That's my sister Eliza with her husband Kevin. That's their son Pete and their baby daughter Madison. She's sitting on my brother's shoulders.
Lily: Aw... She's so cute! How old are they?
Amanda: Pete's 6 years old and Madison is 1.
Lily: And what is your brother's name?
Amanda: Jack. He's a college student. He lives in Florida.
Lily: And who's that?
Amanda: That's my dad, David.

AUDIOSCRIPT

Lily:	Oh, right!
Amanda:	How about you, Lily? Do you have any brothers or sisters?
Lily:	I have a brother.
Amanda:	What's his name?
Lily:	Bruce.
Amanda:	Oh, right! I know Bruce. He plays basketball on the school team!
Lily:	Yes, that's him!

Page 60, Practice

My name is Abigail. This is my daughter Becky. She's 18 years old. She has long, brown hair and brown eyes. She's very outgoing and hardworking. Her favorite sport is soccer.

REVIEW 1

Page 63, Listening

Conversation 1

Man:	This is a nice photo.
Woman:	Yes. That's me with my family. We're in my parents' house. Those are my parents. And that's my sister Liza with her husband Freddy and their two children, Silvia and Paul.
Man:	How old are they?
Woman:	Silvia's 8 and Paul's 5.
Man:	And what are your parents' names?
Woman:	Rafael and Marina.
Man:	And who's that?

Conversation 2

Man:	Excuse me. I need to buy some sunglasses. Is there a department store near here?
Woman:	A department store? Yes. Let's see. There's one on this street, near the station.
Man:	OK. Thanks very much.
Woman:	You're welcome.

Conversation 3

Woman:	What do you do in the morning?
Man:	I get up, take a shower, and get dressed.
Woman:	What time do you get up?
Man:	I get up at 7:30.
Woman:	What time do you take a shower?
Man:	I take a shower at about 8:00.
Woman:	What time do you get dressed?
Man:	I get dressed at 8:15, and then I go to work.

Unit 6 Yesterday

Page 67, Exercise 2

Amelia
I got up at 6:00. I had breakfast, and I took my son to school. I took the bus and got to work at 8:15. I worked all morning and then had lunch. I usually have lunch in the factory cafeteria. Yesterday I had a sandwich in the cafeteria, and then I went shopping. I went back to the factory at 2:00 and finished work at 5:00 p.m. Then I took the bus home. I had dinner at 6:00, and then I watched TV. I went to bed at about 11:00.

Daniel
I got up late, so I didn't have breakfast. I usually walk, but yesterday I took the bus to school. I started work at 9:00. At 12:30, I had lunch in the school cafeteria. Then I taught until 3:30. That's when the students go home. I stayed at school until 4:30, and then I met my wife at her office. We went to a museum and then to dinner at a restaurant.

Tammy
I got to the office at 8:30. I usually have a cup of tea in the cafeteria, but yesterday I had a cup of coffee. I checked my email, and then I had a meeting. Around 1:00, I had lunch at a restaurant in town. Then I went back to the office and worked until about 7:00. I had some plans to finish for the next day—plans for a bridge. I took the train home and took a shower. Then I met my friends in town and we went to a movie.

Page 73, Pronunciation, Exercise 2

started	listened	wanted
walked	liked	completed
played	studied	stayed
decided	shopped	worked

Unit 7 What are you doing?

Page 79, Exercises 2 and 3

Kylie:	Hi, Ben. It's me, Kylie.
Ben:	Kylie! How's it going?

223

AUDIOSCRIPT

Kylie: Good. Really good. I just got home.
Ben: You just got home!? What time is it there in San Jose?
Kylie: Um... it's 1 o'clock in the morning. What time is it in Brisbane?
Ben: It's five o'clock in the afternoon. ... So, what are you doing, getting home at 1 a.m.?
Kylie: Oh, I went to dinner with my Spanish class. It was a lot of fun. We had a great time. And you? What are you doing?
Ben: Not much. I'm just hanging out.
Kylie: Yeah, I can imagine. Is it raining?
Ben: No. Why?
Kylie: It sounds like it's raining.
Ben: Ah! ... No, I'm typing.
Kylie: What! You're typing an email at the same time that you're talking to me!
Ben: Um, no. I'm chatting, actually.
Kylie: Who are you chatting with?
Ben: Well, with... Jasmine.
Kylie: Jasmine? Who's Jasmine?
Ben: Oh, she's my new girlfriend.
Kylie: What? Another new girlfriend? What about Melanie?
Ben: Melanie? She's away for six months, teaching English in Mexico. Anyway, what's the weather like there?
Kylie: Oh, it's hot. Really hot... But, don't change the subject. I want to know about Jasmine!

Page 85, Pronunciation, Exercise 2

1. She's sitting in the first row.
2. I'm moving to New York.
3. We're riding our bikes.
4. He's standing in line.
5. You're writing an email.
6. I'm meeting him at 3 o'clock.

Unit 8 I'm taking a trip

Page 91, Exercises 2 and 3

Kelly: Hello?
Angie: Hi, Kelly? It's Angie.
Kelly: Hi, Angie! How's life in Los Angeles?
Angie: It's great! But I'm calling you because I'm coming to Boston next weekend!
Kelly: You are? That's great! Where are you staying?
Angie: I'm staying at the Park Hotel. Do you know it?
Kelly: Oh, yes! It's a great hotel! The lobby is really big and beautiful! I heard the guest rooms are nice too. So... Let's meet up!
Angie: I would love to! I'm going to my cousin's wedding.
Kelly: When is the wedding?
Angie: It's on Saturday. It starts at three. What are you doing Saturday morning?
Kelly: Actually, Saturday morning I'm busy. Jack and I are taking a tennis class.
Angie: What time does it end?
Kelly: It ends at noon.
Angie: Oh, that's too late.
Kelly: Right... but what are you doing Friday night?
Angie: Let's see... Friday night I'm going to a dinner with my family. Maybe Sunday is the best day.
Kelly: What time do you fly out?
Angie: Let's see... my plane leaves at 2 p.m.
Kelly: Then let's have breakfast!
Angie: OK. That sounds perfect! I can't wait to see you!
Kelly: Me too!

Page 97, Pronunciation, Exercise 2

1. flight
2. alive
3. lock
4. rent
5. pilot
6. deal
7. room

Unit 9 Going out

Page 103, Exercises 2 and 3

The Rose Theater announces their grand opening party on Saturday night at 6:00 in the evening. The new theater has 500 comfortable seats. All of the seats have a good view of the stage. There is also a snack bar in the lobby. The first event at the theater is called The Hairdresser. It's a

AUDIOSCRIPT

wonderful new play by Noah Vega, starring Brad Benson and Paloma Sanchez. The play opens on April 6th and goes until April 27th. Tickets for the opening night party on April 6th are $75 and include tickets to the show.

Buy tickets online at rosetheater.com or at the Rose Theater box office. It is located at 65 Jackson Street in Springfield. The box office opens daily at 11:00 a.m. and closes at 6:00 p.m. The box office is closed on Sundays.

Page 112, Practice

The theater is located at 795 Main Street in Los Angeles. The box office is located at the side entrance of the theater; the side entrance is on 1st Avenue. Tickets go on sale on January 7th.

Unit 10   Let's celebrate!

Page 115, Exercises 2 and 3

Franz: There is an interesting custom in my village. It's connected with the New Year. The idea is to scare away the evil spirits of the old year.
Diana: And what exactly happens?
Franz: Well, there's a group of men...
Diana: A group of men? Are there any women?
Franz: No, there aren't any women in the group. There are men... well, and there are also some boys.
Diana: Uh-huh...
Franz: And the men go from one village to another village, and they have cowbells.
Diana: Uh... What are cowbells?
Franz: You know, like a big bell—ding, dong—for a cow's neck. These bells make a really loud noise, and the evil spirits leave the village because they don't like the noise.
Diana: So, where do people do this?
Franz: Well, it's in Switzerland. They do it in the villages in Switzerland.
Diana: When do people do this? Is it on New Year's Eve?
Franz: Actually, it happens for seven days. The last day is on New Year's Eve, December 31st.
Diana: Every day for a week! Do the men make a lot of noise?
Franz: Yes, they make a lot of noise... all night long. It's very hard to sleep.
Diana: Wow! Have you ever done this?
Franz: Me? No, I haven't.

REVIEW 2

Page 128, Exercises 2 and 3

Andy: Hey, Bill! How was your trip to Mexico?
Bill: Oh, it was amazing, Andy! We went to some great tourist sites and spent time on the beach too!
Andy: How was the weather?
Bill: It was hot and sunny most of the time. It rained one day, so we stayed in the hotel. Then we went to see a concert at a theater that night.
Andy: That sounds great! How was the food?
Bill: The food was delicious! We ate at lots of different Mexican restaurants. Also we were there for Carnival.
Andy: What's Carnival?
Bill: It's a festival. It's the same as Mardi Gras in the United States.
Andy: Oh! How fun!
Bill: Yeah... there were parades, and everyone in the parades wore amazing costumes! It was crowded, but it was really fun!
Andy: It sounds great!
Bill: I bought a couple of masks that I brought home with me. You should come to my house to see them!
Andy: I would love to! So how did you get around there?
Bill: Well, there aren't any trains, so most of the time we rode buses. We also rented a car to go to see the pyramids on the weekend.
Andy: What an adventure! I can't wait to see your pictures!
Bill: Well, we took lots of pictures, so I'll show them to you!

Unit 11   It's a great job!

Page 131, Exercises 2 and 3

Interviewer: Excuse me.
Woman: Yes?

AUDIOSCRIPT

Interviewer: Can I ask you a few questions?
Woman: Yes, of course.
Interviewer: What do you do?
Woman: I'm a financial analyst.
Interviewer: When do you start work?
Woman: Let's see... I usually start work at 7:30 in the morning, but I sometimes start work at 6:00.
Interviewer: Wow! 6 o'clock?! Why do you start work so early?
Woman: Well, I work with people and financial markets all over the world, and we very often have meetings in the morning.
Interviewer: Where does everybody live?
Woman: Well, I live in New York, but I work with people in India, Scotland, and Brazil.
Interviewer: That's amazing! How do you meet with them when they're all over the world?
Woman: Well, we do a lot of work through email and web conferencing. And we often have our meetings over the phone.
Interviewer: Do you ever have meetings in person?
Woman: Not usually. We hardly ever meet in person, but when we do, it's really nice!
Interviewer: Why is it nice?
Woman: Because it's nice to talk to the people you work with in person!
Interviewer: Yes, I imagine it is!
Interviewer: How often do you have meetings in India?
Woman: Actually, we never have the meetings in India. They're always in New York. I'd like to go there sometime.
Interviewer: Me too! And, one more question...
Woman: Yes?
Interviewer: Do you like your job?
Woman: Yes, I do. It's demanding, but it's well-paying and interesting. It's a great job!

Page 138, Exercise 2 11_08

Conversation 1
A: Excuse me.
B: Yes?
A: Can I ask you some questions, please?
B: I'm sorry, but I don't have time.
A: OK. Thanks anyway.

Conversation 2
A: Excuse me. Would you like to try our pizza?
B: No, thanks. I'm not hungry right now.
A: Do you want some coffee?
B: I'm sorry, but I'm in a hurry.
A: OK. Sorry to bother you.

Conversation 3
A: Hey, Brian!
B: Hi, Alison.
A: Do you want to go to the movies?
B: I'm sorry, but I have a lot of homework to do.
A: OK. Maybe another time.

Conversation 4
A: Hey, Jen! Can you help me with my homework?
B: I'm sorry, but I'm busy.
A: OK. I'll ask someone else.

Unit 12   Great vacations.

Page 143, Exercise 2 and 3 12_02

Interviewer: What do you usually do when you go on vacation?
Samantha: Let's see... I like all kinds of vacations! Sometimes I like to be out in nature, and other times I like to be in cities.
Interviewer: What kinds of things do you do when you're out in nature?
Samantha: Usually I like to just go to the beach or the mountains and do nothing. I read, sleep, eat... and that's about it!
Interviewer: That does sound relaxing! Do you like adventure vacations?
Samantha: No, not really. I never go rock climbing or rafting, or anything like that. I like to feel safe and comfortable.
Interviewer: And what do you do when you take a vacation in a city?
Samantha: I usually go sightseeing—like to museums and historical places. Also, I always go shopping when I'm in cities!
Interviewer: When was your favorite vacation?
Samantha: My favorite vacation was in Paris, about two years ago. I went with my friend Marissa.
Interviewer: Ah, Paris. I love Paris! What did you see?
Samantha: A lot of things. We were there for about a week and we went to a lot of museums. And we went sightseeing to the usual places, you know, the Eiffel Tower, a river cruise, Notre-Dame... you name it. We went shopping in some great stores too. You can buy such beautiful things in Paris!
Interviewer: Great. Where did you stay?

AUDIOSCRIPT

Samantha:	We stayed in a small hotel in the center of the city, very near the river.
Interviewer:	And where are you going for your next vacation?
Samantha:	Actually, I'm going to Costa Rica next month!
Interviewer:	Really? How wonderful! What are you going to do there?
Samantha:	Oh, lots of things! We are going to the mountains and the beach!
Interviewer:	That's great! What are you doing when you're in the mountains?
Samantha:	In the mountains, we're going hiking in a cloud forest, where there are unusual birds and animals.
Interviewer:	Wow! That sounds great! And what are you going to do when you're at the beach? Just relax and sunbathe?
Samantha:	Relax and sunbathe, yes, but also we're going snorkeling and windsurfing.
Interviewer:	That sounds exciting! Who are you going with?
Samantha:	I'm going with my sister. It's going to be great!

Page 148, Exercise 4

Host:	And welcome back to "The Talk Show". On today's show, we're going to look at vacation days around the world. We have Brenda Williams here with us today to discuss the issue. Brenda works for an organization called The Benefits Foundation. Welcome, Brenda.
Brenda:	Thank you. I'm happy to be here.
Host:	So how do vacation days differ around the world?
Brenda:	Actually, there's a lot of variation. Most countries have laws about how many days off a year companies must give their employees.
Host:	Really? A law? I don't think that's true in the United States.
Brenda:	You're absolutely right. In fact, the U.S. is one of the only countries in the world that doesn't have a legal minimum for vacation days.
Host:	Wow! One of the only countries? How many days off do other countries require?
Brenda:	Well, there's a lot of variation. An average would be a country like Japan that requires companies to give their employees at least 18 days off a year.
Host:	That's not bad. Most companies in the U.S. only give 10 days off a year.
Brenda:	And that's their decision too. In fact, some U.S. companies only give 5 days or less off a year.
Host:	That's terrible! So what is the highest number of days off around the world?
Brenda	Let's see, Finland and Austria both require a minimum of 35 days off a year. And Brazil has a legal minimum of 30 days a year.
Host:	That's great!
Brenda:	Other countries have lower limits. South Korea, for example, requires 10 days off a year, and Mexico only 7 days off a year. But there is still a legal minimum.
Host:	Well, this has been very interesting. Thank you so much for coming to our show today.
Brenda:	You're welcome! Thanks for having me!
Host:	And up next... [fade out]

Unit 13   Cities around the world

Page 155, Exercise 2

Chul:	Where are you from, Andy?
Andy:	I'm from Sydney.
Chul:	And you live in Seoul now.
Andy:	Yes, that's right.
Chul:	So, do you like living in Seoul?
Andy:	Yes, I do. I like it a lot. It's really interesting. I'm studying at Seoul National University.
Chul:	Ah...right. And what's Sydney like? Is it very different from Seoul?
Andy:	Yeah, it is. A lot of things are different.

Page 155, Exercise 3

Chul:	Ah...right. And what's Sydney like? Is it very different from Seoul?
Andy:	Yeah, it is. A lot of things are different.
Chul:	Like what?
Andy:	Well... the language!
Chul:	Yes, of course!
Andy:	And the climate is more extreme here. It gets a lot hotter here in the summer and a lot colder in the winter.
Chul:	Oh really! I thought it was very hot in Sydney.
Andy:	It is in the summer, but I think it gets hotter here.
Chul:	And what else is different? Is Sydney a big city like Seoul?
Andy:	Yeah, Sydney is the biggest city in Australia, but it's smaller than Seoul. I think there are around 5 million people in Sydney.
Chul:	Wow. Sydney is smaller then, much smaller. I think there are more than 15 million people living in Seoul.

AUDIOSCRIPT

Andy: Really? That many! That's a lot of people. Seoul is definitely more crowded than Sydney. In Sydney a lot of people live in houses, but in Seoul most people live in apartments.

Chul: Yes, there's more space in Australia.

Andy: Yes, but Seoul has things that Sydney doesn't have. I mean, Seoul is so modern, and public transportation is really good. It might be better than in Sydney. A lot of people still use their cars in Sydney, and the traffic can get quite bad.

Chul: And, what about nightlife and eating out? Is it expensive to go to a restaurant?

Andy: Hmmm. Well, it depends on the restaurant, I suppose. Some are cheap and some are expensive. But I think, in general, it's cheaper to eat out in Seoul.

Chul: Yes, there's a lot of choice in Seoul. Speaking of which, I'm hungry. Do you want to get something to eat?

Andy: Sure. Good idea.

Page 162, Exercises 2 and 3 `13_09`

Jack: Which city would you prefer to live in: Los Angeles, Miami, or New York?

Liza: Well, New York is the biggest city. And it's probably the most interesting.

Jack: That's true, but the air is cleaner in Miami, and it's also the warmest city. I really like warm weather.

Liza: I know what you mean. I don't like cold weather. But Miami is also the most dangerous!

Jack: That's so true! I don't want to be unsafe...

Liza: And what about all those hurricanes?

Jack: I see what you mean, but I think people can plan ahead for the hurricanes. So it's not a big problem.

Liza: I don't know about that. There are a lot of problems with the hurricanes every year.

Jack: Yeah, but anyway, I still think I'd prefer Miami. It has a good lifestyle.

Liza: I totally agree. Overall, it's probably a nice place to live.

Unit 14   Wildlife

Page 166, Exercise 3 `14_02`

An animal is endangered when there are not many left. An endangered animal usually becomes extinct due to a change in its environment or danger from other animals or people. Four endangered animals are the Bengal Tiger, the Giant Panda, the Spotted Tree Frog, and the Black Rhinoceros.

The Bengal tiger lives primarily in India. Scientists think that the population is only about 1,500. There is a large wildlife conservation project, called Project Tiger, that is trying to protect the Bengal tiger.

The Giant Panda lives in the mountains in central China. The animal is endangered because the places where it lived were destroyed by people. Many pandas were also hunted and killed by people. Because of strong conservation efforts, the panda population is increasing. There are now about 3,000 Giant Pandas living in the wild.

There are only about 4,000 Spotted Tree Frogs left in the world. The animal is at risk of disappearing forever. These small frogs live in the mountains of Australia. They are in danger because of fish that eat their eggs and changes in the water they live in.

The Black Rhinoceros, an animal that lives in Africa, is not really black. It's the same color as the White Rhinoceros. There are four kinds of Black Rhinoceroses. One kind is extinct.

In 1990, there were only about 2,400 left of the other three kinds. But thanks to conservation efforts, there are now about 3,600 Black Rhinos living in Africa.

Page 167, Exercise 2 `14_03`

Interviewer: So, Nick, can you tell me a little bit about the kakapo?

Nick: Of course. The kakapo is a heavy yellow and green bird. It's a kind of parrot, actually. It can measure up to 24 inches (60 centimeters) long. One thing that makes the kakapo unusual is that it has wings, but it can't fly.

Interviewer: Interesting... And where does the kakapo live?

Nick: It lives on the forest floor in New Zealand.

Interviewer: And what does it eat?

Nick: The kakapo eats plants on the forest floor.

Interviewer: I see... And is it endangered?

Nick: Yes, it is.

Page 167, Exercise 3 `14_04`

Interviewer: And what's the latest news on the kakapo population? Is it good news or bad news?

Nick: Well, right now it's very, very good. We are having a very good season. Last week, four healthy chicks were born. This means that the kakapo population has now reached 60 for the first time in 20 years. And there are another seven eggs waiting to hatch. With luck, this will bring the total population to 67.

Interviewer: Where are the chicks?

AUDIOSCRIPT

Nick: Scientists are looking after the chicks until they are big enough to return to the wild.
Interviewer: And where will they go?
Nick: Well, all the kakapos live on islands off the coast of New Zealand. They are safer there because there are no wild rats or cats. Also, the islands are small, so it's easier to keep an eye on the kakapos.
Interviewer: Can people visit these islands?
Nick: No, they can't. You need permission from the Department of Conservation.
Interviewer: What can people do to help the Kakapo Recovery Program?
Nick: Well, it costs a lot of money keeping the kakapo protected, so we're always happy to get donations. You can send money to: The Kakapo Recovery Program, P.O. Box 10-420, Wellington, New Zealand.
Interviewer: Thanks, Nick, and good luck.

Page 174, Exercises 2 and 3

Conversation 1
Dr. Smith: How tall are you, Maria?
Maria: I'm five feet six inches tall.
Dr. Smith: How much do you weigh?
Maria: I weigh 125 pounds.

Conversation 2
Bill: How much does the kakapo weigh?
Mr. Kim: It weighs about 3.5 kilos.
Bill: How long is the kakapo?
Mr. Kim: It's usually 30 centimeters long.
Bill: And what about the koala? How much does it weigh?
Mr. Kim: A male koala is usually 12 kilos in weight.
Bill: And what is the length of the koala?
Mr. Kim: The male koala is usually about 78 centimeters in length.

Unit 15 All about sports

Page 179, Exercise 2

1 Samantha
I love it. The places you go to are beautiful. You're up in the mountains. Everything is covered in snow. And when you go down, it's really exciting. When you first learn, you fall down a lot. But now I don't fall very much. You don't have to go fast if you're scared. You can choose an easier trail and go slower. But if you like going fast, you can go really fast. The only problem is that there are no mountains where I live, so I have to go during my winter vacation, and that's only one week a year.

2 Masumi
I really enjoy doing this sport. And it's good to know something about how to protect myself. And, it's good exercise. Students must wear special white clothes. I like the clothes, but not everybody does. My coordination and balance are better now than before I started doing it. We do a lot of different moves, like kicks with our feet, and punches with our fists. But we must not hit each other in the head. Mentally it's good, too. It helps you to concentrate better and teaches discipline. One of the rules is that people must not call each other names. I like it very much because it's a very complete sport. I started about eight years ago, and now I'm a black belt.

3 Doug
It's a sport that not many people play. This is too bad because it's such a wonderful game. It's very fast and is really good for your coordination. You don't have to play it on ice. You can play it on grass too. I play on grass, and we use a small ball. When people play on ice they use a flat disc, called a puck. I started playing at school and I still play now. I play for a local team and we have a game every Saturday. I like playing on a team. We always enjoy it, and it doesn't matter if we win or lose!

Page 186, Exercise 2

Receptionist: Welcome to the sports club! Do you have any questions?
Linda: Um... Yes, I do. Is it possible to bring a friend with me?
Receptionist: As a guest?
Linda: Yes.
Receptionist: Guests are allowed, but you have to buy a one-day pass. A pass is $8.00 for the day.
Linda: Wow! That's expensive. Is it cheaper for children?
Receptionist: Actually, children under the age of 12 are not allowed in the gym.
Linda: Ah... I see. And am I allowed to bring my own food to the gym?
Receptionist: It's possible to bring your own drinks into the gym. Food, however, is only allowed in the snack bar, and you have to buy it there.
Linda: Does that include in the changing rooms?
Receptionist: Yes, that's right. Eating in the changing rooms is not allowed either. And smoking is prohibited anywhere in the gym.
Linda: Well, that's no problem. I don't smoke!

AUDIOSCRIPT

REVIEW 3

Page 191, Listening 🔊 15_R3_01

Conversation 1
A: How was the trip?
B: Oh, it was great. The weather was really nice and it's such a beautiful place. The hotel was a little noisy, but we were usually out sightseeing all day.

Conversation 2
A: What's it like?
B: Well, it's about 50 centimeters long and it's green, with red under its wings.
A: Really? But it can't fly?
B: No, it can't. I've never seen one, though…only on the Internet. They live in the mountains in New Zealand.

Conversation 3
A: So tell me more about it. You said it's on the coast?
B: Yes, it is. It's on one of the biggest natural harbors in the world.
A: It must be beautiful.
B: Um…yes, it is. It's close to the mountains too. The population is about three million, I think. So it's quite big. There's a lot to do there, and it's very modern.

PHOTO CREDITS

Cover: *(The Sydney Opera House, Australia)* ©Blend Images/ALAMY, *(Big Ben, London)* ©Image Source/GETTY, *(Grand Canyon, U.S.A.)* ©Michael Clark/GETTY, *(Merlion statue, Singapore)* ©Michael McQueen/GETTY

SS = Shutterstock® Images

2 T ©bikeriderlondon/SS; **3** ©Andresr/SS; **6** T ©AVAVA/SS; B ©Monkey Business Images/SS; **7** TL ©Emely/GETTY, TR ©Tobias Machhaus/SS; **10** (1) ©Tibor Arva/SS, (2) ©Hugo Silveirinha Felix/SS,(3A) ©Serg Zastavkin/SS, (3B) ©Andrey Shadrin/SS; **14** T ©Laurence Mouton/GETTY, **15** ©Tomasz Trojanowski/SS, **16** (Mexican flag) ©Alexander Zavadsky/SS, (U.S. flag) ©megastocker/SS, (Japanese flag) ©Sean Prior/SS, (French flag) ©Neo Edmund/SS, (South Korean flag) ©Sean Prior/SS, (Spanish flag) ©Sasha Davas/SS, (Brazilian flag) ©Sean Prior/SS, (Thailand flag) ©Sasha Davas/SS, (Chinese flag) ©Chen Ping Hung/SS, (Mexican flag) ©Alexander Zavadsky/SS, (A) ©Jose Manuel Gelpi Diaz, (B) ©Eastwest Imaging,(C) ©Andrew Bassett/SS, (D) ©Jozsef Szasz-Fabian/SS, (E) ©Andrey Armyagov, (F) ©Rmarmion, (G) ©Alexander Fedorov, (H) ©DraganTrifunovic; **17** ©Galina Barskaya/SS; **18** L ©Galina Barskaya/SS; R ©Patsy Michaud/SS; **19** T ©zhu difeng/SS; B ©Andresr/SS; **20** ©pixinity/SS; **22** (A) ©ostill/SS; (B) ©Yuri Arcurs/SS; (C) ©Ronen/SS; (D) ©Marten Czamanske/SS; (E) ©Zoom Team/SS; (F) ©Galina Barskaya/SS;(G) ©Yuri Arcurs/SS; (H) ©Schmid Christophe/SS; **23** ©Andrey Kiselev; **25** (1) ©Andrejs Pidjass/SS; (2) ©Schmid Christophe/SS (3) ©VRPhotos/SS; (4) ©WAMVD/SS; (5) ©Kurhan/SS; (6) ©Maksim Shmeljov/SS; **26** (clocks A – F) ©Michael Lawlor/SS, (sun) ©Chud Tsankov/SS;(moon) ©Matthew Cole/SS, B (A) ©michaeljung/SS, B (B) ©Monkey Business Images/SS, B (C) ©AVAVA/SS, B (D) ©Brenda Carson/SS, B (E)©Brian Chase/SS, B (F) ©Majesticca/SS, B (G) ©spaxiax/SS, B (H) ©Monkey Business Images/SS; **28** (1) ©StockLite/SS, (2) ©Poleze/SS, (3) ©Piotr Marcinski/SS, (4) ©ahamrick/SS, (5) ©Phil Date/SS, (6) ©spaxiax/SS, (7) ©iofoto/SS, (8) ©Andrey Arkusha/SS, (9) ©mangostock/SS, (10) ©Monkey Business Images/SS; **29** ©Lasse Kristensen/SS; **30** (Aelef ©Jason Stitt/SS, (Phoung) ©Stephen Coburn/SS; **31** (woman) ©Adrin Shamsudin/SS, (clock) ©STILLFX/SS; **34** ©Anton Gvozdikov/SS; **35** ©ostill/SS; **37** (1) ©Bochkarev Photography/SS, (2) ©Geanina Bechea/SS, (3) ©Alexander Motrenko/SS, (4) ©Gemenacom/SS, (5) ©Monkey Business Images/SS, (6) ©Pavzyuk Svitlana/SS; **38** (A) ©Yegorius/SS, (B) ©Elnur/SS, (C) ©Stephen Coburn/SS, (D) ©Digital Vision/GETTY, (E) ©Diego Cervo/SS, (F) ©liza1979/SS, (G) ©sevenke/SS, (H) ©Elena Elisseeva/SS; **39** (A) ©Robnroll/SS, (B) ©Bedolaga/SS, (C) ©Tatiana Popova/SS, (D) ©Nastya22/SS, (E) ©hunta/SS, (B) ©JungleOutThere/SS; **40** (1) ©Nosha/SS, (2) ©GreenStockCreative/SS, (3) ©Rob Wilson/SS, (4) ©Yarygin/SS, (5) ©Phil Date/SS, (6) ©Nikola Bilic/SS, (7) ©GM Vozd/SS, (8) ©Zibedik/SS, (cash) ©Loskutnikov/SS, (credit card) ©Vladimir Petrov/SS; **41** B ©Christos Georghiou/SS; **44** (escalators) ©prism68/SS; **46** ©iofoto/SS; **49** (1) ©StockHouse/SS, (2) ©Christos Georghiou/SS, (3) ©Elnur/SS, (4) ©Andrey Burmakin/SS, (5) ©Richard Peterson/SS, (6) ©101images/SS; **50** ©oliveromg SS; **51** T ©AVAVA/SS, B ©Gladskikh Tatiana/SS; **53** ©Laszlo Szirtesi/SS; **54** ©Andresr/SS; **58** L ©Stephen Coburn/SS,ML ©Konstantin Chagin/SS, MR ©Dmitriy Shironosov/SS, R ©StockLite/SS; **59** ©Jason Stitt/SS; **60** T ©Julija Sapic/SS, B ©Layland Masuda/SS; **66** (dented car) ©S_E/SS, (bus) ©Tadeusz Ibrom/SS, (old car) ©Xico Putini/SS, (student holding keys) ©Diego Cervo/SS,(row of cars) ©Losevsky Pavel/SS; **67** (A) ©Rainer Plendl/SS, (B) ©Homofaber/SS, (C) ©Zibedik/SS, (D) ©popovich_vl/SS, (E) ©06photo/SS,(F) ©Adriano Castelli/SS, (G) ©Lorraine Swanson/SS, (H) ©Pell Studio/SS; **68** (1) ©George Unger IV/SS, (2) ©James Steidl/SS, (3) ©Monkey Business Images/SS, (4) ©AVAVA/SS, (5) ©Karen Grigoryan/SS, (6) ©Edyta Pawlowska/SS; **69** ©M. Habicher/SS; **70** (girl and dog) ©DNFStyle Photography/SS, (A) ©Phase4Photography/SS, (B) ©Stephen Coburrn/SS; **71** (A) ©Pedro Jorge Henriques Monteiro/SS, (B) ©muzsy/SS,(Jamal) ©Antonio Jorge Nunes/SS; **72** ©Aaron Rutten/SS; **74** (two girls) ©Martin Novak/SS; (hearts and film) ©andkuch/SS; **77** (1) ©ImageryMajestic/SS, (2) ©AlxYago/SS, (3) ©Naiyyer/SS; **78** ©Feng Yu/SS; **79** TL ©IKO/SS, TR ©Yuri Arcurs/SS, (worldmap) ©Jose Emilio/SS; **80** (girl in striped shirt) ©IKO/SS, (A) ©Yuri Arcurs/SS, (B) ©netbritish/SS; (C) ©Yuri Arcurs/SS, (D) ©Ivonne Wierink/SS, (E) ©Alexander Gatsenko/SS, (man on bike) ©Vaclav Volrab/SS, (woman running) ©Gelpi/SS, (girl driving) ©Layland Masuda/SS; **81** ©hartphotography/SS; **82** (from top to bottom): ©sokolovsky/SS, ©olly/SS, ©carlosseller/SS, ©Adriano Castelli/SS; **84** ©Piotr Marcinski/SS; **85** (A) ©Blaj Gabriel/SS, (B) ©ARENA Creative/SS, (C) ©Deklofenak/SS; **89** (woman on couch) ©Rob Marmion/SS, (man at café) ©CREATISTA/SS; **90** (1) ©Lilya/SS, (2) ©Andrew Horwitz/SS, (3) ©Kzenon/SS, (4) ©Dmitrijs Dmitrijevs/SS, (5) ©August/SS, (6) ©Phase4Photography/SS,(7) ©Vladimir Popovic/SS, (8) ©Zastol`skiy Victor Leonidovich/SS; **91** L ©ARENA Creative/SS, M ©Konstantin Sutyagin/SS, (plane) ©James Thew/SS, (woman at front desk) ©Dmitrijs Dmitrijevs/SS, (wedding party) ©Junial Enterprises/SS, (woman in hotel room) ©Jose AS Reyes/SS; **92** (1) ©Lagui/SS, (2) ©akva/SS, (3) ©Bryan Busovicki/SS, (5) ©Rob Wilson/SS, (6) ©Niek, B ©James Weston/SS; **95** B ©Chernetskiy/SS; **96** (A) ©Shuttlecock, (B) ©Paul Turner, (C) (coffee) ©Massman (pita) ©Sergei Platonov, (pastries) ©Alexandr Stepanov,(cheese) ©Aff, (D) ©Massman, B ©Haider Yousuf; **98** (castle) ©leonardo_da_gressignano/SS, (fountain) ©Huang Yuetao/SS, (woman and baby) ©Joel Shawn/SS; **100** (1) ©August/SS, (2) ©Isantilli/SS, (3) ©sonya etchison/SS; **102** (A) ©Ferenc Szelepcsenyi/SS, (B) ©s duffett/SS, (C) ©Pavel Losevsky, (D) ©Megumi,, (E) ©Adriano Castelli/SS, (F) ©Zibedik/SS; **103** (stage) ©aboikis/SS, (couples) ©Konstantin Chagin/SS, (waiter with platter) ©Eric Limon/SS, (box office) ©Danny E Hooks/SS; **104** (A) ©Accent/SS, (B) ©Diane N. Ennis/SS, (C) ©bhathaway/SS,(D) ©vichie81/SS, (E) ©Robert J. Beyers II/SS, (F) ©Losevsky Pavel/SS, (G) ©Alex Staroseltsev/SS, (H) ©Miguel Angel Salinas Salinas/SS, (I) ©3d brained/SS, (J) ©diak/SS; **105** ©Sean Nel/SS; **106** (A) ©Ronen/SS, (B) ©Pavel Losevsky/SS, (C) ©Anne Kitzman/SS, (D) ©Adriano Castelli/SS, (E) ©Jack.Qi/SS, (F) ©Jack Qi/SS; **108** (couple) ©Monkey Business Images/SS, (woman walking) ©Martin Novak/SS, (girl on beach) ©Netfalls/SS, (plane) ©MC_PP/SS, (girl on mountain) ©David Ryznar/SS, (Eiffel tower) ©Ralf Gosch/SS; **110** ©Losevsky Pavel/SS; **111** ©upthebanner/SS; **112** T ©Ginae McDonald/SS, B ©TFoxFoto/SS; **114** TR ©Andresr/SS, (A) ©Jose Gil/SS, (B) ©Dmitriy Shironosov/SS, (C) ©Ramzi Hachicho/SS, (D) ©thefinalmiracle/SS, (E) ©Barnaby Chambers/SS, (F) ©Liviu Toader/SS; **116** (A) ©Karkas/SS, (B) ©gary718/SS, (C) ©Tischenko Irina/SS, (D) ©Olga Lyubkina/SS, (E) ©Brazhnykov Andriyi/SS, (F) ©M. Dykstra/SS, (G) ©Eric Limon/SS, (H) ©Tischenko Irina/SS, (I) ©Tom Grundy/SS, (J) ©posterize/SS; **117** ©Alfredo Schaufelberger/SS; **119** (house) ©Robert Crum/SS, (boy eating corn) ©Suzanne Tucker/SS, (cow)©Margo Harrison/SS, (man with guitar) ©Allison Achauer/SS; **120** (A) ©Arturo Limon/SS, (B) ©Naomi Hasegawa/SS,(C) ©Jupiterimages/GETTY, (D) ©swissmacky/SS, (E) ©sergei telegin/SS; **122** ©AVAVA/SS, **124** ©Frank Spee/SS;**130** LLC ©Golden Pixels /SS, ©Lisa F Young/SS, ©mangostrock/SS, ©Slaven/SS, ©Alexandr Bryliaev/SS, ©rgerhardt/SS, ©MARKABOND/SS,©Paul Matthew Photography/SS, ©mattomedia/SS; **132** ©AVAVA; **134** ©Artifan/SS; **135** ©TomaszSzymanski/SS; **139** ©RAGMA IMAGES/SS; **142** ©kurhan/SS, ©Maxim Tupikov/SS, ©Chubykin Arkady/SS, ©Morgan Lane Photography/SS, ©Alexi Markku/SS, ©Oleg Zabielin/SS, ©Kushch Dmitry/SS, ©Demid/SS, **143** ©KenInness/SS, ©Mark Gabreya/SS, ©Luis Louro/SS, ©Antonio Jorge Nunes/SS, **144** ©Galina Barskaya/SS, ©Vixit/SS, ©Manamana/SS, ©Ekaterina Pokrovsky/SS, ©Svetlana Privezentseva/SS, ©Simon Krzic/SS, ©Benis Arapovic/SS, ©Craig Hanson/SS, **145** ©Khoroshnova Olga/SS, ©Ivan Sazykin/SS, ©Vasiliy Koval/SS, ©Maksym Gorpenyuk/SS, ©Sean Nel/SS, ©bikerriderlondon/SS; **147** ©Brian Maudsley/SS, ©Valery Shanin/SS;**148** ©Paul Frederiksen/SS, ©juampilaco/SS; **150** ©Vivid Pixels/SS; **151** ©upthebanner/SS; **154** ©Amy Nchole Harris/SS, ©s26/SS; **155** ©MountainDeaw/SS, ©Taras Vyshnya/SS; **156** ©Claudio Lovo/SS, ©Jaochainoi_Jaoyingnoi: B. Preecha N. Keasenee/SS; **157** ©Alberto Loyo/SS; **158** ©Taras Vyshnya/SS, ©deb22/SS **159** ©iofoto/SS; **160** ©Tifonimages/SS,©Pchugin Dmitry/SS, ©Ferenz/SS, ©Sapsiwai/SS, ©Maria Gioberti/SS, ©mypokcik/SS, **162** ©Celso Diniz/SS, **163** ©EML/SS, ©Alexey Goosev/SS, **164** ©Monkey Business Images/SS, ©Diego Cervo/SS, ©neelsky/SS, ©Hung Chung Chih/SS, ©Hugh Lansdown/SS, ©turtleman/SS: **167** ©Koshevnyk/SS; **168** ©Daniel Gale/SS, ©Alta Oosthizen/SS, ©mocagrande/SS, ©Antonio Jorge Nunes/SS, ©Eric Isselée/SS, ©Lindsay Dean/SS, ©Noam Wind/SS, ©Eduard Kyslynskyy/SS, **169** ©Leksele/SS, ©Kirsanov/SS, ©Eric Isselée/SS; **170** ©Nick Biemans/SS; **171** ©eugeneharman/SS, ©Allied Computer Graphics,Inc./SS, ©Koshevnyk/SS, **173** ©Stayer/SS, ©Rick Carey/SS, ©FWStupidio/SS, **174** ©covenant/SS, **175** ©CLFProductions/SS, ©Thomas Barrat/SS,©markrhiggins/SS, ©worldswildlifewonders/SS;**178** ©Jian Dao Hua/SS, ©Daniel Goodings/SS, ©Pete Saloutos/SS, ©Jiang Dao Hua/SS, ©muzky/SS, ©Benis Arapovic/SS, ©Michael Macsuga/SS, ©Benis Arapovic/SS, ©iofoto/SS, **179** ©Page2/SS, ©Jiri Hera/SS, **180** ©Ken Inness/SS, ©Stephanie Swartz/SS, ©Cemre/SS, ©mack2happy/SS, ©zimmytws/SS, ©Cemre/SS, ©Alexander Raths/SS, ©Cemre/SS, **182** ©GETTY/Maria/Tama/Contributor/GETTY; **183** ©Vasilkin/SS; **184** ©Nicholas D. Cacchione/SS; **185** ©Bruce Amos/SS; **187** ©Wolfe Larry/SS.

231

AUDIO TRACK LIST

Takeaway English, Student Book 1

Track	Unit	Section	Exercise
01_01	Unit 1	Start	1
01_02	Unit 1	Listening	2
01_03	Unit 1	Vocabulary	1
01_04	Unit 1	Vocabulary	2
01_05	Unit 1	Vocabulary	3
01_06	Unit 1	Vocabulary	4
01_07	Unit 1	Reading	2
01_08	Unit 1	Song	4
01_09	Unit 1	Pronunciation	1
01_10	Unit 1	Pronunciation	2
01_11	Unit 1	Conversation	2
02_01	Unit 2	Start	1
02_02	Unit 2	Start	2
02_03	Unit 2	Listening	2, 3
02_04	Unit 2	Vocabulary	1
02_05	Unit 2	Vocabulary	3
02_06	Unit 2	Reading	2, 3
02_07	Unit 2	Culture	2, 3
02_08	Unit 2	Pronunciation	1
02_09	Unit 2	Pronunciation	2
02_10	Unit 2	Conversation	1
02_11	Unit 2	Conversation	2
03_01	Unit 3	Start	1
03_02	Unit 3	Start	2
03_03	Unit 3	Star	3
03_04	Unit 3	Listening	3, 4
03_05	Unit 3	Vocabulary	2
03_06	Unit 3	Reading	2, 3
03_07	Unit 3	Song	3
03_08	Unit 3	Pronunciation	1
03_09	Unit 3	Pronunciation	2
03_10	Unit 3	Conversation	2
03_11	Unit 3	Test	Example
03_12	Unit 3	Test	Practice
04_01	Unit 4	Start	2
04_02	Unit 4	Listening	2
04_03	Unit 4	Vocabulary	1
04_04	Unit 4	Vocabulary	3
04_05	Unit 4	Reading	3, 4
04_06	Unit 4	Culture	3
04_07	Unit 4	Pronunciation	1
04_08	Unit 4	Conversation	2
05_01	Unit 5	Start	2
05_02	Unit 5	Start	3
05_03	Unit 5	Listening	2, 3
05_04	Unit 5	Vocabulary	1
05_05	Unit 5	Vocabulary	2
05_06	Unit 5	Reading	2, 3
05_07	Unit 5	Song	2, 3
05_08	Unit 5	Pronunciation	1
05_09	Unit 5	Pronunciation	2
05_10	Unit 5	Conversation	2
05_11	Unit 5	Test	Example
05_12	Unit 5	Test	Practice
05_R1_01	Review1	Listening	
05_R1_02	Review1	Reading	
06_01	Unit 6	Start	1
06_02	Unit 6	Start	3
06_03	Unit 6	Listening	2
06_04	Unit 6	Vocabulary	1
06_05	Unit 6	Grammar	2
06_06	Unit 6	Reading	2, 3
06_07	Unit 6	Culture	1
06_08	Unit 6	Culture	3
06_09	Unit 6	Pronunciation	1
06_10	Unit 6	Pronunciation	2
06_11	Unit 6	Conversation	1
07_01	Unit 7	Start	1
07_02	Unit 7	Start	2
07_03	Unit 7	Listening	2, 3
07_04	Unit 7	Vocabulary	2
07_05	Unit 7	Grammar	1
07_06	Unit 7	Grammar	2
07_07	Unit 7	Reading	2, 3
07_08	Unit 7	Song	3, 4
07_09	Unit 7	Pronunciation	1
07_10	Unit 7	Pronunciation	2
07_11	Unit 7	Conversation	2
08_01	Unit 8	Start	2
08_02	Unit 8	Listening	2, 3
08_03	Unit 8	Vocabulary	2
08_04	Unit 8	Grammar	2
08_05	Unit 8	Reading	2
08_06	Unit 8	Reading	3
08_07	Unit 8	Culture	3, 4
08_08	Unit 8	Pronunciation	1
08_09	Unit 8	Pronunciation	2
08_10	Unit 8	Conversation	2
09_01	Unit 9	Start	2
09_02	Unit 9	Listening	2, 3
09_03	Unit 9	Vocabulary	2
09_04	Unit 9	Grammar	2
09_05	Unit 9	Reading	2, 3
09_06	Unit 9	Song	2, 3
09_07	Unit 9	Pronunciation	1
09_08	Unit 9	Pronunciation	2
09_09	Unit 9	Conversation	2
09_10	Unit 9	Test	Example
09_11	Unit 9	Test	Practice
10_01	Unit 10	Start	2
10_02	Unit 10	Listening	2, 3
10_03	Unit 10	Vocabulary	2
10_04	Unit 10	Reading	2, 3
10_05	Unit 10	Culture	2, 3
10_06	Unit 10	Pronunciation	1
10_07	Unit 10	Pronunciation	2
10_08	Unit 10	Conversation	2
10_R2_01	Review2	Listening	2, 3
10_R2_02	Review2	Conversation	2
11_02	Unit 11	Start	2
11_03	Unit 11	Listening	2, 3
11_04	Unit 11	Vocabulary	2
11_05	Unit 11	Reading	3
11_06	Unit 11	Song	3
11_07	Unit 11	Pronunciation	1
11_08	Unit 11	Conversation	2
12_01	Unit 12	Start	2
12_02	Unit 12	Listening	2, 3
12_03	Unit 12	Vocabulary	2
12_04	Unit 12	Grammar	2
12_05	Unit 12	Reading	2
12_06	Unit 12	Culture	2
12_07	Unit 12	Culture	4
12_08	Unit 12	Pronunciation	1
12_09	Unit 12	Pronunciation	2
12_10	Unit 12	Conversation	2
13_01	Unit 13	Start	2
13_02	Unit 13	Listening	2
13_03	Unit 13	Listening	3
13_04	Unit 13	Vocabulary	2
13_05	Unit 13	Reading	2
13_06	Unit 13	Song	3, 4
13_07	Unit 13	Pronunciation	1
13_08	Unit 13	Pronunciation	2
13_09	Unit 13	Conversation	2, 3
14_01	Unit 14	Start	2
14_02	Unit 14	Start	3
14_03	Unit 14	Listening	2
14_04	Unit 14	Listening	3
14_05	Unit 14	Vocabulary	2
14_06	Unit 14	Grammar	3
14_07	Unit 14	Reading	2
14_08	Unit 14	Culture	2
14_09	Unit 14	Culture	3
14_10	Unit 14	Pronunciation	1
14_11	Unit 14	Pronunciation	2
14_12	Unit 14	Conversation	2, 3
15_01	Unit 15	Start	2
15_02	Unit 15	Listening	2
15_03	Unit 15	Vocabulary	2
15_04	Unit 15	Reading	2, 3
15_05	Unit 15	Song	2
15_06	Unit 15	Pronunciation	1
15_07	Unit 15	Pronunciation	2
15_08	Unit 15	Conversation	2
15_R3_01	Review3	Listening	
15_R3_02	Review3	Reading	